BUILDING BLOCKS
in Science

GARY PARKER

First printing: December 2007
Second printing: November 2013

ISBN-13: 978-0-89051-511-2
Library of Congress Catalog Number: 2007925408

Cover design by Bryan Miller
Interior design by Diana Bogardus

Unless otherwise noted, all Scripture is from the King James Version of the Bible.

Printed in the United States of America

Please visit our website for other great titles: www.masterbooks.net

For information regarding author interviews, please contact the publicity department at (870) 438-5288.

Please consider requesting that a copy of this volume be purchased by your local library system.

Illustrations & Photo Credits:
A=All, T=Top, M=Middle, B=Bottom, L=Left, R=Right

Photos:
NASA Jet Propulsion Labratory: 6T
NASA: 7, 13TL, 80
Dr. and Mrs. Parker: 36, 13B, 19, 56, 60, 91BR
The Great Alaskan Dinosaur Adventure, Master Books: 57
Secrets of the Ica Stones and Nazca Lines, Dennis Swift: 58B
www.bible.ca: 91BR, 94T, 94BL
Science Photo Library: John Reader/Photo Researchers 125TL, 125TR; Des Bartlett /Photo Researchers 125TM;
    James King-Holmes /Photo Researchers 139TL, 139TR

Other photos: istockphoto.com, photos.com

Illustrations:
Bryan Miller: 20T, 20BR, 23BR, 29TR. 29BL, 39BR, 46B, 47, 48BL, 49TR, 55B, 56. 58T, 62BR, 65B, 68-69B,
    70BL, 71T, 74R, 76MR, 77B, 78, 82-83, 90B, 92TL, 92BL, 103BR, 104B, 112B,
Earl & Bonita Snellenberger: 27, 28T, 49B, 51T, 66L, 91T, 136T,
Institute for Creation Research: 84L

Table of Contents

4   **Unit 1: War of World Views**

8   **Ch.1 – The Classic Debate**
Evolutionist's Opening Remarks

12   **Ch.2 – Creationist's Opening Remarks**
What a Difference!

18   **Ch.3 – The Nature of Science**

22   **Ch.4 – Evolution vs. Science**

26   **Ch.5 – Historical Time-lines**
Classic Creationist Model
Classic Evolutionist Model

38   **Ch.6 – Scientifically Testable Predictions**
Philosophic Presuppositions: Assumptions, Assertions, and Implications

44   **Unit 2: Dinosaurs!**

46   **Ch.7 – Dinosaurs, Creation, and the Fall**

54   **Ch.8 – Dinosaurs, the Flood, and the Gospel**

62   **Ch.9 – Dinosaurs, Evolution, and Science**
Creation vs. Evolution
Dinosaur Reconstructions

68   **Ch.10 – "Terrible Lizards" or "Terrible Reptiles"**
Dinosaurs as Reptiles
Dinosaurs and Reptilian Subgroups

74   **Ch.11 – Dinosaurs and Birds?**

80   **Ch. 12 – What about Dino Extinction and an "Age of Dinosaurs"?**

90   **Ch.13 – Dinosaurs in Recorded History**
Mankind and Dinosaurs: The Fossil Evidence
The Good News

98   **Unit 3: Human Origins**

100   **Ch.14 – "Cave Men" and "Human Evolution"**
Neanderthal "Cave Men"

108   **Ch.15 – Enormous Errors in the Evolutionist's Evidence**
Evolutionary Racism
Piltdown Man (*"Eoanthropus dawsoni"*), Java Man ("Pithecanthropus")

116   **Ch.16 – Nebraska Man and the Scopes "Monkey" Trial**

124   **Ch.17 – Australopithecines**

130   **Ch.18 – "Away from Evolution"**
Science vs. Human Evolution
More Science vs. Human Evolution: Classification
Anatomy

138   **Ch.19 – Dating Fossils of Apes and People**
Radiometric Dating
Stratigraphic Dating
Molecular Dating

146   **Ch.20 – In God's Image**

Unit 1: War of World Views

Have you ever faced questions like these? "You say you believe the Bible. Well, where did dinosaurs come from? Did Noah have dinosaurs on the ark? Where did Cain get his wife? Isn't it embarrassing to believe in a six-day creation about 6,000 years old when scientists can see galaxies millions of light years away and measure the age of fossils and rocks with carbon-14 and uranium dating?"

Or, how about this? "You say you're a Christian. If God created just two people, what color were they? Where did all the races come from? If 'creation' should be taught in schools, do you believe in equal time for Muslim and Buddhist creation stories, too?"

Or, "If there's an all-powerful, all-loving God who created everything, why do we have the AIDS virus and birth defects? Why do fossils show millions of years of struggle and death, and mass extinctions? Who'd want to pray to a 'god' who wiped out 99 percent of all the species he/she/it supposedly created?"

Maybe you've wondered about some of these questions yourself. Perhaps you have a personal relationship with Jesus Christ and you love the spiritual truths in the Bible and its promise of life in heaven forever. But privately, almost subconsciously, you've wondered, "Is the Christian faith any more real than other faiths? If I'd been born in a Muslim country, would I be a Muslim? Is the Bible really any different from the 'holy books' of other religions? Hasn't science really shown it's foolish to take the Bible literally?"

Or, maybe you have a solid foundation for your own faith, but you have friends, family, and people you love who just won't accept the free gift of new life in Christ, and you wonder how to reach them. Lots of religions promise a "warm, fuzzy feeling," many with far fewer demands than "dying to self and living for Christ." Is there any reason to think the Christian faith enables us to understand ourselves and our world any better than other faiths do? Are there answers for people who excuse their disbelief by saying science has disproved the Bible and the Christian faith?

If you don't need this *Creation Foundations* series to strengthen your own faith, you may need it to be a more effective witness in a world steeped in evolutionism. God, through the apostle Peter, commands us to "be ready always to give an answer to every man that asketh you a reason of the hope that is in you . . ." (1 Pet. 3:15). And God through the apostle Paul warns us how evolutionary humanism and philosophic naturalism ("science falsely so-called") has been a stumbling block keeping many from coming to Christ: "O Timothy, keep that which is committed to thy trust; avoiding profane and vain babblings and oppositions of science falsely so called: which some professing have erred concerning the faith" (1 Tim. 6:20).

I certainly needed a "creation evangelist" in my own life. From a young age through my first few years as a professor of biology, I was a naturalistic evolutionist. I believed and taught, enthusiastically, that all life — including yours and mine — was produced by time, chance, and millions of years of struggle and death, NOT by the plan and purpose of some so-called "Creator God." Indeed, I thought and taught that God was a figment of the human imagination, created in our image when we reached a stage in evolution where our minds could project dreams of an ideal future and create a god to lead us to victory (often over the corpses of other human beings who had made up images of different gods).

"Science" was my god. While philosophers and politicians struggled with less and less success over older and older questions, scientists conquered diseases and put mankind on the moon and were on the way to conquering aging and poverty and reaching onward to the stars! At age ten, I wrote a constitution for the first government of Mars, hoping I would be among the scientists leading the conquest of space. As a college freshman, I tried to found a new discipline, "experimental philosophy," convinced that science could finally determine what truly produced human happiness. In all this, I was considered a "nice guy" and actually felt sympathy for Christians who hoped for heaven and believed "love conquers all." But I wanted my students to realize that it was millions of years of struggle and death that had brought all life, including ours, into existence, and only science — *not* some god of our own imagination — could finally lead us past the

Sagan and Viking: Famous for his television series *Cosmos*, evolutionist Dr. Carl Sagan poses with a model of the Viking lander in Death Valley, California. Image Credit: NASA Jet Propulsion Laboratory

era of struggle and death into a new evolutionary age of universal happiness and peace.

Then a chemistry professor (Dr. Charles Signorino) at the college where I was teaching invited me to his home for a Bible study. I had no desire to study a dusty, outmoded, pre-scientific book like the Bible — but I did have a real desire for free coffee and donuts, so my wife and I began attending the Bible study. What followed was an incredible three-year "war of the world views" raging in my mind, paralleling the great debate that has raged in the hearts and minds of thinking people in the world during the past 200 years.

At bottom, there are two and only two possible views for the ultimate origin of the universe — time, matter-energy, and space. Either (1) the universe made itself, or (2) the universe was made by transcendent power outside the limits of time, matter-energy, and space.

These two are *mutually exhaustive* (i.e., they cover all possibilities), and they are *mutually exclusive* (i.e., one is true and the other is false). One view can be described by the pithy phrase attributed to Carl Sagan, "The cosmos is all there is or was, or ever will be," and the other in the often-quoted first verse of the Bible, "In the beginning, God created the heaven and the earth" (Gen. 1:1).

On a less ultimate plane, this "war of the world views" has centered on the classic debate between scientists building on the *biblical record* of the earth's history and scientists espousing what's called either *evolutionary humanism* or *philosophic naturalism*. As is popular today, we'll call proponents of these opposing viewpoints "creationists" and "evolutionists," respectively (and respectfully).

In this *Creation Foundations* series, we'll examine both creationist and evolutionist perspectives, their *assumptions* and *implications*, and most especially differences in their understandings of *scientific evidences* related to origins. Can either of these views sustain a burden of proof? Are compromises between these two views possible or desirable? I hope you conclude, as I did, that *what we see in God's world agrees with what we read in God's Word!*

As a "preview of coming attractions," let's look at the stark contrast between creationist and evolutionist positions summarized in opening remarks of "the classic debate."

The Classic Debate

Evolutionist's Opening Remarks

Anyone here a Christian? Anyone believe the Bible? Well, you won't after this lecture is over. Evolution's a fact, and science can prove it.

Now let me ask you an easier question. Anyone here want to sail around the world? That was an opportunity given to a young man named Charles Darwin. Darwin hadn't succeeded in medical or ministerial schools, but he really loved collecting bugs. So, his father booked him as ship's naturalist aboard the *H.M.S. Beagle*, departing England in 1831 for a five-year voyage around the world.

His stop at the Galapagos Islands, 600 miles (900 km) west of Ecuador in the Pacific, was destined to change the world. Darwin arrived as sea turtles were hatching from eggs in the beach sands. Gulp! Gulp! Perhaps 97 in 100 of the turtles were eaten by birds and other predators before they got their first taste of seawater. Of the three that made it to the sea, perhaps two were eaten, leaving only an average of one survivor among 100 hatchlings.

Darwin began to wonder how an "all-powerful, all-loving" Creator could be so cruel, wasteful, and inefficient. (His growing disbelief in a powerful, loving Creator may have been pushed over the line when his daughter died at the innocent age of nine.) Everywhere he looked, Darwin was confronted with what he later called the "struggle for survival." The ship's Captain Fitzroy professed to be a Christian, but when young Darwin asked him how God could be so cruel, he had no answer.

Darwin did notice the incredible beauty and diversity of life on his voyage, too. For a young man from England, the astonishing variety of tropical plants, birds, and bugs must have been awe-inspiring. Yet it was over 20 years before Darwin finally put variety and struggle together into the

revolutionary/evolutionary concept that burst the bonds of Victorian Christianity: "survival of the fittest." His concept was simple, yet profound, a logical conclusion based on a few observations. Darwin observed (1) that only a few of each species came through the struggle for survival, and (2) that each species included individuals with a variety of traits. Logically, (3) some varieties would be more likely to survive than others — survival of the fittest! Add it up for yourself!

$$
\begin{aligned}
&\quad\ 1.\ \text{struggle} \\
+\ &\quad\ 2.\ \text{variety} \\
\hline
=\ &\quad\ 3.\ \text{survival of the fittest}
\end{aligned}
$$

Based on analogy to artificial selection practiced by plant and animal breeders (including himself), Darwin called this "three-step process" *natural selection.*

Evolutionists saw almost immediately that Darwin had discovered the means by which nature itself, not some capricious Creator, would continuously produce ever more varied and improved organisms — the appearance of design, without a Designer! Darwin summarized his theory with these words in the closing paragraphs of his *Origin of Species,* published in 1859: "Thus, from the war of nature, famine, and death, the production of higher animals directly follows."

Natural selection, the *"war of nature"* that originally drove Darwin from God, now replaced God as the author of all living things.

Think about it for yourself. Is there a struggle for survival? Yes. Is there variety among living things? Yes. Are some varieties more likely to survive than others? Yes. 1 + 2 = 3: struggle + variety = survival of the fittest. No wonder people think Bible-believing Christians are foolish. They can't count to three. Evolution's a fact. Most Christians accept evolution, and the Church is embarrassed by biblical literalists today just as it was in Galileo's time. Evolution's a fact; we see it going on all around us today.

The amount of evolutionary change seen in a human lifetime or even a century is slight, like the change in the wing color of peppered moths that followed the Industrial Revolution in England. But imagine what would happen if natural selection continued, trait after trait, for millions and billions of years. Random changes in DNA, called mutations, would increase hereditary variability immensely. The many harmful mutations would be eliminated by natural selection, but the beneficial ones would be saved for countless generations.

Biblical literalists are stuck with a six-day creation that only goes back 6,000 years, but evolution is based on "geologic time" confirmed by radioactive decay dating that goes back to the earth's beginning, 4.6 billion years ago. Charles Lyell, lawyer and amateur geologist working in England in the early 1800s just ahead of Darwin, was the first to push past the biblical "time limit." He noticed the slow rates of sediment accumulation and erosion. Simple calculations show it would take far more than biblical time to build up the rock layers at the Grand Canyon, then cut through them a mile deep. Besides, argued Lyell, scientists should base their judgments of what happened in the past on their observations of the present, a principle called uniformitarianism, often summarized as "the present is the key to the past." Lyell provided the time required for the small changes produced by natural selection to add up to big evolution changes, from molecules to mankind! As the late great Carl Sagan once put it, "The secrets of evolution are time and death." Over eons of time, the continuous death of the less fit paves the way for continuous evolution of the more fit.

Laboratory experiments, such as those of Stanley Miller, and our exploding knowledge of DNA show us how chemical evolution from non-life to life could have occurred. Nothing supernatural appears to have been involved, but only time, chance, and the particularly suitable conditions of the ancient earth. Recent meteorite evidence suggests life may have evolved even earlier on Mars, and it's the height of narrow-minded religious bigotry to believe that similar processes would not have produced life on many of the millions and billions of other planets in our universe. What a waste of space if life exists only here.

Man is the first animal on earth to look back over his evolutionary history. As we do so, we learn things that

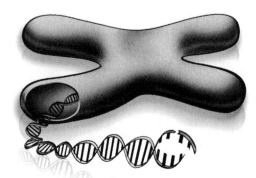

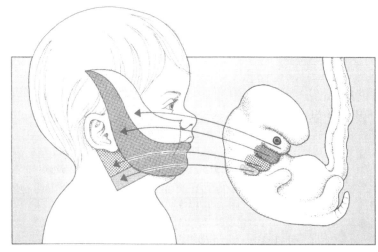

The structures in an embryo that evolutionists call gill slits actually have important developmental and adult human functions.

help us understand ourselves. Why do we have useless organs (vestiges) like the appendix and tailbone? They functioned in our ancestors. Why does the human embryo have *gill slits* and a *yolk sac*? We shared a common ancestor with fish and reptiles, which also explains why the bone pattern in our arm is like that in the forelimb of a whale, a bat, and a bear (homology).

More importantly, why do we do things that are harmful to other people? It's not "sin" or failure to live up to some "god's" moral code; it's the war of nature that brought us into being in the first place.

Charles Lyell

Fossils allow us to trace the evolutionary history of life on earth through the geologic column. The first abundant fossils show us life on earth over half a billion, perhaps 530 million, years ago, consisted only of simple sea creatures, like trilobites and lampshells. About 400 million years ago, the first land plants and animals appeared in the fossil sequence. Dinosaurs ruled from about 220 to 65 million years ago. Fossils such as "Lucy" show how mankind evolved from ape-like ancestors during just the last 3½ million years. If the whole 4½ billion years of earth's history were condensed into a film one year long, our fragile species would not appear until the last second before the end of the movie. Surely the earth was not created as man's dominion, as the Bible says.

But we're not without hope. We've reached a level of consciousness that enables us to direct our own further evolution. We're already taking control of DNA, the molecule of heredity. Perhaps we can remake ourselves into our own image of what mankind really ought to be. We're reaching for the stars. There's simply no limit to what mankind can do.

As we look ever deeper into space, we're looking ever further back into time, back ultimately to the big bang that brought our universe into being. Biblical literalists embarrass themselves and other Christians by trying to claim God created a universe 6,000 years ago that includes galaxies billions of light years away! As we continue to search the heavens, inevitably we'll encounter other life forms, some undoubtedly more intelligent than our own. It may be in deep space that we find the final links in the evolutionary chain that turned particles into people, people like you and me who can finally appreciate the stardust from which we came. It was the laws of science and properties of matter that transformed dust into life, not the whimsical plan of some mythical "creator," and we are responsible only to ourselves. There is an awesome grandeur in this view of life that far transcends what is offered by the tribal god of the Hebrews and his son; evolution is an exhilarating push for discovery to expand the frontiers of scientific knowledge, "to boldly go where no one has gone before"!

* * * * *

Wow! Never underestimate the power or appeal of evolution! But is there an alternative to evolution more consistent with the scientific evidence? Most of the major scientific disciplines were founded in the two centuries *before* Darwin by scientists who considered themselves creationists. Let's see how a classic creationist looks at origins questions today.

Form your foundation.

The author once believed what evolutionists still teach, that all life (including yours!) came from millions of years of struggle and death (Darwin's "war of nature") and not from the plan and purpose of a caring Creator.

100 A+

Which of these questions is used to challenge the Christian faith and belief in the Bible?

- ☐ Did Noah take dinosaurs on the ark?
- ☐ If God created only Adam and Eve, where did their son Cain get his wife?
- ☐ If creation should be taught in schools, should Muslim and Buddhist views be taught as well as Christian?
- ☐ Why would an all-powerful, all-loving God create the AIDS virus and allow birth defects?
- ☐ If fossils and living things show struggle and death, does that mean God used millions of years of struggle and death to create?
- ☑ All of the above

The author began his college biology teaching career as an enthusiastic evolutionist; what enticed him to study the Bible and the evidence for creation?

- ☐ the scientific search for truth
- ☐ a spiritual encounter with Jesus Christ
- ☐ a promise he made if God would get him out of trouble
- ☐ intellectual honesty and academic curiosity
- ☑ free coffee and donuts
- ☐ none of the above

1. Match each Bible quotation below with one of the three Bible references below.

   Genesis 1:1   1 Peter 3:15   1 Timothy 6:20

   _____ a. "In the beginning God created the heaven and the earth."
   _____ b. ". . . avoiding profane and vain babblings of science falsely so-called. . . ."
   _____ c. "Be ready always to give an answer to every man that asketh you a reason of the hope that is in you."

2. Darwin believed evolution was produced by the " _war_ of nature," a ceaseless " _struggle_ for survival," plus " _variety_ " among members of a species which, he said, led to "survival of the _fittest_."

Which of these arguments was NOT used by the "classic evolutionist" in his/her opening remarks?

- ☐ Experiments show DNA and living cells could evolve without help from God.
- ☐ People and other animals harm each other because of the struggle for survival, not because of sin.
- ☑ The human body contains no useless, leftover parts, because evolution eliminated all of them.
- ☐ Fossils and radioactive decay dating show the earth is way older than the Bible allows.
- ☐ We must look to science, not God, to make the world a better place to live.
- ☐ None of the above; the evolutionist made all the claims above.

3. Ultimately there are only two views about the origin of the universe: either the universe _created it's self_ or the universe was made by _God_. In the classic and current debate, the first view is held by (creationists/evolutionists) _evolutionary humanism_ and the second by _philosophic naturalism_ (creationists/evolutionists).

Chapter

1

Creationist's Opening Remarks

Let's take a look now at the scientific evidence of creation. Evidence of creation? Isn't creation something you either believe or don't believe? Sometimes even Christians believe you can't really talk about evidence of creation. I would like to suggest, however, that nothing is easier or more natural for scientists (and other people) than finding and recognizing evidence of creation.

Imagine you are walking along a streambed on a sunny summer day, idly kicking at the pebbles. You pick up one that reminds you of a mini-Christmas tree. But as you roll it around in your hand, you notice lines of wear in the pebble follow lines of weakness, and softer material is worn away more than harder material. In spite of some appearance of design, you conclude the unusual pebble is just a product of time, chance, and natural processes of weathering and erosion.

But then you find an arrowhead. The chip marks go both with and against the grain, and harder and softer materials are cut through equally. Immediately you recognize evidence of creation, matter shaped and molded by a plan that gives it a special purpose. I'm only talking here about human creation, of course. But imagine if we found arrowheads or pottery fragments on Mars. Without knowing who or what the creative agent was, scientists would logically conclude that those objects were the products of plan, purpose, and special acts of creation (even if it were Martian intelligence instead of Earthlings!).

Note that you don't have to see the creator, and you don't have to see the creative act, in order to recognize evidence of creation. What does it take to recognize evidence of creation? The ordinary tools of science: logic and observation. "Creation" is simply the logical inference from our observations of certain patterns of order — and that is true whether the creative intelligence is human, Martian, or the transcendent Creator God of the universe! The famous evolutionist Carl Sagan spent millions of public and private dollars

on SETI (the Search for Extra-Terrestrial Intelligence). He was convinced scientists could detect unseen creative intelligence in the difference between wave patterns produced by physical processes and those sent with deliberate intent. The Bible puts it this way: "God's invisible qualities . . . have been clearly seen . . . from what has been made" (Rom. 1:20; NIV).

We all (scientists and everyone else), then, ordinarily recognize two quite different patterns in the world around us. One pattern is produced by the properties of matter "doing what comes naturally" (inherent order, we'll call it); the other pattern is imposed on matter by purposeful choice producing properties of organization ("exherent" order, to coin a term, or "mind over matter"). Which kind of pattern do we find among the molecules in a living system: the kind resulting from time, chance, and natural processes of evolution, or the kind that reflects plan, purpose, and special acts of creation?

The two "parts" in the tumbled pebble and the arrowhead we compared were hard and soft materials. The two basic "parts" of every living system are DNA and/or RNA, molecules of heredity, and proteins, molecules of structure and function. DNA and protein molecules are both chains of repeated links. The links in protein chains are amino acids, and the coding parts of links in DNA chains are bases. In all life forms, from viruses to people, inherited chains of bases "tell" the living cell how to line up amino acids to form each structural and/or functional protein molecule.

Since nothing is more natural than a chemical reaction between acids and bases, you might think time, chance, and chemical processes would naturally evolve a system in which series of bases produce series of acids. Exactly the opposite! The problem is that the natural base-acid relationship is the wrong relationship as far as living things are concerned. The distinctive part of each amino acid is an R-group that may be an acid, a base, a short chain, a long chain, a single ring, a double ring, etc.! There is *no* natural chemical tendency for a series of bases to line up a series of highly variable R-groups. The genetic coding relationship is one no chemist would ever predict

from time, chance, and the properties of matter! It's using a series of bases, taken three at a time, to "tell" the cell how to line up a series of R-groups. That relationship has to be imposed from the outside by deliberate choice. At this most fundamental level, then, we see evidence that life on earth is a result of plan, purpose, and special acts of creation.

Consider a simpler example. Did you ever wonder what it takes to make an airplane fly? The wings don't fly; the engines don't fly; the person in the cockpit doesn't fly. Try not to think about this on your next flight, but an airplane is a collection of non-flying parts! What does it take to make an airplane fly? The answer is something every scientist can logically infer from observations: creative design and organization. Flying is a property of purposeful organization, not a property of mindless matter. Nothing supernatural occurs during the *operation* of an airplane, but trying to explain the *origin* of airplanes without reference to creative design would be both unscientific and futile.

Now think about a living cell. Not a single molecule in a cell is alive. A living cell is a collection of non-living parts. What does it take to make a cell alive? The answer is something every scientist can logically infer from observation: creative design and organization. Living things are made up of ordinary chemicals ("dust of the ground"), and so are dead cells. "Life" is not a property of mindless matter, but a property of purposeful organization! Nothing supernatural happens during the *operation* of a living cell, but trying to explain the origin of life without considering intelligent design would be unscientific and has been futile. The most logical inference from our current scientific knowledge is that life is the product of plan, purpose, and special acts of creation!

Evidence of creation is seen at many other levels, too: the "pre-planning" in embryonic development; mosaic patterns of structural similarity (convergence and homology); and adaptations that could originate only with many parts working together simultaneously (compound traits or irreducible complexity). Our knowledge of DNA and the laws of heredity allow scientists both to define the boundaries of the created kinds and to understand the tremendous built-in variability that enables descendants of each biblical kind to "multiply and fill" the dazzling diversity of environments on earth (*entelechy*).

But the perfect world God created was ruined by mankind. The Bible tells us (Gen. 3; Rom. 8) that man's willful rejection of God's love and God's gifts brought suffering, struggle, disease, death, and disaster into the world God had created "very good." Scientists see evidence of this corruption of creation in the random mutations that damage DNA and produce defects, disease, and disease organisms. As mutations damaged instincts for limiting populations and changed diets and behaviors, predator-prey relationships replaced territorial population control and the struggle for survival began. Publishing 24 years before Darwin, a creationist (Edward Blyth) showed how natural selection would help both to reduce harmful changes and also to explain how and where living things survived as they multiplied and filled a fallen world. Mutations and Darwin's "war of nature" could never act onward and upward to explain evolution; instead, they operate outward and downward to help explain diversification within created kinds and the origin of defects — disease, disease organisms, and decline.

In fact, the violence and corruption that filled the earth because of man got so bad that God resolved to destroy the world with a flood, to give it a fresh start with Noah and those with him on the ark. Scientists studying the volcanic eruptions of Mount St. Helens in 1980 and 1982 observed a miniature "laboratory model" of the major geologic forces at work on a larger scale in the catastrophe of Noah's flood. Like the Flood, the eruption of Mount St. Helens began when "the fountains of the great deep burst forth." Highly pressurized, extremely hot water in molten magma flashed into steam, blowing the top 1,300 feet off the mountain in the first eruption. The resulting mudflow rushed into Spirit Lake, creating a gigantic wave that sheared off a million trees in a matter of moments. The sediment layers produced, complete with upright trunks, form patterns like scientists see in coal layers — except coal seams can run from Pennsylvania to Kansas, suggesting a catastrophe much more awesome than Mount St. Helens!

Volcanic eruption of Mount St. Helens

The second eruption formed thick, finely layered deposits in minutes, and then pyroclastic flows gouged out a *miniature grand canyon*, a 1:40 scale model of the Grand Canyon, in less than five days! Tilted and sheared rock layers, embedded boulder flows, gaps of "millions of evolutionary years" with insufficient evidence of erosion, cross-bedded submarine dunes, a nautiloid mass kill event, lava flows in "reverse time" order, and many other geologic evidences show us the layers of the real Grand Canyon were formed and cut quickly — *a lot of water,* NOT a lot of time. Evidence of catastrophe even extends into our solar system and beyond, where telescopes show us pockmarked planets, comets breaking up, and "the heavens …will all wear out like a garment" (Heb. 1:10–11; NIV).

Fossils confirm the biblical outline of earth's history: creation followed by corruption and catastrophe. Among the fossils first buried in abundance ("Cambrian") are members of all the major animal groups living today, including those with the most complex organs (brains, hearts, eyes, etc.). This "Cambrian Explosion," as scientists call it, seems to point back to a prior act of creation producing a multitude of life forms, all well designed to multiply after kind. Fossil discoveries since Darwin have only sharpened the boundaries between kinds, leaving his missing "intermediate links" still missing. But fossils are dead things, and they tell us also about man's corruption of God's creation, bringing death, disease, and a decline in the variety and sizes of almost all major groups, the opposite of evolution.

And fossils did not and could not form slowly and gradually, here and there, over millions of years. Evolutionists agree that most fossils form under flood conditions, and vast fossil graveyards, huge oil deposits, so-called "mass extinctions," seashells atop the highest mountains, carbon-14 imbalance, and helium deficiency all testify, along with many other evidences, to the worldwide catastrophe of Noah's flood. The fossil sequence (geologic column) is not from few and simple to many and complex, but from complex and varied sea life to near shore life, to complex and varied upland life — burial of different life zones around the world in the rising waters of the Flood.

But with every trial and judgment, God provides a way of escape. Just as God provided the ark to save all who would turn to Him, and a remnant of all life to restore the earth, so God provides His Son, Jesus Christ, to save us from death and to provide a "new heavens and a new earth" (2 Pet. 3:13) where "there shall be no more death" (Rev. 21:4).

According to evolution, it's millions of years of struggle and death, until death wins. According to the Bible, life wins — new life in Jesus Christ. As a professor of biology, it took me three years of tough mental battle to finally conclude that science makes it hard to believe in evolution, and "easy" to believe the Bible. What we see in God's world (science) agrees with what we read in God's Word (the "four Cs"): (1) God's perfect *creation*, (2) ruined by mankind (*corruption*), (3) destroyed by Noah's flood (*catastrophe*), and (4) restored to new life in *Christ*.

I hope your study lifts you above the limits of space, time, and cultural bias into the living presence of the eternal Creator, the God of all peoples, all times, and all places, who can bring you to new life — rich, abundant, and forevermore — in Christ!

What a Difference!

It's certainly obvious from their opening remarks that the "classic evolutionist" and "classic creationist" have drastically different ideas about the origin, history, and destiny of life on earth!

Is it millions of years of struggle and death until death wins, or does Jesus Christ conquer death and bring new life, rich and abundant forevermore? Do fossils show us a long, slow, generally progressive evolution of ever more complex and varied life forms, or are fossils largely the remains of creatures buried during the year of Noah's flood after man's sin corrupted God's perfect creation? Are the words of men guided by our knowledge of present processes the best and only guide to answering these questions, or does the Word of God give us the true outline of earth's history from before the beginning to after the end? The key differences between classic creationist and evolutionist perspectives are summarized in Table 2.1.

Ideas have consequences, and it's certainly obvious that creationist and evolutionist ideas suggest radically different answers to key questions. Most of the questions considered in this *Creation Foundations* series will be scientific and historical. Can we expect science to settle the creation/evolution question for us?

Form your foundation.

Scientific evidence in God's world supports the historical record in God's Word, the Bible: God's perfect creation, corrupted by man's sin, destroyed in Noah's flood, restored to new life in Jesus Christ — summarized in four Cs: Creation, Corruption, Catastrophe, and Christ.

Table 2.1: Comparing Creation and Evolution

Classic Positions of Creationists	Classic Positions of Evolutionists
1. God is eternal and made the universe at the beginning of time.	1. Matter (mass-energy) is eternal, and the universe made itself.
2. God created life from the dust of the ground and left evidence of plan, purpose, and properties of intelligent design.	2. Time and chance produced life from simple elements ("dust of the ground") based on the properties of matter.
3. Struggle and death followed man's sin, which corrupted God's perfect creation with defects, decline, and disaster.	3. Struggle and death resulted in survival of the fittest, which produced ever more complex and varied life.
4. Lots of built-in variability (entelechy) was expressed as created kinds multiplied and filled the earth, but only variation within kind.	4. Mutations and natural selection change one species into others, from a few simple species in the past to many complex ones today.
5. Most fossils were formed during Noah's flood; their sequence shows stages in the burial of successive life zones in a year-long worldwide catastrophe.	5. Fossils accumulated slowly and gradually over millions of years; their sequence shows stages in evolution of increasing life.
6. Mankind was created in God's image and charged with the care of the earth. There is only one race of human beings; all died in Adam, and all can be made alive in Christ. There is one God of all peoples, times, and places.	6. Man is an animal that evolved from ape-like ancestors through once-missing links like "Lucy." Races may represent different stages in evolution. There are many gods made in men's images, or no God.
7. The study of radioactive decay, and of features and processes in geology and astronomy, support the concept of a young earth and recent creation.	7. The study of radioactive decay, and of features and processes in geology and astronomy, prove the earth and universe are billions of years old.
8. The universe ends with a loud noise (a "big bang") when Christ returns to restore eternal peace and harmony in a new heavens and new earth.	8. The universe began with a big bang and ends with a whimper when the last of useful energy is converted to random, chaotic motion and death conquers all.
9. Science makes it hard to believe in evolution and supports what the Bible says about God's perfect Creation, ruined by man's sin (Corruption), destroyed in Noah's flood (Catastrophe), restored to new life in Christ.	9. Science makes it hard to believe in the God of the Bible and supports what evolutionists believe, which means there's nothing greater than man's intelligence and no absolutes beyond human opinion.

Building Inspection

1. Use an arrowhead (or example of your choice) to show how scientists can use logic and observation to recognize evidence of creation without seeing either the creator or the creative act.

2. What is there about the properties of matter vs. the properties of organization (mind) that suggest a created origin for both airplanes and living cells?

3. Associate each of the four Cs of biblical earth history below with one reference from God's Word below and one example from God's world:

   Creation   Corruption   Catastrophe   Christ

   Creation ___ a. "The invisible things of him from the creation of the world are clearly seen . . ." (Rom. 1:20).

   Christ ___ b. ". . . there shall be no more death . . ." (Rev. 21:4).

   Corruption ___ c. ". . . the creation itself will be set free from its bondage to decay . . ." (Rom. 8:20; RSV).

   Catastrophe ___ d. "In the six hundredth year of Noah's life . . . were all the fountains of the great deep broken up" (Gen. 7:11).

   Catastrophe ___ e. Fossils are found as billions of dead things buried in rock layers laid down by water all over the earth.

   Corruption ___ f. Mutations (chance changes in DNA and heredity following sin) have produced birth defects, diseases, disease organisms, and even death.

   Christ ___ g. Practicing biblical principles, medical doctors, and others can heal and set right things man's sin ruined in God's perfect creation.

   Creation ___ h. Just like it takes plan and purpose to combine non-flying parts together to make a flying airplane, it takes plan and purpose to put non-living molecules together to form a living cell.

4. When it goes beyond scientifically repeatable observation, creationists and evolutionists often view the same evidence differently. Associate the following with creationists (C), evolutionists (E), neither (N), or both (B):

   B a. In today's world there is tremendous variation within a species and a constant struggle for limited resources, so some varieties are more likely to survive than others — a fact usually called "survival of the fittest" or "natural selection."

   E b. Generally speaking, fossils show a net increase in variety and complexity over millions of years.

   B c. Most fossils begin to form under flood conditions, rapid burial under a heavy load of water-borne sediment.

   C d. Examining both living cells and arrowheads, scientists find evidence of order produced by properties of organization (mind), not by properties of matter.

   N e. Hardly anyone cares about when, where, and how life came into being, so we should not waste time in science class trying to study ideas about origins and history, such as creation and evolution.

Chapter 2

The Nature of Science

Did you ever dream of finding new life forms in a deep ocean trench, finding a cancer cure in a fungus growing high in the rainforest canopy, tracking down a murderer through a little DNA left at the crime scene, or designing the life support system for a long voyage into space? Those are all things scientists do. Their domain (area of interest) is the physical universe, and for biologists it's the living world. Their goal is to find patterns of order in nature so that they can make statements (theories) that predict the behavior of nature and allow people to control, influence, understand, or just enjoy the wonders of our world.

Science has made our lives better in so many ways that we sometimes think science can do anything. It can't. Scientific knowledge has progressed so dramatically largely because *science limits itself* to questions that can be objectively answered by repeatable and verifiable observations.

Like many other human activities, building concepts and theories in science begin with hunches, dreams, wishful thinking, educated guesses (hypotheses), serendipity (lucky accidents), or some subjective flash of insight. But the concept or theory earns the right to be called "scientific" if (and only if) it makes testable predictions that are verified by direct or indirect observations in the field or laboratory. And other scientists must repeat the tests and get the same results. That's the scientific method: an ever-widening cycle of subjective ideas tested objectively by repeated observations in the scientific community.

In science, majority vote doesn't count. The majority of scientists once believed leeches could suck bad diseases out of the blood, and George Washington died for that view. Fame doesn't count, either. Albert Einstein, Nobel Prize winner and the most famous scientist of the 20th century, once said that new evidence smashed one of his theories like a hammer blow. In science, it's not the popular or famous scientists or those who go along with the crowd who decide scientific truth; it's the scientist with the verifiable, observable evidence to support his/her hypothesis.

Albert Einstein

Objective tests based on observations and procedures that can be repeated by others are called empirical. For this reason, real science or scientific science — science

(and most do enthusiastically) with reaching the next best approximation of the truth.

Science progresses partly because certain kinds of questions are deliberately ignored. Scientists choose to leave to non-scientists vitally important questions of right and wrong, politics, art, and personal choice. Although science can help us understand issues in other areas, scientists acting as scientists cannot tell you what music to enjoy, who's the best person to be president, or whether another person is really in love with you.

Most science textbooks and teachers do a good job of explaining the nature, strengths, and limits of the scientific method. But the boundaries of science often get blurred when it comes to the origin and history of the cosmos and life on earth.

Using the methods of empirical science, scientists can tell us (in increasingly intricate detail) how living cells operate, but science cannot tell us how cells first originated. A scientist can explain how an automobile operates by means of controlled gasoline explosions moving pistons

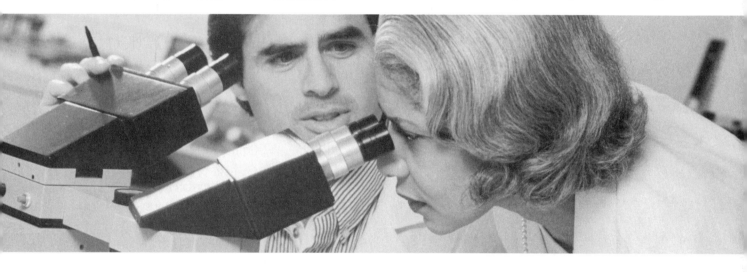

based on the scientific method — is called empirical science. In this book series, the word *science* will mean empirical science, unless otherwise noted.

Because it limits itself to empirical tests, empirical science has made tremendous progress. The works of Greek philosophers who wrote before Christ are still studied in colleges, as are the centuries-old writings of Shakespeare and the music of Mozart. But a science book written even 100 years ago seems almost comic compared to the progress that has been made.

Science progresses by continually discovering new information; however, the conclusions of science are always tentative. Absolute truth lies ever beyond the reach of scientific theories, and scientists must content themselves

up and down and the crankshaft, gears, and wheels round and round — but no scientist believes automobiles originated by the same mechanism (controlled explosions) that now operates them. An extraterrestrial scientist with no knowledge of coke, coffee, or American culture might never figure out the function of those numerous empty cylinders that flip into and out of view in our cars (those things we call "cup holders").

Even though it's just common sense, few biology textbooks make the important distinction between how life operates and how it originated. You may be a whiz at operating computer software, but you need different knowledge to know how computers originated and how to build one. A book is made *of* ink and paper; that does not

19

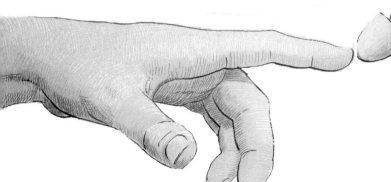

mean it was made *by* ink and paper. Similarly, a living cell is made *of* chemicals; that does not mean it was made *by* chemicals.

How do scientists know how life originated, then? They don't. Scientists are human beings, and science is a human endeavor. That means scientists are finite; they don't and can't know everything, and they definitely can't be sure — scientifically — what happened on earth before scientific records were kept. Many scientists believe chemicals evolved into life on earth; some scientists, such as Francis Crick (who shared the Nobel Prize for helping to discover DNA's structure), believe life was seeded here from outer space. Neither view is science; both are story lines or scenarios. Neither view is fact; both rest on faith.

Francis Crick

Many people believe science is based on fact, not faith. Empirical science does depend on repeatable, observable, objective facts far more than most any other approach to knowledge, but it takes a lot of faith to believe, as evolutionists do, that the laws of science have never changed (especially over presumed billions of years); to believe that no process ever happened faster or on a grander scale in the past than at present; or to believe that a three-pound (1.3 kg) chunk of mostly fat (the human brain) thrown together by time, chance, struggle, and death can come to the right conclusions about anything, including its own origin.

Discovering that science is based on assumptions accepted by faith does not mean there's anything wrong with it. People of many different backgrounds accept the basic assumptions of science: that there is order in the universe, that our senses are generally reliable, and that sensory input can be processed by the human brain to correctly comprehend that order. The Bible actually provides a firm basis for accepting the basic assumptions of science, and it's no surprise that science reached its highest expression in partnership with the Christian faith.

Form your foundation.

Without seeing either supernatural creative acts or assumed evolutionary events in the unrecorded past, scientists can compare the merits of creation vs. evolution by running repeatable, observable (empirical) tests on their predictions about patterns and processes in the present.

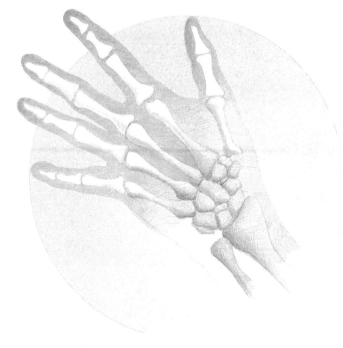

1. _Scientists_ don't just collect facts about nature; they are looking for patterns of order to make and to use _theories_ which are statements that predict the behavior of nature.

2. A theory can begin with a hunch, dream, wishful thinking, educated guesses, or blind luck, but a theory can be called scientific if and only if:

   a. most scientists agree with it.

   b. it contains no reference to God or design or anything that might be called religious.

   c. it is a proven fact.

   (d.) it is supported by observations and/or experiments made repeatedly by many scientists (and challenged by little or no contradictory evidence).

   e. all the above.

3. Mark the following true (T) or false (F):

   _T_ a. Observations suggest ideas (hypotheses and theories) which can be tested by experiments and further observation, and science proceeds as an ever-widening circle of observation — idea — observation . . . or experiment — theory — experiment. . . .

   _T_ b. A scientific theory can never be proven, although it can be disproven.

   _F_ c. Scientific method can be applied equally well to questions about both the origin and operation of living things.

   _F_ d. The practice of science requires no faith or assumptions, but just the facts.

   _T_ e. In science, one researcher with the evidence to support his/her theory overrules opinions of the majority of scientists.

   _F_ f. The only absolute truth is scientific truth.

4. Scientists have done so many wonderful things for mankind that we sometimes forget scientific method cannot answer all the questions we have. Mark the following questions as answerable by science (S) or not (N).

   _S_ a. Are antibiotics effective against the AIDS virus?

   _S_ b. Will long exposure to loud rock music damage nerves required for hearing?

   _N_ c. Is rock music superior to opera?

   _S_ d. Can runoff from ammonia and phosphate in fertilizer and detergent stimulate fish-killing algal blooms?

   _N_ e. Should families who use too much detergent be fined, put in jail, or sentenced to community service?

   _N_ f. Was the decline and fall of the Roman Empire caused by lead in its water pipes?

   _N_ g. Does he/she really love me?

5. Write one question you'd like to see scientists answer, and write one question important to you that scientists cannot answer.

   If evolutionists belive life came from a chemical reaction, How did the chemicals get in the water! Can you completely prove evolution?

Chapter **3**

Evolution vs. Science

Without a doubt, the greatest propaganda triumph in the last 150 years has been convincing much of the world that creation is religion and evolution is science. Nothing could be further from the truth! In the molecules-to-man sense, evolution is not science, never was science, never will be science, and never could be science.

Evolution is a belief about the past, a value system that puts human opinion above God's Word, a story purporting to describe a unique time-line of events by which evolution produced our galaxy, our sun and planet earth, life, sea creatures, land animals, apes, and man. Unless otherwise stated, "evolution" will be used in this book series to refer to, as most people think of it, the postulated molecules-to-man sequence often called macroevolution.

Science can investigate the recent past by using the scientific records of human observers and assuming scientific laws and processes have not changed. But evolutionists claim to go back much further than that, back before (they claim) there were any human observers, back to when conditions on earth (they assert) were quite different, back so far that assuming no change in scientific laws or process rates is either incorrect, unwise, or merely self-serving!

Evolution is certainly a bold belief with personal and global consequences that deserve serious study, but (apart from a time machine!) evolution never was, never will be, and never could be scientific. Evolution belongs to the domain of history and historical method, not of science and the empirical scientific method. Historical method involves gathering unique bits of data, weaving them into a time-line of events, and defending one's story against others to see if any can be subjectively established "beyond a reasonable doubt." For example, there are many historical theories for the fall of Rome and tons of evidence (writings, artifacts, etc.), yet we cannot rerun Roman history to see which theory is correct, as empirical science would require.

But don't fossils allow us to investigate the past scientifically? Well — *yes* and *no*. The description of a fossil, its possible identity, and its position relative to other fossil and mineral deposits can be studied scientifically — but its role in past events cannot be.

Consider the famous group of fossil dinosaur eggs discovered with the bones of a dinosaur spread out over them. The dinosaur was named *Oviraptor* ("egg eater") because it was thought to have been caught in the act of eating dinosaur eggs. That was the first story. The second story, now popular, is that the bones are those of a mother dinosaur trying desperately to save her eggs as all are engulfed in sudden burial. Same evidence, but two different stories about what happened in the unrecorded, unobserved past. How does a scientist decide which, if either, of these stories is true? A scientist can't. To reach a decision based on scientific method, one would need repeated observations of the behavior of partially known creatures now presumed extinct. To solve mysteries like these, we must turn from the methods of scientists to the methods of historians and lawyers.

Almost any story sounds good — as long as you hear only one side. Think about a murder trial. After the prosecuting attorney presents his/her case, the jury may think it's obvious the defendant is guilty. But then the defense attorney tells the rest of the story, bringing up other evidence and offering different explanations for the evidence already presented. Now each juror has to think it through. Has all the relevant evidence been presented? Which story explaining the evidence makes the most sense? What can be established "beyond a reasonable doubt"?

If evolution is such good science, students must wonder why it seeks legal protection from contrary evidence and contrasting views; why freedom of speech and academic freedom extend to neo-Nazis and the Ku Klux Klan but not to the science classroom; why award-winning science teachers have been fired just for discussing scientific challenges to evolution; why most science textbooks rigorously censor any view but evolution. The answer, of course, is that evolution is not science; it's a belief about the past used to justify certain values in the present and promote a particular philosophy about the future.

Evolution is a historical story line or scenario, not a scientific theory, but it still belongs in the science classroom. Why? There are several reasons. (1) Evolution does produce scientifically testable deductions (most of which, as we shall see, have been falsified). (2) The historical investigation of evolution involves scientific terminology and processes. (3) Discussion of evolution provides excellent opportunities (a) to explore the nature, strengths, and limits of science; (b) to distinguish fact from faith and assumptions and assertions from evidence; (c) to consider whether or not to base one's world and life view on creation or evolution; (d) to build bridges of understanding and respect for ideas from people with many different backgrounds; and (e) to help you make an informed choice on what to believe about your own ultimate origin and destiny, and why you believe it.

Evidence is very important in the study of origins, of course, but historians and lawyers use a *different kind* of evidence than the scientist uses. To decide a murder case, scientists would need to have the murder committed over and over again in the presence of qualified observers who would be expected to agree objectively on just what happened and who did it — empirical evidence. Historians and lawyers are usually "stuck" with circumstantial evidence — incomplete bits of information that can be subjectively interpreted in a variety of ways. In science, majority vote, popularity, and fame count for nothing; in history and law, majority vote, popularity, and fame all too often award the debate victory to the best storyteller, sometimes in spite of the evidence.

Because it's restricted to variable subjective interpretations of circumstantial evidence, evolution belongs to the domain of historical science, not empirical science. The difference is extremely important, since historical science cannot claim anywhere near the objectivity and degree of certainty that empirical science can. Comparing evolution with empirically testable theories like gravity or atomic theory is done either out of ignorance or in a deliberate attempt to bolster a weak idea by associating it with strong ones (a common propaganda technique).

Stories about what might have happened in the past are correctly and increasingly called scenarios or models. They should not be called scientific theories, since they cannot be tested empirically. However, hypotheses based on various scenarios or models may be scientifically testable. That's true of both the classic evolutionary scenario and the creation model of earth's history.

Models can also be used to suggest historical time-lines or scenarios, which can be tested using the methods employed by historians and lawyers. An origins model is a broad conceptual framework for interpretation, then designed to stimulate research directed toward a fuller understanding of the origin, history, and destiny of life and our universe.

The goal of an origins model is expansively philosophical; it's the discovery or assignment of meaning to existence. An origins model incorporates both historical and philosophic goals. The historian's goal is to properly reconstruct a unique chronology of events and to offer a plausible explanation for the flow of events that can be defended in terms of logical consistency and fit with the circumstantial evidence.

The goal of the scientist is quite different from that of either the philosopher or historian — the scientist is much more pragmatic. The scientist's goal is to make and to use theories, which, to the scientist, are empirical, testable statements that predict the behavior of nature under its present conditions. Although creation and evolution are primarily philosophic and historical models, both suggest numerous scientific hypotheses that can be empirically tested, and both offer scientific laws and evidence as key arguments for accepting the superiority of their different models!

In this *Creation Foundations* series, we will emphasize differences between creation and evolution models that are scientifically testable. But remember, both the creation and evolution models extend far beyond the domain and testability of science. Both extend into the realms of history and philosophy, where subjective interpretation, circumstantial evidence, and personal presuppositions play crucial roles. Origins, therefore, is a truly interdisciplinary study that offers superb opportunities to explore different ways of learning and knowing and to relate the search for knowledge with the search for meaning in powerfully personal, professional, and practical ways.

Consider the Search for Extra-Terrestrial Intelligence (SETI). Is SETI a philosophic, historical, or scientific endeavor, or some combination of these? The goals are clearly philosophic, relating to the meaning of existence. Some think SETI will prove the God of the Bible is no more than a minor, sub-planetary deity, not worthy of worship in the space age. Some hope SETI will provide the cure for cancer, the formula for world peace, and the fountain of eternal youth. Others are just curious, and think SETI is fun. Most involved in SETI subscribe to the big-bang view of cosmic history. They just assume life started "out there" and should be coming here; they don't even consider that life started here and may have been originally intended to move "out there." So, like the broader creation and evolution models, SETI involves all

three major approaches to knowledge: philosophic, historic, and scientific.

Science has not been kind to SETI. The suggestion that fossils of Martian life were found in a meteorite was disproved by scientific study. Science showed the first so-called "message" from outer space was the result of physical process, not extra-terrestrial intelligence. Scientific measurements of gravitational time dilation and the youthful appearance of so many cosmic structures have been used to support a biblical world view.

As a prelude to comparing their merits, let's review the creation and evolution models, then look at scientifically testable deductions and the philosophic/historical assumptions and assertions, contrasting their:

(1) historical time-lines,

(2) scientifically testable predictions, and

(3) philosophical implications, assertions, and assumptions.

Form your foundation.

Evolution is not science, never was science, never will be science, and never could be science. As a story about the past promoting human opinion above God's Word, evolution is really philosophic naturalism — "humanism dressed up in a lab coat," or "science falsely so called" (1 Tim. 6:20).

1. __C__ "Creation is religion; evolution is science." This often-repeated statement best represents the triumph of (choose one): (a) reason, (b) open-mindedness, (c) propaganda, (d) scientific method, (e) biblical interpretation, (f) constitutional law, (g) all the above.

2. As popular "molecules-to-man macroevolution," evolution is not science, never was science, never will be science, never could be science. Describe three aspects of empirical science that support this statement (then, if you disagree, give your reasons).

   a. Observability - almost nothing in evolution story line has Been Seen or recorded

   b. Domain - Evolutionists attempt to establish a time sequence, Scientist attempt to establish theories

   c. Goal - Scientist have Goals such as healing disease. Evolutionists want people to accept evolution - Not GoD

3. __E__ Scientific theories are defended by open discussions of evidence, but non-scientific evolutionary belief may be defended in American classrooms by (a) censoring opposing evidence, (b) threatening grades of students who oppose evolution, (c) intimidating teachers who allow open discussion, (d) using lawyers to enforce a false view of separating church and state, or (e) all of the above.

4. Explain differences between empirical vs. circumstantial evidence, and relate these to differences between methods used by scientists vs. historians.

   empirical- can be continuously, directly + repeatedly observed

   circumstantial evidence- tidbit of info. thought to be related

5. Evolution is a (philosophic/scientific/interdisciplinary) _____ study, which means the influence of world view is (greater than/less than/the same as) _____ the effect of world view in theories in empirical science.

6. cannot be tested
   Why is it wrong to compare the evolutionary scenario with gravitational or atomic theory? Why would anyone want to use such a false comparison?   can be tested

   propaganda technique

7. Even though molecules-to-man evolution is not empirical science, give three reasons (including reference to SETI) why creationist and evolutionist ideas and evidence about origins *should* be discussed in the science classroom.

   ① Both can be tested scientifically
   ② Free open Discussion about both Views promote understanding or change
   ③ SETI-proves that there is differences in patterns

Historical Time-lines

Classic Creationist Model

Before the Beginning — Before, during, and after time is the transcendent "I AM" (Exod. 3:14), the triune God eternally existent in three persons as the Father, the Lord God, Maker of heaven and earth; the Holy Spirit (Gen. 1:2, et al.); and the Son, Jesus the Christ, described thus in John 1:1–14:

In the beginning was the Word [divine plan, ultimate reason], and the Word was with God and the Word was God. The same was in the beginning with God. All things were made by him; and without him was not any thing made that was made. . . . And the Word was made flesh, and dwelt among us, (and we beheld his glory, the glory as of the only begotten of the Father), full of grace and truth.

Jesus is further described as the One "which is, and which was, and which is to come" (Rev. 1:8) and as the One "by [whom] all things consist [hold together]" (Col. 1:17).

With the interacting parts of His universe complete, God pronounced what He had created in six days "very good" (Gen. 1:31). There was no suffering, disease, violence, or death of sentient creatures (*nephesh*, in Hebrew); all animals and people were created to eat only plants.

Man and woman (Adam and Eve) were created supremely intelligent, "programmed" with language and many other skills, living in the Garden of Eden ("Delight"), talking daily with their Creator, and learning more about their duties as God's chief stewards, caretakers of His creation.

Corruption of Creation — Rejecting God's love and perfect provision, our first parents willfully ate the one fruit God told them not to, and their self-serving decision brought death, decline, and disaster. As the apostle Paul said, "The creature was made subject to vanity . . . [and] the bondage of corruption" (Rom. 8:20–21). The first person born (Cain) killed his brother (Abel); some animals, created as vegetarians, began to kill and eat other animals; thorns and thistles flourished, and cultivating beneficial plants became difficult.

Chapter 5

At the Beginning — "In the beginning God created the heaven and the earth" (Gen. 1:1). The first thing created was time, and during six days (like those we experience today), by means of special, completed, supernatural acts, the Lord God created from nothing beyond himself (*de novo* or *ex nihilo*; Hebrews 11:1–3) the universe with all its interdependent and interacting parts:

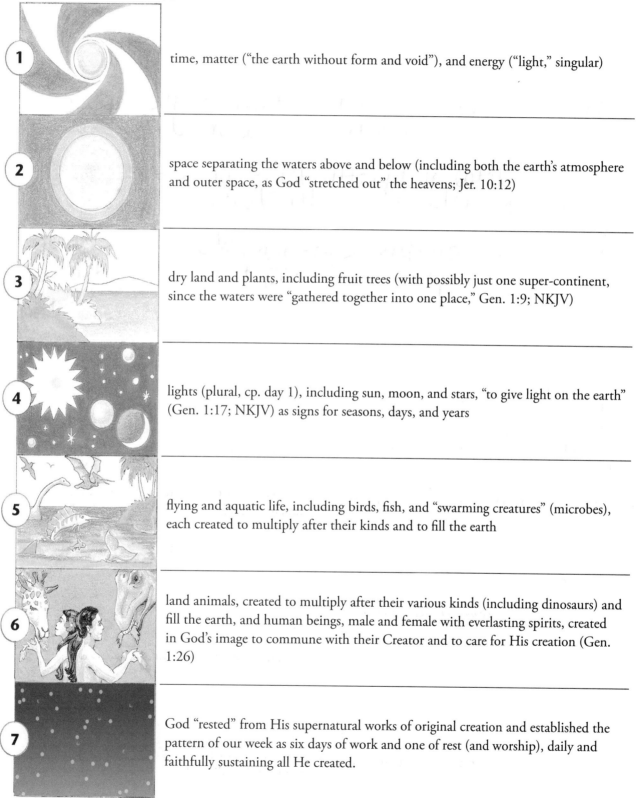

1 — time, matter ("the earth without form and void"), and energy ("light," singular)

2 — space separating the waters above and below (including both the earth's atmosphere and outer space, as God "stretched out" the heavens; Jer. 10:12)

3 — dry land and plants, including fruit trees (with possibly just one super-continent, since the waters were "gathered together into one place," Gen. 1:9; NKJV)

4 — lights (plural, cp. day 1), including sun, moon, and stars, "to give light on the earth" (Gen. 1:17; NKJV) as signs for seasons, days, and years

5 — flying and aquatic life, including birds, fish, and "swarming creatures" (microbes), each created to multiply after their kinds and to fill the earth

6 — land animals, created to multiply after their various kinds (including dinosaurs) and fill the earth, and human beings, male and female with everlasting spirits, created in God's image to commune with their Creator and to care for His creation (Gen. 1:26)

7 — God "rested" from His supernatural works of original creation and established the pattern of our week as six days of work and one of rest (and worship), daily and faithfully sustaining all He created.

However, even after the fall into sin brought what Darwin later called "the war of nature," people (and some animals like large dinosaurs?) lived to be over 900 years old. The post-Fall/pre-Flood world still had a mild climate pole to pole (maintained, perhaps, by a water vapor canopy and/or higher levels of CO_2). Spring-fed rivers and mist from an underground watering system brought minerals up to plant roots, encouraging lush vegetation to spread quickly over the land (perhaps then one super-continent). There was considerable ecological variety, but no vast deserts or ice sheets. There was much greater variation and larger sizes among pre-Flood groups of plants and animals. Mutations were much, much rarer than they are today, but they did probably begin to produce defects, disease, and disease organisms.

Although the post-Fall/pre-Flood world retained much of the created Edenic grandeur, "the earth also was corrupt before God, and the earth was filled with violence" (Gen. 6:11) at an accelerating rate; the violence may have threatened earth's survival, and it certainly "grieved [God] at his heart" (Gen. 6:6), and brought on the judgment of Noah's flood. Not willing that any should perish (2 Pet. 3:9), God let Noah preach repentance for 120 years (Gen. 6:3), and He would have spared the earth, as He spared Nineveh after Jonah's preaching, but the people did not turn back to God. So God destroyed that first world in a global flood, giving the earth a fresh start with Noah's family (eight people; 1 Pet. 3:28)

and two of every kind of land animal (seven of each "clean kind") that God brought to Noah on the ark (Gen. 7:2).

Catastrophe, Cool Down, and Confusion — The Flood began when "all the fountains of the great deep [were] broken up" (Gen. 7:11). Cataclysmic eruption of volcanoes would release tremendous quantities of pressurized, superheated water into the atmosphere ("juvenile water"). Scores of volcanoes went off simultaneously along what we now call the mid-Atlantic Ridge, perhaps initiating rapid continental separation (plate tectonics).

The waters continued to rise (and the land to sink) for 150 days (about five months; Gen. 7:24), until finally the waters covered the tops of the highest pre-Flood mountains (Gen. 7:19–20). First buried in greatest abundance by the eroding sediments were the heavy-shelled, slow-moving, bottom-dwelling sea creatures, but examples of all the major groups of sea creatures were buried with them in what have been later called Cambrian deposits. The sudden appearance of varied and highly complex sea life in the lowest known fossil-rich deposits has been called the Cambrian Explosion, but it does not record the sudden appearance of complex life (since life had been created earlier and had already multiplied and filled the earth); instead, the Cambrian records an explosion of disaster bringing death, destruction, and decline worldwide!

As the Flood waters continued to rise during a five-month period, their sediments successively buried near shore, lowland, the upland life, with fossils of sea creatures extending in some places through all the sedimentary layers, as water eventually covered the whole earth, as it had in the third day of the creation week. The ark could have floated over any point of earth without touching bottom (see Gen. 7:19–20).

Then the waters began to recede as God, repeating what He did on day 3, caused the mountains to rise and the valleys to sink down (Ps. 104:8). For another 150 days (five months) the waters drained off the newly rising continents into the sinking ocean basins (Gen. 8:3). Fossils of seashells and underwater pillow lava were raised to the highest peaks in the post-Flood world, the Himalayan Mountains. Much of the top layer of sediment, including remains of the upland environments that were most likely the chief pre-Flood habitat for mankind and flowering plants, were heavily eroded away.

The ark came to rest in a highland area now called the "Mountains of Ararat" (in eastern Turkey). As that

area dried out and vegetation grew up in the post-Flood soil, God opened the doors of the ark to the new post-Flood world. Fish trapped in draining pools of water and carrion (dead animals) provided food for animals that were, or would become, predators or scavengers, and God even told mankind (Noah's family) that, although they had been created vegetarian, they now could eat meat. That was a year and ten days (Gen. 7:11 and 8:13) after God had closed them up in the ark, over 1,600 years (from adding patriarchal ages) after mankind's sin had corrupted God's creation, and (from biblical and other historical records) about 4,500–5,000 years B.P. (Before Present, or "years ago").

The new post-Flood world was dramatically different, a marred reflection of pre-Flood conditions. Heavy rains washed minerals away from plant roots in the newly formed sedimentary soils, and there was no widespread underground watering system to bring minerals up to the roots as there once had been. In other areas, "rain shadows" of the higher post-Flood mountains produced vast desert areas where only patches of xeric (dry) habitats had once existed. Whatever radiation protection the pre-Flood world experienced (perhaps a vapor canopy and/or stronger magnetic field) declined substantially, allowing mutations to occur at much greater rates, quickly coming to visible expression in the initially small post-Flood populations. Disease, disease organisms, and various genetic defects spread rapidly, and mutations probably contributed significantly to declining life spans — dropping from 950 for Noah into the 800s, 600s, 400s, and 200s, until Moses finally writes (Ps. 90:10) that the average human life span is only 70–80 years.

The climate changed drastically. Seasons (annual variations in day length) were established at creation (Gen. 1:14), and there were patches of warmer and cooler and of wetter and drier environments in the pre-Flood world, especially with altitude and soil variation, but the overall temperature had been mild from pole to pole (with fossils of alligators and palm trees buried near both North and South Poles). A vapor canopy would have held in the earth's heat and perhaps doubled

atmospheric pressure. The higher atmospheric CO_2 levels for which plants are designed would have acted like the glass in a greenhouse to bottle up the sun's heat, keeping the whole earth warm. At the time of the Flood, a vapor canopy would have collapsed, and the CO_2 level would drop drastically (to its present 0.03 percent!) as carbon (in buried fossils, coal, oil, and limestone rock) was not recycled to the atmosphere.

The sudden drop in levels of greenhouse gases at the end of the Flood would have the effect of throwing off a blanket on a cold night. Land cools off much more quickly than water, so moisture evaporating abundantly from the warm oceans fell as snow at higher latitudes and altitudes, eventually producing sheets of ice (in places over

two miles deep) that covered 30 percent of the continental surface within perhaps 500 years after the Flood. Earth never fully recovered from the "Chill" or "Ice Age," since 10 percent of the earth's surface is still covered with ice. The extreme temperature differences, greater moisture variation, and higher mountains also helped to generate colossal storms, including super hurricanes or hypercanes, and ice and super storms produced considerable regional catastrophism that continued for several centuries after the worldwide catastrophe of the Flood itself.

Continental splitting, ice, and storms also influenced migration patterns followed by animals moving away from Ararat. The two continents hardest to reach, and the two with the most "unbalanced fauna" suggesting recent

migration, are South America and Australia. At first, human beings were reluctant to follow God's command to migrate, to multiply, and fill the earth again. Instead, they stayed together and built a huge tower, the Tower of Babel, to "reach unto heaven" (Gen. 11:4). So to force them to migrate outward, God did "confound the languages" (Gen. 11:9). This confusion produced many different "tribes and tongues and nations," but not different races. There's only one race, the human race, and we're all part of that one race (Acts 17:26)!

Christ and Coming Again — Just as that one race was subjected to disease, disaster, and death by the willful sin of its founders, Adam and Eve, so any human being can be restored to new life — rich, abundant, and everlasting — through Jesus Christ, God's only begotten Son, the "Last Adam," our Savior and Lord. By allowing himself to be born as a human being, living a sinless life for us, and laying down His life on the Cross, He paid the death penalty for sin we each deserve. But He rose from the dead and has prepared a place in heaven for any and all who believe, and He's coming again! Our present, fallen heaven and earth, or corrupted creation, will disappear suddenly with a "great noise" (2 Pet. 3:10; a "big bang" at the end of time). Then God will make a "new heavens and a new earth, wherein dwelleth righteousness" (2 Pet. 3:13). There, believers will have billions upon billions of years, a nearly infinite amount of time to explore an infinite amount of space to learn an infinite amount about the truly Infinite God who made us!

In the creation model, the "millions of years" are not in the past where they do us no good; they are in our future! And the "millions of years" are not filled with struggle and death; they are filled with unspeakable joy! "Even so, come, Lord Jesus" (Rev. 22:20).

Highlights with dates for the classic creationist historical time-line are given, alongside the classic evolutionist time-line, in Table 5.1.

Biblically, the sweep of history can be summarized in three generations:		
GENERATION	**DEGENERATION**	**REGENERATION**
Or as "Seven Cs," such as:		
Creation	**Corruption**	**Catastrophe**
Confusion	**CHRIST**	**Cross**
Consummation		

Classic Evolutionist Model

It's a commentary on our times, and a credit to evolution teaching through schools, museums, TV nature programs and magazines, national parks, etc., that the evolutionist's historical time-line is much better known by more people than the creationist's biblical time-line.

Before the Beginning — Before the beginning was absolutely nothing. The following words were emblazoned on the cover of *Discover* magazine for April 2002:

> **Where Did Everything Come From?** The universe burst into **something** from absolutely **nothing** — zero, nada. And as it got bigger, it became filled with even more stuff that came from absolutely **nowhere.** How is that possible? Ask Alan Guth. His theory of inflation helps **explain everything.**

At the Beginning — The universe began perhaps 8–16 billion years ago, when matter, energy, time, and space exploded into being in what's called the big bang. Radiation, then gas and dust, rushed outward in an awesome expansion reflected now in the red shift and cosmic background radiation. Under the relentless force of gravity, matter collected to form galaxies. Within those initial galactic clouds, stars began to shine. Around those stars, cooling clumps of matter collected to form planets.

Among the billions of planets that must have been formed in a manner like that, one is this tiny chunk of rock we call home, the Earth, one of the planets circling an average star (the sun) in one of the spiral arms far from the center of an average spiral galaxy (the Milky Way).

At its birth about 4½ (4.61) billion years ago, the earth was a hot, molten blob. Stupendous volcanic erup-

Table 5.1: Historical Time-lines

Creation Model
Before beginning
Eternal God, "I AM" and "Word"

Evolution Model
Before beginning
Nothing (or eternal matter)

Big Bang and Cosmic Evolution
About 8–16 billion years ago (B.P.): *"Explosion" produced time and expanding matter, energy, and space. Gravity produced galaxies, stars, and planets, including our solar system.*

Ancient Earth Formed
4.61 billion years ago: *Reducing atmosphere or methane (CH₄) and ammonia (NH₃) with no oxygen. Hot, with lots of volcanic action and lightning storms.*

Chemical Evolution
About 3.8 billion years ago: *Time, chance, and chemical combinations in the "primordial soup" produced the first life as self-reproducing proto-cells.*

Biological Evolution
Struggle for survival plus chance mutations produced survival of the fittest, or natural selection — time, chance, struggle, and death ("TCSD") produced an increasing variety of better adapted species.

Fossil Evidence
570 mya (million years ago): *"Cambrian explosion" — sudden appearance of abundant fossils of sea life following evolution of hard parts.*
470 mya: *First land plants and animals.*
220 mya: *first dinosaurs.*
65 mya: *Asteroid impact destroyed dinosaurs and allowed rapid "adaptive radiation of mammals."*
4.2 mya: *Apes evolved into people.*
about 100,000 years ago: *Modern mankind.*

The universe at about 10³⁴ seconds — ACTUAL SIZE
The universe burst into something from absolutely nothing. And as it got bigger, it became filled with even more stuff that came from absolutely nowhere.
Claim on cover of *Discover* magazine, April 2002

Creation
First 6 days, about 6,000 years ago: *Completed supernatural acts, established all parts of universe in harmonious working order ("all very good") during creation week:*
(1) time, matter, energy
(2) space
(3) dry land and plants
(5) aquatic life and birds to multiply after kind
(6) land life and mankind
(7) rest.

Corruption ("Fall"):
Mankind's sin brought suffering, disease, disaster, and death into God's perfect world.
Time, chance, struggle, and death (TCSD) (Darwin's "war of nature") began to ruin the design, beauty, and harmony God created.
Some animals, created vegetarian, began to kill and eat others.

Catastrophe: Flood and Fossils
About 4,500–5,000 years ago:
Brought on by violence and corruption that filled the earth.
Worldwide flood destroyed all land life, except those on the ark with Noah.
Produced worldwide layers of fossils deposited in 150 days.
(1) Early Flood: complex sea creatures
(2) Middle Flood: complex near shore and lowland life (and sea)
(3) Late Flood: upland life and man
(4) Erosion of upper layers as waters recede 150 days
(5) After 371 days in ark, people and animals free to multiply after kind and fill the earth (Cool Down Chill "Ice Age").
Build up of ice sheets, violent storms, and regional catastrophes followed Flood.

Confusion
Languages confused at Tower of Babel; disobedient people forced to migrate.

Christ
Conquered sin and death at the Cross, and was to bring new life.

Coming Again (Consummation)
New heavens and new earth at Christ's return, and everlasting life for all who believe.

Creation Model

Evolution Model

Future
Most species become extinct in 5 million years; will mankind?
Sun expands and earth will be destroyed.
Universe ends with Big Whimper (random scatter) or Big Crunch (another explosion).

tions finally released enough water to cool and cover its surface. Lightning flashed back and forth in a strange reducing atmosphere of methane (CH_4) and ammonia (NH_3), producing amino acids, sugars, and other pre-biological molecules that rained down into the ancient lifeless oceans, forming a "primordial soup."

It was perhaps two billion years before finally, just by chance, a group of molecules got together that could reproduce, and life on earth began. As the experiments of Miller, Fox, and others have shown, the origin of life was a purely chemical process, called chemical evolution. Nothing supernatural appears to have been involved, but only time, chance, and the properties of matter. Mars should have produced life even before the earth did, and we can be sure that there are countless other worlds in our galaxy and beyond populated with beings in several states of evolution, some much further advanced than ours.

The first simple life forms to evolve on earth may well have been the blue-green algae, also called cyanobacteria, that built layered structures, called stromatolites, preserved in rocks in Western Australia that may be 3.8 billion years old. It is likely that earlier, non-fossilized, soft-bodied proto-cells survived by feeding, animal-like, on the primordial soup. But plants evolved the ability, called photosynthesis, to harness sunlight energy to make food and to release oxygen (O_2) into the atmosphere, and the oxygen revolution provided much more energy for evolution.

As the earth began to fill with life forms, two new players appeared in the unfolding drama of evolution: (1) the struggle for survival based on competition for limited resources, and (2) hereditary variation based on imperfect copying of the newly evolved molecule of heredity, DNA, and on continuing changes, called mutations, occurring in the hereditary code. It would be over three billion years before evolution would finally produce a creature that could understand the evolutionary process that brought all microbes, plants, and animals, including people, into being.

In 1859 Charles Darwin published the book, *Origin of Species,* which first explained in scientific detail how (1) the struggle for survival acting on (2) hereditary variation would produce a ceaseless, gradually progressive (3) survival of the fittest. He summarized his three-part theory, called natural selection, with these words:

"Thus, from the war of nature, from famine and death, the production of higher animals directly follows."

Early forms of evolving life were soft-bodied and only occasionally left fossil remains. But about 530 million years ago, several quite different animal groups evolved members with hard parts, producing a sudden dramatic surge in fossil preservation, the so-called "Cambrian Explosion."

The first organisms fossilized were only sea creatures, but about 400 million years ago, land plants and animals first appeared in the evolutionary sequence. About 220 million years ago, the first abundant fossil, the trilobite, became extinct, and the famous dinosaurs first appeared on land. Dinosaurs ruled the earth for over 150 million years, until they were destroyed — along with a high

Archaeopteryx

percentage of all earth species — by an asteroid that hit the earth about 65 million years ago.

During the "Age of Dinosaurs" (the Mesozoic Era), two new kinds of creatures had evolved from reptile stock: birds and mammals. *Archaeopteryx,* a reptile-bird found in 1860, was the first so-called "missing link" to be found, and its features showed how dinosaurs evolved into birds. Further evidence for the dinosaur/bird transition is presently being uncovered in China. Another important series of fossils show how other reptiles gradually evolved into mammal-like reptiles and then into full-fledged mammals, including the platypus as an egg-laying reminder of the mammal's reptilian past.

When the asteroid wiped out their dinosaurian competition, the few surviving birds and mammals rapidly evolved to fill the void. As a stupendous example of adaptive radiation, the small, shrew-like, insect-eating mammals living with dinosaurs 65 million years ago evolved within perhaps five million years, a blink of the eye in "geologic time," into flying bats, swimming whales, burrowing moles, climbing squirrels, giant elephants, and running horses. The best-documented examples of mammalian evolution are (1) the transition from land animals to walking whales to swimming whales, and (2) the gradual change from small "horses" with many hooves and a short face with browsing teeth to today's large horse with one hoof per foot and a long face with grazing teeth!

Somewhere between 2 and 5 million years ago, a group of chimpanzee-like apes in Africa produced mutant forms that began to walk upright. Bipedal gait freed the hands to use tools, and tool-using favored selection for larger brain sizes. The fossil called "Lucy" (*Australopithecus afarensis*) shows an early stage in this ape-to-man evolutionary scenario. DNA studies show that the various races of modern human beings (*Homo sapiens*) still have about 98 percent of their DNA in common with chimps (and a few international organizations think that chimps, and perhaps orangutans also, should be offered the same civil rights as human beings).

Mankind is the first species on earth that can look back over the history of its own evolutionary development. It's a humbling experience. If all of earth's 4.6 billion years were condensed into a movie that would run for one year, mankind would not appear until one second before midnight on the last day of the year! We are certainly not the center of the universe, and we have not yet proven ourselves as fit to survive as the dinosaurs. Indeed, it seems few species survive longer than 5 million years; extinction is the rule, and that may well apply to mankind. Beyond that, the sun will expand and incinerate all life on earth. The universe itself will end in oblivion, with either a "Big Whimper" that leaves only scattered, random chaotic motion or a "Big Crunch" if gravity pulls matter back together for another explosion.

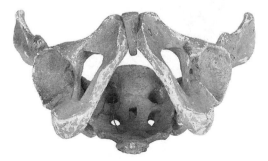

Until the final end, however, we have a responsibility to understand ourselves and our world. We must recognize that greed and a "me first" urge are built into people, not because of "sin" against some god who must be appeased, but because of the ceaseless struggle for survival that brought us into being. We can and must learn to redirect those instincts toward preservation of our species and of others on which our fragile lives depend. There is no god beyond our own imagination to help us, but we are beginning to take control of that molecule of heredity, DNA. And we're listening to, and reaching for, the stars. There is simply no limit to what mankind can do, as science continues to unlock the mysteries of life and to pave the way for a brave new world of our own making. Let's reach for the stars together. as we all continue to evolve. (See Table 5.1 for creationist vs. evolutionist time-lines.)

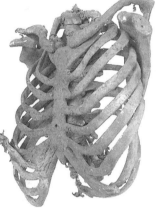

Form your foundation.

Different time-lines are built on different foundations.

Building on belief that today's natural processes have always acted very slowly, evolutionists imagine millions of years of struggle and death changing a few simple life forms into more complex and varied ones — until death finally wins.	Building on the Bible as the eyewitness record of earth's 6,000-year history, creation scientists relate design to God's perfect creation in six days about 6,000 years ago, struggle and death to man's sin, fossils to the worldwide flood, and restoration to Christ — life wins!

Bonus Project

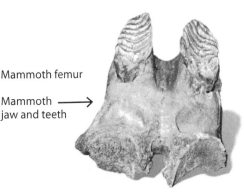

Mammoth femur

Mammoth jaw and teeth

Dr. and Mrs. Parker helped to excavate fossils of a mammoth family a mile up the Peace River from their Creation Adventures Museum in Arcadia, Florida, and replicas of the lower jaw, tusk, and femur of the young mammoth are on display there.

A. Think of at least five questions about these mammoth fossils that could be answered by the methods of empirical science — and three that could not be.

B. Think up examples of circumstantial evidences a "paleo-historian" might hope to find to weave a story about why and how the mammoth family died — then offer a different story to explain the same evidence.

C. Give examples of four points about the mammoth fossils on which you expect creationists and evolutionists to agree, and two on which you expect them to disagree.

1. To indicate His eternal nature as the One who is, always was, and always will be, God told Moses to call God by the name ___I AM___ (Exod. 3:14).

2. What person is described in the Bible as (a) the Word who was with God in the beginning, (b) the God who became flesh and dwelt among us, and (c) the One who was, who is, and who is to come? ___Jesus___ (See John 1:1, 1:14, and Rev. 4:4.)

3. Cite the day of the creation week (1 to 6) on which each of the following were created:

   __4__ a. sun, moon, stars   __5__ c. sea life and birds   __2__ e. atmosphere and space

   __3__ b. dry land and plants __1__ d. time, matter, light   __6__ f. land animals and man

4. List in order the "seven Cs" of biblical earth history, then match each with a description at right:

   __Creation__ __4__ a. the "Ice Age" begins

   __Corruption__ __5__ b. Tower of Babel; language groups begin

   __Catastrophe__ __2__ c. struggle and death begin

   __Confusion__ __6__ d. death conquered; Cross and Resurrection

   __Christ__ __1__ e. marriage begins in perfect environment

   __Consumation__ __3__ f. Noah's flood

   _____ __7__ g. new heavens and new earth

5. first dinosaurs   first fruits   first stars

   first birds   first death   first continent

Leaving out "first," list the six things above in the order of their appearance in history — according to:

creation ___Continent, fruits, stars, birds, dinosaurs, death___

evolution ___stars, continent, death, dinosaurs, birds, fruits___

6. Associate the paired completions below with either creation or evolution:

	Creation	Evolution
a. The war of nature, struggle, and death make things (better/worse).	Worse	better
b. The "big bang" in the universe comes at the (beginning/end) and produces (order/disorder).	end disorder	beginning order
c. Mutations produce defects and disease (and also/but never) new and improved kinds of genes.	but never	and also
d. Living things are (put together/torn apart) by random chemical reactions.	torn apart	put together
e. The sequence of fossils in the geologic column (1) show (simple/complex) beginnings with the "Cambrian Explosion";	complex	simple
(2) progress from (simple to complex/sea to land);	sea + land	simple + complex
(3) formed in about (1/500,000,000) year(s).	1	500,000,000
f. "Missing links" are (always disproven/sometimes found).	always disproven	sometimes found
g. Mankind's selfishness and greed result from (sin against God/struggle for survival).	sin against God	struggle for survival
h. Billions of years lie in the (past/future) and are filled with (struggle and death/new and everlasting life).	future new everlasting life	past struggle for death

Scientifically Testable Predictions

Creationists and evolutionists certainly have radically different concepts of earth's history and the time-line of events! Were there billions of years of struggle and death before man's existence, or are the billions of years in the future for mankind's exploration of God's restored creation? Are fossils mostly a few thousand years old, largely buried during the year of Noah's flood, or are they millions of years old, representing stages in evolution? Does Darwin's war of nature (time, chance, struggle, and death) make things worse or better?

The creation and evolution models involve elements of history and philosophy that lie beyond the reach of science, but both also make predictions about the kinds of evidence found in our world that can be tested by repeatable observation and the methods of empirical science. Table 6.1 contrasts scientifically testable predictions deduced from creation vs. evolution models in several categories.

Most of this *Creation Foundations* series will be concerned with scientific study of contrasting creationist and evolutionist hypotheses, those in Table 6.1 and many more. As you look over Table 6.1, please note one astonishing thing: Both creationists and evolutionists want to use observations of the same facts (observations) to support their radically different concepts! In biology, both sides look at the evidence from DNA, the laws of heredity, systematics, and human variation. In paleontology, they offer different scientifically testable explanations for the same fossils and rock layers — and for the same geologic processes and astronomical observations! (Author's note: If predictions of the creation and evolution models were compared side by side in high school science classes, over 90 percent of the time would be spent presenting and learning evidences [features and processes] both sides share — and a landmark educational study done by R.B. Bliss shows students will learn evolution better if it's contrasted with creation than if it's taught as just a dusty collection of "facts" to memorize.)

How can that be? How can such different concepts be built from the same evidence? You've heard the old saying, "The facts speak for themselves." Nothing could be further from the truth! Facts don't say anything. In science, facts are just features or processes that can be repeatedly observed and on whose description observers agree. What the facts mean — that's another story.

Scientists are not just fact collectors; they're thinkers. They're looking for patterns of order in their observations, hoping to make and/or use theories that will correctly predict the behavior of nature, or at least infuse it with some sort of meaning. That's terrific, and that's scientific. But when the goal involves reconstruction of a historical time-line, and the evidence shifts from empirically observable in the present to historical and circumstantial, then the scientist — just as every other human being — needs to consciously be aware of his or her philosophic presuppositions, his or her basic assumptions and assertions, and their implications and applications.

Philosophic Presuppositions: Assumptions, Assertions, and Implications

As the prosecutor weaves a story about the facts in evidence, it's obvious the defendant is guilty — until a defense attorney tells a different story about the same evidence. Or suppose you've known the defendant well for a long time. The tight web of evidence that seems to convict your friend only convinces you that she has been cleverly framed. "Knowing in your heart" that your friend is innocent, you look for other evidence or for different ways to interpret the evidence at hand.

In a creation/evolution debate, an Australian atheist once said that even if Noah's ark were found, even if the ark were placed in his backyard, that would only prove the Hebrews were clever at making up stories and perpetrating hoaxes. The atheist was 100 percent prejudiced. He already "knew in his heart" that the idea of God was only a myth and that the

story of Noah's ark was only a fairy tale. No matter how much evidence for the existence of God or for Noah's ark was presented, he would always try to find other evidence or a way to explain away the evidence at hand.

Similarly, a Christian who "knows Jesus in his/her heart" is sure the Bible is true. When "evidence" (more often an assertion or popular opinion) is contrary to what the Bible teaches, the Christian tries to find, or asks a more knowledgeable Christian, whether or not the alleged evidence really is factual, and, if so, what it might mean in biblical perspective.

In short, every person who begins to look at questions of origin comes to the evidence already starting, consciously or not, with certain basic life assumptions or presuppositions, a paradigm or world view. That's simply part of being human, and finite, and it should cause people to respect and tolerate each other. Perhaps the only bad or dishonest assumption is the assumption that you're not making any assumptions, which is demonstrably false. The question, then, is not whether presuppositions are at work in you before you look at the evidence; the question is, rather, what presuppositions are the best and why?

What roles, then, do logic, experience, and evidence play in our personal world view? The happiest people (most "blessed," to use the biblical term), it seems, are

Table 6.1: Scientifically Testable Predictions

Creation Model	Evolution Model
A. Biology	
1. DNA and the genetic code will have the kind of design that logically implies plan, purpose, and acts of creation.	1. DNA and the genetic code will have the kind of pattern produced by time, chance, and the chemical properties of matter.
2. Biological processes will limit recombination, mutation, and selection to "sideways" variation within kind and to "downhill" changes (defects, disease, and disease organisms).	2. Mutation and natural selection will produce limitless genetic expansion, sufficient to transform one or a few products of chemical evolution into all forms of life today.
3. Complete and complex traits will be distributed in a mosaic pattern reflecting creation according to a common plan.	3. Traits and partial traits will be distributed along branching lines of descent reflecting evolution from a common ancestor.
4. All human variation could develop from two people within the past 6,000 years, and there is only one race, the human race.	4. Fossils will show human beings evolved from ape-like ancestors within the past 2–5 million years, and the various races may have evolved at different rates in different places.
B. Paleontology (Fossils)	
Fossils in each group will show . . .	**Fossils will show . . .**
1. Initial complexity	1. Initial simplicity
2. Disease, death, and decline in variety and size	2. A steady increase in variety within and among groups
3. Rapid burial on a large scale	3. Burial by local floods and small-scale events like those we see today
4. Mass extinction	4. Steady replacement of less fit forms with those more fit
5. Persistence of criteria for classification	5. Blurring of modem distinctions in classification
6. Sharper boundaries between kinds, with "missing links" not found	6. Finding more and more "missing links" to document evolutionary transition
7. Sequence of eco-sedimentary zones representing stages of burial during the year of Noah's flood	7. Sequence of time zones representing evolution from a few simple life forms to many complex life forms
8. Index fossils that lived in restricted pre-Flood environments	8. Index fossils that lived in restricted evolutionary time periods
C. Geology	
Studies of geologic features and processes will show . . .	**Studies of geologic features and processes will show . . .**
1. Most land forms are relics of a tremendous burst of energy in the past, now changing only by processes that could not produce them.	1. Land forms from the past can be explained by the same slow and gradual processes occurring today.
2. Both coal and oil deposits formed rapidly and recently in globally cataclysmic processes.	2. Both coal and oil deposits were formed by gradual processes occurring over millions of years.
3. Splitting of the continent was initially very rapid and plates are now slowly skidding to a stop.	3. Splitting of the continents has been occurring slowly and steadily, about 1–2 cm/year, over the past 200 million years.
4. The Grand Canyon formed rapidly and recently as a "breached dam."	4. The Grand Canyon was produced slowly over millions of years by river erosion.
5. The "Ice Age" was initiated by a sudden global catastrophe that left the earth with warm oceans and cold continents, an unstable condition now abated.	5. The most recent Ice Age began about one million years ago, and ice advanced and retreated with gradual climate changes.
6. The vast majority of global processes that could date the earth will indicate a young maximum age.	6. Radiometric dating will indicate fossil deposits are millions of years old, dinosaurs became extinct 65 million years ago, and the earth is billions of years old.

D. Astronomy	
1. Studies of other planets in our solar system will highlight how unique the earth is, and contradict the big bang theory.	1. Studies of our solar system will suggest many stars have planets, many with life, and that the earth is nothing cosmically special.
2. Clusters of stars and galaxies, spiral galaxies, and gravitational time dilation will suggest a universe that is big but young.	2. The red shift, cosmic background radiation, and the time it takes light to reach earth from distant galaxies will suggest a very old universe.

E. Laws of Science	
1. Information theory will show that formation of the genetic code required outside intelligence.	1. Chaos theory will show that order can arise from pure chance.
2. The second law of thermodynamics will show the universe could not have made itself, since there would be no energy source outside the system.	2. The second law of thermodynamics will show that the sun has supplied the energy for the evolution of life on earth.

those whose world view, logic, experiences, and evidences are all in agreement. Evidence can never force a person to change his/her world view, but evidence (and logic and experience) can encourage a person to rethink his/her basic beliefs. In Christian terms, evidence can be used as a witnessing tool to encourage someone to reexamine his/her basic beliefs; but it's the Holy Spirit's job (somehow operating in conjunction with our responsibility) to convict and convert.

This *Creation Foundations* series could be studied by both Christians and those not yet Christians. Creationist speakers have often seen Christians bursting with joy as they see how the evidences from God's world fit so neatly with the truths of God's Word, bringing their presuppositions, evidence, logic, and experience into exhilarating harmony. Many scientists (myself included) remember when they were evolutionists fighting long battles over lots of evidence until somehow, mysteriously and miraculously, a change in perspective fit all that evidence into a new pattern — one pointing away from millions of years of struggle and death until death wins, to one pointing toward new life in Christ!

There is a battle for the mind going on. But the weapons in the battle for the mind (and heart) need not be barbaric; they need not be weapons of power meant to cut down, but weapons of persuasion meant to build up. The battle for the soul is not won by crushing the enemy, but by building up your opponents until perhaps — for their own good reasons — they willingly join your side, ultimately God's side: the God who made them, who loved them while they were yet sinners, and who restores them to full fellowship with Him in new life, rich and abundant and everlasting.

How should such a "battle of persuasion" be waged? By treating each person with respect, looking freely at all the evidence available, people sharing what they believe and why they believe it. As the apostle Peter put it, we should "be ready always to give an answer to every man that asketh [us] a reason of the hope that is in [us] with meekness and fear" (1 Pet. 3:15).

If creationists win the debate over public education, we'll have *two winners*, because evolutionists will also win. Evolutionists will still be able to present all their evidences, but they'll hear the "rest of the scientific story," too. *Open discussion of all the relevant evidence in an atmosphere of mutual respect — isn't that what good science and good education is all about?*

As we look more deeply into the contrasting historical time-lines and differing scientific predictions of creationists and evolutionists, you will come face-to-face with their strikingly different presuppositions or world views. As you read over the contrasting philosophic assumptions and implications in Table 6.2, think about how you would answer the questions now — then come back to answer them again after you complete this series.

Form your foundation.

Creation and evolution both require assumptions and faith far beyond what human beings can directly observe. But both also make predictions about the present that can be tested by empirical science. Good science and good education demand respectful discussion of all evidence and willingness to listen to others.

Table 6.2:

Creation Model	Evolution Model

ASSUMPTIONS

1. Where's the best place to begin studying the origin of the world, life, and humankind?

The best beginning is the Word of God, the Bible, the infallible, eyewitness record of the acts of God in history from before the beginning to after the end. The Bible's truths are absolute and never-changing, a firm foundation.	The only place to begin is with the words of man, human opinion, since there is no higher authority. Humans are fallible and finite, so "truth" is relative and ever-changing, but there's no other option.

2. What's the basis for science, and what role does it play in the study of origins?

Science is based on two assumptions, both based on the Bible: (1) the universe is orderly, and (2) the human mind can understand that order. Science is best for learning the operation of nature and applying that knowledge, but science can also test some ideas about origins.	By requiring that ideas be tested by repeatable observations, science provides a system of checks and balances that limit the extremes of human opinion. Although science cannot deal directly with origins, only naturalistic beliefs that exclude the supernatural should be called "scientific."

ASSERTIONS

1. How did the universe (time, matter, energy, space) originate?

The eternal, transcendent God whose name is I AM made the universe from nothing (*de novo* or *ex nihilo*).	Everything came from absolutely nothing, or the universe made itself by a "big bang" in eternal matter.

2. How did life originate?

With plan and purpose, God gave chemicals He had created (e.g., "dust of the ground") special properties of organization that do not derive from nor reduce to properties of matter (somewhat like people made in their Creator's image can give the organizational property of flying to non-flying parts in a 747).	Thanks to time, chance, and the natural chemical properties of matter, random collisions among molecules continued for millions of years until finally a group of molecules got together that could reproduce, and life began — and began Darwin's "war of nature" as reproductive variants struggled for nutrients.

3. How did fossils originate, and what do they show?

Most fossils are the remains of created life forms subjected to Darwinian struggle and death by man's sin and buried during the year of Noah's flood (about 5,000 years ago) in a sequence generally from complex and varied sea bottom life through near shore and lowland life to complex and varied upland life.	Fossils form best under flood conditions, and many small floods over millions of years preserved fossils showing a general increase in variety and complexity, occasionally recording evolutionary links from one species to another.

4. How did human life originate?

Created in a loving relationship and given charge of earth as a Garden of Delight (Eden), people were created in God's image, creative and with free moral choice. All of us are descendants of Adam and Eve, so there's just one race, the human race. Unfortunately, we followed our first parents into sins of selfishness and arrogance, but, praise God, all can be forgiven and we can receive new life in Christ!	Human beings evolved as a result of struggle and death among their ape-like ancestors, beginning with "Lucy." Different races may represent different stages in evolution. The harmful things people do to one another result from the "war of nature" that brought us into being (not from "sin"), and only human reason (not "god") can save us from our animal instincts.

IMPLICATIONS

1. What value is there to human life?

Each person has an absolutely unique place in God's plan, and we can and should help each other become all we can be in Christ.	Tempered by "enlightened self-interest," competition is the rule, and the only absolute values are winning or losing the struggle for survival.

2. What does the future hold?

Christ conquered sin that brought death at the Cross, and His Coming again will bring a new heaven and earth and new life with endless billions of years of bliss for His followers: life wins!	Darwin's "war of nature" continues ceaselessly, replacing old species — even mankind — with new ones, until finally the sun and stars burn out and even the universe dies: death wins.

Building Inspection

1. "Since it tests ideas against repeatedly observable evidences and processes, science is a great way to learn about nature." With this concept of science in mind, mark the following true (T) or false (F):

___ a. Love and respect for science as an excellent tool for studying nature is an enthusiasm shared by both creationists and evolutionists.

___ b. Both creationists and evolutionists make statements about nature that they explain and defend using evidences and processes in biology, paleontology, geology, astronomy, and other sciences.

___ c. If creation and evolution were openly compared in science classrooms, most of the time would be spent discussing (and learning about) scientific evidences and processes.

___ d. Science works just as well with circumstantial evidence about past origins as it does with empirical evidence about present operations in nature.

___ e. Science is not influenced by a person's basic beliefs or world view, because scientists just let the "facts speak for themselves."

2. Since both creationists and evolutionists are looking at the same scientific evidences in the present, why do they come to such different conclusions about what happened in earth's past?

_____

_____

3. On what basic assumptions about science and nature do creationists and evolutionists agree? . . . disagree?

_____

_____

4. Where does "God" fit in the classic evolutionist's view?

_____

_____

5. According to the classic creationist, what global acts of God in earth history must be taken into account to understand scientific evidences and processes in the present?

_____

_____

6. Classic creationists and evolutionists agree that absolute truth lies beyond the reach of finite and fallible mankind, but creationists believe the absolute truth that sets people free from the limits of space, time, and culture can be found _____.

7. The "weapons" for waging the "War of the World Views" should be (a) lawyers and courts, (b) majority opinion, (c) censorship, (d) persuasion, (e) propaganda, (f) all of the above. _____

8. How can there be "two winners" in the "War of the World Views"?

_____

_____

9. Think about the contrasting "Assumptions, Assertions, and Implications" in Table 6.2, then mark your present preference for C or E (classic creation or evolution) — then come back after completing this book to see if your choices changed._____

Chapter
6

Unit 2: Dinosaurs!

DINOSAURS! Few things are more exciting to children than dinosaurs! Children watch dinosaurs on TV, eat cookies shaped like dinosaurs, play with dinosaur molds (even robotic ones), play dinosaur video games, and go to movies about dinosaurs. Adults flock to movies about dinosaurs, too. Whether consciously or not, many adults act as if understanding dinosaurs is the key to understanding the origin, history, and destiny of life on earth.

Surprisingly, scientists didn't get interested in the study of dinosaurs until the 1800s — the same century in which the modern evolutionary belief began to take shape. In the early 1800s, the lawyer Lyell proposed uniformitarian belief as a way to stretch earth's history beyond the biblical "time limit." In 1859, Darwin offered natural selection, "the war of nature, famine, and death," to explain all appearance of design without a Designer, and in 1871, he began to interpret human "races" as stages in evolution. The latter 1800s saw the "dinosaur wars," an intense (and not always fair or friendly) competition for fame among scientists (especially Marsh and Cope) to find dinosaur fossils and fill their museums with reconstructions to tantalize the public and titillate the media.

For evolutionists (and even some Christians), discovery of fossil dinosaurs meant the end of taking the Bible literally. If God had created such awesome creatures, how could the Bible fail to mention them? Or how could a caring Creator allow such magnificent animals to go extinct? Most importantly for evolutionists, dinosaur fossils "proved" there were millions of years of struggle and death before some mythical Adam's sin brought death into God's "perfect world" and necessitated the death and mythical resurrection of a Jewish teacher called Jesus. Dinosaurs seemed to provide such powerful support for evolution that a few Christians began to believe (incorrectly) that dinosaurs were all fakes, or maybe bones put in the ground by Satan to test the Christian's faith!

In the face of widespread belief that dinosaurs disprove the Bible, what's the faithful Christian to do?

Dinosaurs, Creation, and the Fall

Actually, if you only knew what the Bible says about dinosaurs, you would know more about dinosaurs than many who have spent years collecting bits and pieces of dinosaur fossils, trying to figure out what they mean.

The word *dinosaur* itself is not in the Bible, simply because that word wasn't made up until 1841; the Bible was written and translated into English long before that! Even though the word *dinosaur* is not in the Bible, however, there are creatures whose descriptions match those of known kinds of dinosaurs. The best known of these is behemoth, described in Job 40:15–24.

Job is famous as the person who endured the most extreme of all suffering without turning away from God. But he did cry out to speak with God, to plead his case. God answered Job out of a whirlwind. To contrast himself as Creator with Job as creature, God recounted many of the wonders of creation: the stars he calls by name, the wild horse, ostrich, and other familiar animals. But then, beginning in Job 40:15, God described an animal "chief of the ways of God" (i.e., the land creature most awesome in size). Job knew the creature well, but the translators didn't know what it was, so they just made its Hebrew name pronounceable in English: "behemoth."

The Bible tells us behemoth had bones like tubes of bronze or rods of iron; its strength was in the muscles of its belly; it could hold its mouth against the mighty Jordon River at flood stage; and it had a tail like a cedar tree (a symbol of strength throughout Scripture).

Some modern "translations" (and at least a couple of television quiz shows) claim behemoth is a hippopotamus. A hippo does have an interesting tail (a manure-spreading propeller), but it is nothing at all like a cedar tree! Some say behemoth is an elephant, but an elephant's tail is more like a rope or reed than a cedar.

There is an animal known to us now, however, that was not known to the first Bible translators: a "long-neck" sauropod dinosaur, such as *Diplodocus*, *Apatosaurus*, or *Brachiosaurus* (including *Ultrasaurus* and *Seismosaurus*). A dinosaur such as one of these does have a tail like the thick trunk of a cedar tree! Hippos and elephants flee a flooding river, but these sauropod dinosaurs would not have to! The name *Diplodocus* means "double beam"; its strength was literally in "the [muscles] of its belly" (Job 40:16), so that it could move its long head and neck on one end and its long tail on the other. Once again, it looks as if scientists have only discovered recently (the late 1800s) what those who accepted God's Word, the Bible, would have known a few thousand years earlier!

And there's more. If the man named Job recognized a behemoth dinosaur as easily as he recognized a wild horse or ostrich, that means mankind and dinosaurs once lived together! Evolutionists find that outrageous, because they believe (and assert over and over and over again through textbooks, television, magazines, and museums) that dinosaurs died out 65 million years ago. Partly because of the success of evolutionary propaganda, even some Christians find it hard to believe dinosaurs could have been created with mankind on day 6. After all, wouldn't such "terrible lizards" just step on people or eat them up?

In my dinosaur talk, I like to hold up a plastic 16-inch (40 cm) sauropod and then ask the audience how many believe it's a life-sized model of the mighty behemoth dinosaur that once stalked the earth. Few, if any, raise their hands. Then I tell them that it is a life-sized model of a dinosaur — when it first hatched out of its egg!

Thanks to evolutionary propaganda, most people just assume dinosaurs are huge monsters. But behemoth dinosaurs like *Diplodocus* hatched out of eggs.

None of the dinosaur eggs yet found are larger than a football, and most are much smaller. In fact, dinosaur eggs found in Argentina show a behemoth dinosaur would be almost exactly the size of my model when they first hatched. Imagine that! Even though a long-neck sauropod might eventually grow over 100 feet (30 m) long and weigh over 50 tons, when it first hatched, a child could hold it, pet it, even put a string around its neck and take it for a walk in the park!

According to the fossil evidence, some dinosaurs grew

None of the dinosaur eggs yet found is larger than a football, and most are much smaller.

47

had huge jaws and big teeth with serrated edges, and the baby probably had impressive teeth, too.

But do sharply pointed teeth with cutting edges belong only to vicious predators that kill live animals and eat them? Absolutely not! Look at the close-up picture of a fruit bat's face below. Notice the sharp, recurved, cutting teeth in the fox-like face. A March 1983 issue of *National Geographic* tells us that those ferocious-looking teeth are for "ripping and slashing into mangoes and papayas." The animal is the "fruit bat" or "flying fox." It's just a fruit eater!

The four-legged, bushy-tailed fox, like our dogs, is a member of the group called carnivores, which means "meat-eaters," and it will eat meat, but it also eats grapes and other berries and fruits. Grizzly bears, other members of the so-called carnivore group, catch and eat fish and other animals, but 80–90 percent of their diet is plant material! Polar bears enthusiastically eat lettuce and carrots, and will take time out from performing for an audience (which they seem to enjoy!) to snack on a huge carrot (like a teen might chew up a candy bar). Pandas are also bears with "carnivorous teeth" (falsely so-called), but they just eat bamboo and plant material. A grizzly's claws can be used to snatch fish from a river (or a camper from his/her

no larger than chickens. (If they hadn't died out, maybe we could dine on Kentucky Fried Dinosaur!) Astonishingly — and contrary to popular misinformation — the average dinosaur was only the size of a pony. Some were the size of cattle, hippos, and elephants. Only a few kinds got to be really big — and even those hatched from eggs you could easily hold in your hand!

Consider *T. rex*, star of television, the movies, and *Jurassic Park*. When *T. rex* first hatched out of its egg, you could hold it in your hand, pet it, even let it perch on your shoulder like a parrot! *Wait a minute*, you might be thinking, *it might bite my neck or rip my ear off! Something terrible might happen!*
Certainly the adult *T. rex*

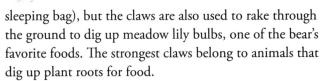

often to strip away the tough coat that surrounds seeds that fall into the river!

Remember, too, that not all meat-eaters (carnivores) are predators. A predator is an animal that hunts down and eats its prey, and usually eats them while the prey's meat is still "fresh." A scavenger is an animal, like a buzzard, that eats animals that are already dead; their meat has often rotted and softened up. Jack Horner, science expert for the *Jurassic Park* films, thinks the real *T. rex* (not the computer animated version) was probably a scavenger rather than a predator (but who would go to a movie about the world's biggest buzzard?).

Could *T. rex* have been a vegetarian? Knives with serrated (toothed) edges are not used just to cut steaks; they are used to cut tomatoes, celery, and bread, too! Some animals with teeth like *T. rex*'s are plant eaters. The uakari is a South American animal the size of a mountain gorilla, but its *T. rex*-like teeth (Figure 7.1) are used as banana peelers! Wire basket fruit pickers have rows of "teeth" to rake fruit from trees. Scientists now believe *T. rex* walked around with its head down near the ground and its tail sticking out, acting as a counterbalance. Is it possible the big teeth and jaws of *T. rex* were designed to rake through ground vegetation, snaring watermelons, cantaloupes, and pumpkins?

sleeping bag), but the claws are also used to rake through the ground to dig up meadow lily bulbs, one of the bear's favorite foods. The strongest claws belong to animals that dig up plant roots for food.

The strong, hooked beaks and sharp talons of hawks and eagles are often touted as fearsome weapons of death, but parrots have hooked beaks and sharp talons as strong or stronger, and they eat seeds! Most people know that piranhas in the Amazon River can shred a huge carcass in seconds with their razor-sharp teeth; very few people know that they use these teeth more

Figure 7.1

6'

The Bible tells us two things scientists can use to understand animal diets. First, the Bible tells us that both mankind and animals were created to eat only plants:

And God said, Behold, I have given you every herb bearing seed, which is upon the face of all the earth, and every tree, in the which is the fruit of a tree yielding seed; to you it shall be for meat. And to every beast of the earth, and to every fowl of the air, and to every thing that creepeth upon the earth, wherein there is life, I have given every green herb for meat: and it was so (Gen. 1:29–30).

There was no suffering or death of sentient beings in the created world God called "very good" and certainly no predators chasing down prey, ripping them to shreds, and eating them alive.

But if you're thinking about your last hamburger, don't panic. The Bible also tells us that after Noah's flood, God allowed mankind to eat meat (Gen. 9:3) — possibly because deterioration in soil and climate conditions after the Flood reduced the nutritional value of plants, and because the greater complexity in cell biochemistry and digestion required for a plant diet was ruined by mutations. No doubt some animals and some people had already begun to kill and eat animals after man's sin corrupted God's perfect creation, even before the Flood.

Scientists studying Darwin's "war of nature" in our present fallen world probably would not have figured out that all animals were once vegetarian. But we have an infallibly accurate historical record (the Bible) that tells us there was a dramatic, non-uniformitarian change in the flow of history when the creation was corrupted by man's sin, so that struggle and death, including predation, became a part of our world. It was not the structure of teeth and claws that changed; it's what animals did with their teeth and claws (their behavior) that changed. Shirley Strom, a scientist who lived with normally vegetarian chimpanzees, for example, witnessed a male chimp kill a sick, old gazelle. The blood seemed to taste good especially to females, and soon males began chasing down other sick animals. Dr. Strom thought she was witnessing a behavioral change producing a new predator, even though no change in teeth or claws (fingernails) had occurred. But then the chimps stopped killing old and sick animals (the ones most predators kill) and went back to their plant-eating habits (with occasional insects for dessert).

Given the historically accurate biblical record, scientists can understand both how dinosaurs could have all once been vegetarian (even *T. rex*) and also how some (including *T. rex*) could later become meat-eaters, even with no change in teeth or claw structure.

So, if a scientist can't tell by teeth or claws what an extinct animal ate, how can he or she figure out the diet? The answer is coprolite, or "petrified poo"! Believe it or

Coprolites (fossilized animal droppings)

Sloth

Dinosaur

Shark

Dinosaur Slice →

Turtle

Alligator

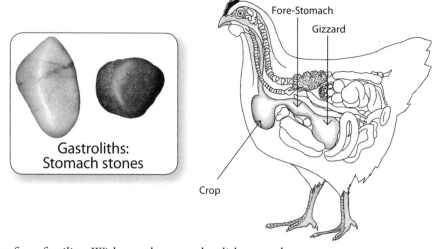

Gastroliths:
Stomach stones

Fore-Stomach

Gizzard

Crop

not, feces fossilize. With a rock saw and polisher, a paleo-scatologist can slice and polish petrified dinosaur dung, examine it under the microscope, and see what the animal ate! Herbivore coprolite will contain bits and pieces of leaves, twigs, grass, seeds, etc.; carnivore coprolite will contain bits and pieces of broken bone or shells. Some dinosaurs were omnivores (like human teenagers are), eating just about anything plant or animal.

Woodsmen today can easily tell the difference between droppings left by rabbits, deer, coyotes, turtles, alligators, horses, cattle, etc. With less certainty, paleo-scatologists usually assume dinosaur droppings go with the dinosaur that left the most bones nearby.

Gizzard stones or stomach stones called gastroliths also provide clues to dinosaur diet. Some reptiles and birds today swallow stones that they hold in a muscular food-grinding organ called a gizzard. (You may have seen a chicken gizzard with its giblets, and gizzards are also eaten as meat.) Gastroliths help the gizzard's muscular action to grind up food. The grinding action also polishes the gastroliths so that after a while, their high polish gives the

gastroliths what looks like a smooth waxy or oily coating, making them quite distinct from ordinary pebbles found nearby. Gastroliths are especially useful in grinding up wood in the diets of herbivores.

Alligators may swallow rocks for ballast to adjust their buoyancy, somewhat like a scuba diver will add weights so that he or she can float effortlessly at a certain depth under-water. Some fish secrete minerals, forming smooth (but not highly polished), normally symmetrical "rocks" (mineral deposits) called ballast bones. Ballast rocks and ballast bones do not have the combination of irregular shape and high polish that gastroliths have, and they are not clues to diet like gastroliths are.

Sometimes, smaller fossils are found inside a larger one. These are sometimes interpreted as food and clues to diet, sometimes as unborn baby animals, and sometimes as one animal crushed under another.

How would a creationist put together the bits and pieces of historical/biblical and scientific dinosaur evidences we've looked at so far? All the kinds of land dinosaurs, including the long-necked sauropods and *T. rex*, would have been created from the elements in the ground on creation day 6, the same day God created man from the dust of the ground. Creation from the same material at the same time may have been implied when God said to Job, "Behold now behemoth, which I made with thee" (Job 40:15).

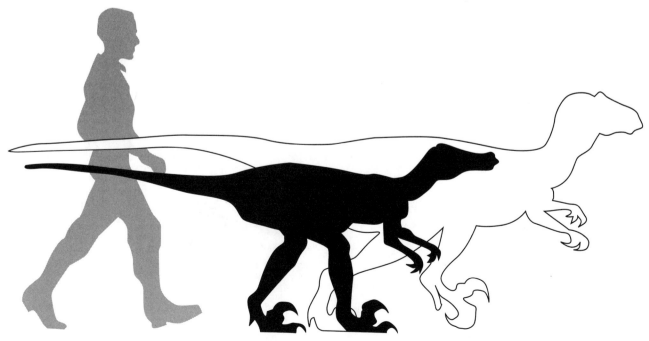

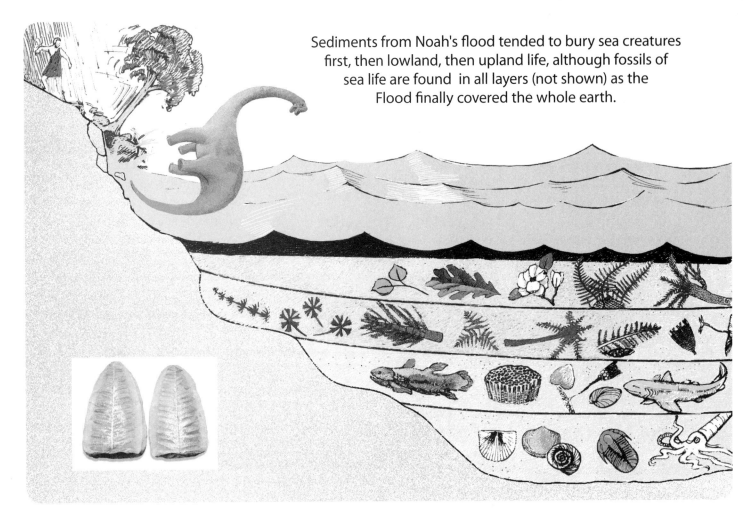

Sediments from Noah's flood tended to bury sea creatures first, then lowland, then upland life, although fossils of sea life are found in all layers (not shown) as the Flood finally covered the whole earth.

Some may gasp in disbelief: "You could never have man and dinosaurs living together! Dinosaurs would crush us, eat us, and destroy our homes!" That fear comes from seeing *Jurassic Park*, watching Godzilla tramp out Tokyo, or listening to too much evolutionary propaganda in textbooks and television nature programs. Remember first that dinosaurs come in all sizes, from chicken-sized to the 100-foot (30 m) sauropods, with the average dinosaur only the size of a pony. Most dinosaurs were smaller than elephants, yet elephants in India are used as farm animals and children ride on their backs. The largest land dinosaurs were much smaller than today's great blue whale, but man nearly hunted to extinction blue whales whose volume could hold two of the largest dinosaurs! (When man and large animals live together, it's usually the large animals that are in trouble!)

Form your foundation.

Dinosaurs have been used to "preach" millions of years of struggle and death, contrary to the gospel. But the Bible has man and dinosaur both created on day 6, dinosaurs before sin, eating only plants (like many animals with sharp teeth and claws today are vegetarians), and the Bible even describes two giant reptiles (behemoth and leviathan), both much larger than the pony size of the average dinosaur. Man and dinosaurs together? No problem!

Building Inspection

1. Why do Christians need to learn about dinosaurs?

   _____

   _____

2. Why isn't the word "dinosaur" in the Bible? Are animals like dinosaurs described in the Bible?

   _____

   _____

3. Explain why "behemoth" (described by God to Job in Job 40:15–24) is probably a long-necked dinosaur (sauropod) — and definitely not a hippo or elephant.

   _____

   _____

   _____

4. If *T. rex* dinosaurs were still around, could you let one perch on your shoulder? When (or why)?

   _____

   _____

5. What did the first *T. rex* eat? How can you be absolutely sure?

   _____

   _____

6. God created all animals to eat only plants, but some animals began to eat meat after struggle and death were brought into God's world by _____. Although some may have begun earlier, God gave man permission to eat meat after _____.

7. Evolutionists believe meat eaters have been around for millions of years and can be identified by teeth and claws or beaks and talons. But scientists have discovered many animals that eat mostly or only plants, despite "carnivorous" features — "falsely so-called." Give five examples:

   _____

   _____

8. Since teeth and claws can't identify a carnivore, what kind of fossil must a paleontologist find to tell what an extinct animal ate? _____

9. Although scientists wouldn't discover all animals were created vegetarian by looking at today's world, if scientists found an eyewitness account (the Bible) that recorded a vegetarian creation, would a scientist be able to explain how some herbivores (after sin) become carnivores?

   _____

   _____

10. How big were dinosaurs — small, medium, large, or all of these? _____ Were any full-grown dinosaurs smaller than chickens? _____ How big was the average dinosaur (compared to a living animal)? _____ Name three animals today larger than the average dinosaur: _____, _____, _____. Name an animal living today twice as big as the largest dinosaur: _____ How big was the biggest dinosaur when it first hatched? _____

53

Dinosaurs, the Flood, and the Gospel

Remember that animals were created vegetarian. After sin corrupted God's perfect creation, some dinosaurs did become meat eaters, but man has been much more effective in killing large meat eaters (even great white sharks, lions, and tigers) than the other way around. Cultures from around the world record "mighty hunters" who killed large scaly beasts whose descriptions resemble those of dinosaurs.

If mankind and dinosaurs once lived together, what happened? Evolutionists have proposed all sorts of explanations for the disappearance of dinosaurs: dinosaurs ate too much; they ate too little; mammals ate their eggs; earth got too hot; it got too cold; there was a dinosaur virus plague; they died of constipation when a laxative plant in their environment died out; etc.! But all those explanations would affect only some dinosaurs in some environments at some times. After a century of trying little-by-little, slow and gradual uniformitarian explanations, most evolutionists now blame dinosaur demise on a worldwide catastrophe: an asteroid got them!

Some think that a chunk of rock 5–10 miles (8–16 km) in diameter slammed into the ocean (off Mexico's Yucatan Peninsula is the currently popular location). Scientists have calculated that such an impact would, in addition to the blast wave, slosh waves of water over all the continents. Dinosaurs are often found in "graveyards," huge deposits of jumbled bones in thick layers of water-laid rocks. Even evolutionists will often say it must have taken colossal flooding to tear apart and bury so many big animals so deep and so fast that they are preserved for us to find today.

A worldwide, watery catastrophe (Noah's flood) has always been part of creationist thinking. Scientists agree that flood conditions are the ideal and most common conditions for forming fossils.

The Bible certainly does not say God used an agent like an asteroid to trigger Noah's flood, but it doesn't necessarily rule it out, either. At least evolutionists and creationists agree that it would take a worldwide watery catastrophe to bury the last of the many different kinds of dinosaurs in so many different places around the earth, all at the same time.

But, according to evolutionists, the asteroid that killed off the last of the dinosaurs hit earth 65 million years ago. The record of earth history in the Bible suggests that Noah's flood occurred about 4½–5 thousand years ago. If most of the dinosaurs we find as fossils were buried in the Flood, then dinosaur fossils would only be thousands of years old, not millions. Is that possible?

Actually, there are several lines of evidence that suggest dinosaurs lived on earth and got buried and fossilized only thousands of years ago, not millions. Consider the famous *T. rex* named Sue that was dug up in South Dakota in the 1990s. Jack Horner and his team of scientists found red blood cells in Sue's bones! In 2005, soft tissues including bone and blood cells and stretchable blood vessels were reported from another *T. rex,* this one found in Montana. Under ideal conditions, cells might survive thousands of years, but never millions. Protein and DNA molecules are also found in some dinosaur bones, and those molecules rot or decompose far too quickly to last for millions of years. Evolutionists once claimed that DNA recovered from fossils might be used as clues to the past, but now they are claiming all the reports of DNA and protein in fossils must be contamination because those molecules can't last for millions of years. Maybe the evidence is just telling us the fossils are not that old!

Carbon-14 and other radioactive decay dating techniques are becoming friends of the creationists. Carbon-14 has a short half-life (5,730 years), meaning half the amount in a specimen at death disappears every 5,730 years. If fossils with carbon of "dinosaur age" really were millions of years old, there would not be enough C-14 left in them to measure. But the C-14 is there, and it's well above the minimum level modern techniques can detect, and it's in fossils that show no evidence of C-14 contamination! Carbon-14 is telling scientists — and it should be telling students, teachers, media, museums, and the public — that dinosaur fossils are only thousands of years old at most, not millions!

But, can Noah's flood be used to explain extinction of dinosaurs? Not quite. If dinosaur fossils are largely the remains of dinosaurs buried in Noah's flood, then where were two of every kind of land dinosaur? On the ark? If a dinosaur stepped on the ark, wouldn't it just tip up, flip over, and sink? Many people think it's comically ridiculous to think there were dinosaurs on Noah's ark! But that popular disbelief in dinosaurs on the ark is based on two very common misconceptions. First, dinosaurs were nowhere near as big as people think. Second, the ark is much bigger than most people realize.

We don't have to guess how big the ark was; its dimensions are given in Scripture. Converting biblical cubits (forearm length of about 18 inches or 45 cm) into feet and meters, the ark was approximately 450 feet long by 75 feet wide and 45 feet high, or about 135 x 23 x 14 meters. That means the ark was as long as 1½ American football fields, as wide as a six-lane highway, and higher than a four-story building! Its volume was over 13,600,000 cubic feet or c. 400,000 m³; 50,000 sheep-sized animals could be packed onto one of its three decks! Figure 8.1 gives you some idea of the ark's enormous size.

Figure 8.1

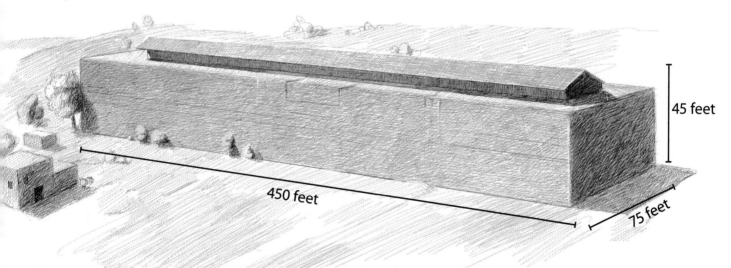

450 feet

75 feet

45 feet

If Noah had wanted to cheat, he could have gotten all the dinosaur kinds on the ark in four bushel baskets. How? By taking the eggs! But that would be cheating. God's purpose in bringing land dinosaurs to the ark was to have them multiply and fill the earth again after the Flood. So, He would bring Noah neither the very young nor the very old, but young adults in their reproductive prime. Remember, even the very largest dinosaurs hatched from eggs no bigger than footballs. And, like many reptiles and fish today, dinosaurs would no doubt be ready to lay eggs and reproduce long before reaching maximum size. An alligator or

dinosaur in just one corner of the huge ark. Remember, too, the average dinosaur was only the size of a pony or a big dog, and some dinosaurs were no bigger than chickens. There was lots of room on the ark for dinosaurs — not just two dinosaurs, but two of each of the different kinds of dinosaurs (two *Diplodocus* types, two *T. rex*, two *Triceratops* types, two chicken-sized "compies," etc.).

But if land dinosaurs were on the ark, they got off the ark. So, what happened? Why don't we have as many dinosaurs on earth today as there were in the pre-Flood world? Two major factors probably contributed to the dinosaurs' decline: (1) a dramatic climate change after the Flood and (2) overhunting by people.

Factors associated with Noah's flood generated the so-called "Ice Age." Before the Flood, higher levels of CO_2 (carbon dioxide) in the atmosphere acted like the glass in a greenhouse to trap heat and keep earth's temperature warm and mild pole to pole. But the Flood trapped coal, oil, fossils, shells, and limestone deep in the earth so the carbon in these things could not be easily returned to the atmosphere as CO_2. Land cools much more quickly than water does, so water evaporated from the warm oceans fell as snow at the higher latitudes and altitudes on the continents. For perhaps 500 years, ice sheets built up until they covered about 30 percent of the continental land mass. Cooling oceans slowed down the post-Flood "snow machine," and some of the ice sheets melted back. But we're still in the so-called "Ice Age": At the Ice Age maximum, perhaps 500 years after Noah's flood, 30 percent of the continents were covered; today, 10 percent of the continents are still covered with ice, some two miles (3 km) deep. Earth has never gotten back its pole-to-pole mild climate.

How Big Are Dinosaurs?

tortoise can lay eggs, for example, while still young and small, although it will continue to grow bigger and bigger as it grows older (unlike human beings or mammals). A long-necked behemoth dinosaur that hatched from an 8-inch (20-cm) egg, for example, might eventually grow to over 100 feet (30 m) in length, but it was probably a reproductively mature adult at less than 20 feet (6.5 m), most of that being neck and tail.

Reproductively mature mammals such as the elephant, giant ground sloth, and bear were probably bigger than the young adult dinosaurs of the largest kinds. Figure 8.2 shows a full grown human being (Shem?) and a young adult of the largest kind of

Judging by the fossils, much of the pre-Flood world was covered with spore-bearing plants, the ferns and "fern allies," and not as much with seed plants like conifers and flowering plants. The proportions of seed to spore plants reversed after the Flood. Similarly, the percentages of "cold-blooded" (ectothermic)

Figure 8.2

Collecting bones at the bone bed. We dug down several feet through coal and shale to find the frozen bones. Some were petrified, and others were lightweight showing little petrifaction.
The Great Alaskan Dinosaur Adventure

Buddy looking over his "Branchiosaurus" in the sand.
The Great Alaskan Dinosaur Adventure

amphibians and reptiles were greater before the Flood, shifting to a greater percentage of "warm-blooded" (endothermic) birds and mammals after the Flood. The post-flood environment seems harder for spore-bearing plants, amphibians, and reptiles, and comparatively easier for seed-bearing plants, birds, and mammals. The cooler post-Flood environment with greater seasonal temperature extremes and reduced amounts of spore-bearing and tropical vegetation may have been particularly hard on the dinosaurs. They needed to eat far more to keep up their body temperature, but it's likely they had far less of their favorite vegetation on which to feed. Fossils show us that alligators and palm trees both once lived near the poles, but now they live in a far smaller area of the world.

Dramatically fresh-looking, unmineralized bones of dinosaurs have been discovered on the North Slope of Alaska. Five creationist adventurers (including both ICR graduate and Cedarville College geologist John Whitmore and dinosaur sculptor and "creation gospel" musician Buddy Davis) brought back over 200 pounds (90 kg) of unfossilized dinosaur bones preserved in the permafrost along the Colville River. Obviously, these bones were not 65 million years old, and no evolutionist could claim they were preserved in ice for 65 million years, because evolutionists believe that area had subtropical climate for 64 of those 65 million hypothetical years! The fresh dinosaur bones were collected under federal permit, and a few approved specimens are on display at the Creation Adventures Museum in Arcadia, Florida.

The unmineralized bones may be the partial remains of dinosaurs migrating away from the ark. Continental ice build-up after the Flood lowered sea level almost 900 feet (nearly 300 m), producing a broad land bridge across

what is now the Bering Strait between Siberia and Alaska. During at least the first couple of hundred years after the Flood, the land bridge would probably have had a somewhat moderate climate and considerable vegetation, at least in the summers. The dinosaurs whose bones are found may have migrated (in one or several generations) from the ark to Alaska, only to starve, die in an early snowstorm, or be killed by animals or people seeking food.

All scientists freely admit that human beings hunted and killed mammoths and mastodons, types of elephants larger (and perhaps smarter and more agile) than the majority of dinosaurs. Florida was once home to many mammoths, mastodons, giant ground sloths (heavier and taller than *T. rex*), saber-toothed cats, rhinos, camels, llamas, giant bison, and other animals larger than the average dinosaur. Scientists at the state museum in Florida have concluded the last of these large animals were killed off by the Indians (Native Americans) in Florida about 4,000 years ago — the same time period a creationist would give for the demise of these post-Flood creatures. (Even today, the Pygmies in Africa kill elephants for tribal food — one man with one spear for one elephant!)

If people killed the last of large Ice Age mammals in the harsh, early post-Flood world, it's possible they also killed off the last of some kinds of dinosaurs. Cultures all over the world have records of people killing fearsome, scaly creatures whose descriptions are similar to those of different kinds of dinosaurs. Chinese records even tell of animals being reared from eggs and put into service for the emperor. All scientists recognize that peoples drew pictures of Ice Age mammals like woolly mammoths, yet there are some paintings that are just as clearly dinosaurs (Figure 8.3). Apparently Job, who lived in the early post-Flood

University (and an eloquent creationist): "Dinosaurs are missionary lizards" (or "missionary reptiles").

For years, evolutionists have been using dinosaurs to "preach" their view, but dinosaurs can be used more effectively as missionaries to tell the gospel message of God's perfect creation, ruined by man's sin, destroyed by the Flood, restored to new life in Jesus Christ: *Creation, Corruption, Catastrophe,* and *Christ.*

(1) When dinosaurs are found as fossils and the evidence is complete enough, they are recognized as specific kinds of dinosaurs, complete and complex, with no "links" to other types of life or even to other kinds of dinosaurs. Nor are there links between land dinosaurs and flying pterodactyls or the swimming marine reptiles like plesiosaurs and ichthyosaurs. When fossils are found within dinosaur eggs, they are little baby dinosaurs. In short, dinosaurs were created on day 6 as dinosaurs: well designed to multiply after kind — creation (Gen. 1, John 1).

(2) But dinosaur fossils are dead things. Some show evidence of bite marks and disease, the effects of time, chance, struggle, and death. The "war of nature" evident in

years, was not the only person who saw live dinosaurs! The pioneering work of Paul Taylor (*The Great Dinosaur Mystery and the Bible* book and video)[1] and later work by Bill Cooper (*After the Flood*)[2] document many historical encounters between man and dinosaur.

That just leaves one final question: What is a dinosaur? Perhaps the most intriguing definition was provided by Dr. Paul Ackerman, Professor of Psychology at Wichita State

Figure 8.3
Dinosaur
Petroglyph

---

1. Paul Taylor, *The Great Dinosaur Mystery and the Bible* (Denver, CO: Accent Books, 1998).
2. Bill Cooper, *After the Flood* (West Sussex, UK: New Wine Ministries, 1995).

dinosaur fossils does not point toward upward evolution, as Darwin supposed; rather, it points downward to the ruin of creation by man's sin — corruption (Gen. 3, Rom. 8).

(3) Dinosaurs are often found in colossal graveyards, thousands of creatures suddenly buried in thick layers of cement-rich sediment and rapidly preserved in stone before scavengers or rotting could completely destroy them. Noah's flood would produce such deep, rapid burial on a worldwide scale, and the climate and environmental changes, including the "Ice Age," caused by Noah's flood would help explain the decline in size and variety of those awesome creatures. Although they get the date wrong (as usual), even evolutionists blame the final demise of dinosaurs on a worldwide catastrophe (Gen. 8:6–9; 2 Pet. 3).

(4) But, God provided a way of escape from judgment: the ark. In it, God preserved all people who trusted in Him (eight souls) and reproductive pairs of all the dry land animals, including dinosaurs, to repopulate earth. Many dinosaurs were small, and young adults of the largest dinosaurs would not have been the biggest animals on the ark, so there was plenty of room for the various kinds of dinosaurs and a total of perhaps 50,000 land animals! Dinosaurs got off the ark and began to repopulate the earth. Some (perhaps identified by the fresh dinosaur

Form your foundation.

Dinosaurs are four C "missionary reptiles," showing:

Creation: separate and complex kinds

Corruption: struggle and death after sin

Catastrophe: rapid, recent burial worldwide

Christ: preservation aboard the ark

bones preserved in Alaskan permafrost) may have died from the climatic and environmental changes; others may have been overhunted by people, like the mammoths in Florida were. Post-Flood peoples, including Job and persons from many different cultures around the world, knew and drew dinosaurs, and some (even a few evolutionists) think there might be some dinosaurs still living in parts of the world today. The ark, a provision for deliverance from judgment and catastrophe, is a "type" of the deliverance from sin, death, and the final judgment by fire provided by Jesus, and believers can look forward in joyful anticipation to a new heaven, a new earth, and a new life — rich, abundant, and eternal — in Christ!

Bonus Project

Mrs. Parker is shown teaching home school families how to plaster jacket the dinosaur fossils they are excavating.

A. What problems do you think scientists would have in putting together reconstructions (including flesh) of the dinosaurs that left the bones? Do you think crime scene investigators could do a better job with human bones? Why or why not? (Compare your thoughts with what you'll be reading later.)

B. Suppose a few of the dinosaur bones were found with blood and bone cells and stretchable blood vessels inside. How might a "paleo-historian" "explain" that discovery? How might the explanation change if human tools were found entombed in the same rocks?

C. The dinosaur fossils are found in very thick layers of water-laid sedimentary rock far from any large body of water. What different explanations for these fossil layers might be offered by creationists vs. evolutionists?

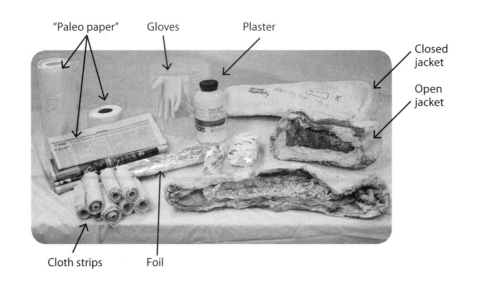

"Paleo paper" Gloves Plaster Closed jacket Open jacket Cloth strips Foil

1. Did dinosaurs appear on earth the same day as humankind (creation day 6), or millions of years before people? _____

2. Would it be scary for people and dinosaurs to live on the earth at the same time? Why or why not?

   _____

   _____

   _____

3. Most, perhaps all, dinosaurs are now extinct. According to evolutionists, what caused their extinction about 65 million years ago? _____ According to creationists, what caused the death of most dinosaurs about 4,500 years ago? _____

4. Explain how (a) Alaskan fossils, (b) dinosaur blood, and (c) carbon-14 provide evidence that most dinosaurs died and most dinosaur fossils formed only thousands of years ago, not millions. Although many dinosaurs died and were fossilized during Noah's flood, the Flood did not cause the extinction of dinosaurs. Why not?

   _____

   _____

   _____

5. Was there room for two of every kind of land dinosaur on Noah's ark? Explain.

   _____

   _____

   _____

6. Name two things that happened after Noah's flood that made it hard for dinosaurs to continue living into the present.

   _____

   _____

   _____

7. Use dinosaurs as "Missionary Reptiles" by illustrating each of the four Cs of earth history with something about dinosaurs:

   Creation: _____

   _____

   Corruption: _____

   _____

   Catastrophe: _____

   _____

   Christ: _____

   _____

Chapter
8

Dinosaurs, Evolution, and Science

Creationists think that dinosaur fossils point us back to the ruination of creation by man's sin and the restoration of creation in Christ — life wins. Evolutionists believe dinosaurs tell us about millions of years of struggle and death that for dinosaurs (and, ultimately, all other creatures) ends in extinction — death wins.

The general story evolutionists tell about dinosaurs is so familiar from constant repetition that many people just take it for granted without even asking about the evidence.

The story of dinosaur evolution begins long, long ago when, evolutionists assert, the only four-legged land animals (tetrapods) were amphibians, the group including frogs, toads, and salamanders today. Evolutionists believe time, chance, struggle, and death (mutation and natural selection) changed some amphibians into reptiles, although no missing links have yet been found, and no one has described the stages through which moist skin became dry scales or by which a free-swimming tadpole eating algae became a food-absorbing embryo enclosed in a shelled egg laid on land.

About 220 million years ago, the evolutionary story continues, time, chance, struggle, and death converted some more generalized reptile type(s) into a variety of the more specialized types we call dinosaurs. During the next 155 million years, the story goes, a variety of dinosaurs abruptly appear and disappear from the rock layer sequence called "Mesozoic" or the "Age of Dinosaurs." These dinosaurs lived among, and their herbivores fed upon, spore-bearing plants (ferns and fern allies) and on seed-bearing gymnosperms (especially conifers and cycads). Flowering and fruiting plants appeared near the end of the dinosaur age, not long before an alleged asteroid impact 65 million years ago produced a worldwide catastrophe that ended the reign of the "ruling reptiles" and paved the way for flowering plants and furry mammals to take over the world.

(Most evolutionists believe dinosaurs died out completely, but a vocal minority believes, as discussed later, that some dinosaurs sprouted feathers and are flying among us as birds.)

According to traditional evolution, dinosaurs lived and died millions of years before mankind appeared on earth, so their death could have nothing to do with man's sin or Noah's flood. Furthermore, evolutionists assert, records of encounters between mankind and dinosaurs in the Bible and in the writing and traditions of cultures around the world must all be myths, fables, or superstitions. Most importantly, evolutionists and their lawyers loudly proclaim, academic freedom, the American Constitution, and the survival of science require that no historical record or scientific evidence contrary to the evolutionary scenario can ever be presented or tolerated by anyone in any of the science classrooms in any of our tax-supported "public" schools.

But is the oft-repeated evolutionary story of dinosaurs really good science, or is it really just good propaganda — based on dodging the real science? What does science tell us about dinosaurs? Can the scientific method tell us how dinosaurs originated and what happened to them?

Creation vs. Evolution

Notice again what dramatically different stories evolutionists and creationists tell, both using the same evidence! Why? To answer that question, first answer another question: When do fossils exist, past or present? When Ken Ham asks that question, it's amazing how many in an audience say, "Past." But, of course, fossils exist in the present (otherwise we wouldn't be able to dig them up and study them!). So scientists (paleontologists) who dig up dinosaur bones are not digging up the past; they are digging up evidence in the present and making up stories

Dinosaur Reconstructions

Scientists (anatomists) may compare the shapes of joint surfaces and the locations of bumps, grooves, openings, etc., in dinosaur bones with similar features in living reptiles and attempt to reconstruct how a whole dinosaur skeleton would fit together. A tremendous amount of expert knowledge and talent is required of scientists who attempt such reconstructions. Despite the enormous amount of praiseworthy effort and ability put into such reconstructions, however, the results are only "semi-scientific" and subject to considerable reinterpretation.

Perhaps the most famous error in dinosaur reconstruction was committed by the scientist Marsh, who produced "Brontosaurus" by putting what turned out to be the head of one dinosaur on the body of another. So what was once perhaps the best-known dinosaur turned out to be a mistake, although the parts do seem to belong to real dinosaurs. An even greater mistake was putting the head of an ichthyosaur, a marine reptile, on the body of a bird! Less dramatically, a bone found in the fossil of one of the first named dinosaurs, *Iguanodon,* was first thought to be a spike on its nose, but now is considered a spike on the thumb.

At least we can all sympathize with the great difficulties faced by those trying to reconstruct dinosaur skeletons. Fossil evidence usually consists of some broken bone fragments from several creatures mixed together and scattered through or over a large amount of rock!

(scenarios or models) of what they believe may have happened in the past to produce the evidence we find only in the present!

Scientists can make objectively verifiable and repeatable descriptions and measurements of the shapes and locations of dinosaur fossils, but these observable facts do not speak for themselves. Stories about the past lives of dinosaurs go way beyond the scientific method and necessarily involve historical and philosophical assumptions and methodology — and these are strongly influenced by personal prejudice, presuppositions, and world view. It is no wonder, then, that we have different stories about the same evidence.

Creationists think the Bible gives them a head start in understanding dinosaurs, because it's an infallibly accurate eyewitness account of real events in earth's history. Both creationists and evolutionists, however, want their models to explain the scientific evidence we have about dinosaur fossils. So, although no one can run a scientific experiment to decide which view of the past (if either) is correct, scientific study of present dinosaur evidence may be used to defend one view or the other, somewhat like opposing lawyers might use accurate but circumstantial evidence to argue for one's story and against the other's.

Let's look first at the evidence about dinosaur fossils. Then we'll contrast the evolutionist and creationist ideas about what the historical and scientific evidence mean.

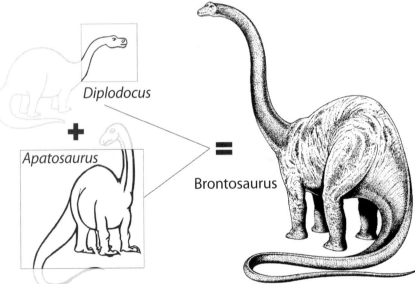

Diplodocus

+

Apatosaurus

=

Brontosaurus

64

Suppose you smashed a wine goblet, soda bottle, and drinking glass and then mixed some fragments of each in a bucket of sand. If you then gave the bucket of mixed fragments to someone without telling them what you put in it, you can imagine it would be difficult and time consuming to put the fragments together in a correct reconstruction — especially if the person doing it had never seem complete examples of the glassware involved, and many pieces were missing!

The problems in anatomical reconstruction can be demonstrated more realistically (and with far less danger or cut fingers) with owl pellets. Owl pellets are hairballs full of undigested bones spit up by owls that have eaten mice, moles, and other small animals. Sterilized owl pellets with instructions for use can be purchased for an excellent lab exercise. Even with the help of pictures of the bones and of the whole animals, however, reconstruction takes effort and careful observation. Paleontologists trying to put dinosaurs together don't have pictures of the bones and live animals to use, so their task is much more difficult and much more subject to error.

Fortunately, however, there are some deposits that include huge numbers of bones from primarily one kind of dinosaur, like fossil herds of hadrosaurs (duck-billed dinosaurs). There are even a few cases where nearly whole dinosaur skeletons are found almost intact. Skeletal reconstruction in such cases is much

Owl Pellet

more reliable than it is in those many cases in which a dinosaur name is given to a few teeth and/or fragments of broken bone.

Even when skeletal material is fairly complete, interpretations can change dramatically. The big, four-legged, long-necked sauropods, for example, were first reconstructed with their legs spread to the side somewhat like a crocodile's, and it was thought that they were slow-moving and may have spent much time wading so that water would help support their huge bodies. Now they are pictured with their legs under the bodies, providing strong support and a much faster gait. Their tails were originally pictured dragging on the ground behind them; now the tails are pictured sticking out, held up in the air as a counterbalance to the long neck, and some think they could lean back on their tails (as in *Jurassic Park*) to reach leaves even higher in the trees than their long necks could reach. (Notice, incidentally, that even the largest dinosaurs could hide in a forest; they were not taller than oaks, maples, or the larger pines, in spite of what you see on the Saturday morning cartoons!)

No matter how complete or reliable the skeletal reconstruction, however, it is primarily artists, not scientists, who supply the flesh, skin color, and "facial expressions" to dinosaurs. A person has the same bones, for example, both before and after they gain or lose 110 pounds (50 kg), and the bones do not tell you whether a person is usually frowning or always smiling, bald or hairy, ill-tempered or mild-mannered, eats mostly hamburgers and fries or is a strict vegetarian, has full or thin lips, broad or narrow nostrils, free or attached ear lobes, ripply muscles or flabby skin, round or "slanted" eyes, dark or light skin, high or low IQ, gravelly bass voice or melodic soprano, etc.!

You may be thinking, "Wait a minute! A CSI (crime scene investigator or forensic scientist) can figure out a person's skin color, eye shape, body hair, and lots of other things from the skeletal remains of a murder victim. Why

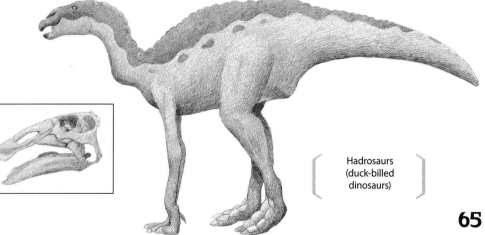

Hadrosaurs (duck-billed dinosaurs)

Sir Richard Owen, famed anatomist and founder of the British Museum of Natural History, originated the name *Dinosauria*.

Based upon the few fossil remains of *Iguanodon* found at first, Sir Richard Owen mistakenly placed a thumb spike on its snout in this early reconstruction.

can't paleontologists do that with dinosaurs?" The answer is simple: CSI forensic scientists observe lots of different people living in the present. They do statistical studies on large numbers of living people, relating what they can repeatedly observe of external fleshly features to subtle variations observed in hundreds of bone samples from known groups of people. Totally unlike the CSI forensic scientist working with large numbers of repeatable observations in the present, the dinosaur paleontologist — and his/her artist companion — must try to imagine the appearance, demeanor, color, etc., of an animal in the complete absence of detailed scientific description.

Because there is no objective scientific evidence to guide, artists have produced a variety of different views about dinosaur appearance. Early pictures portrayed dinosaurs as sluggish, stupid, and "swamp-colored" in dull grays and greens. Now they are pictured as alert, intelligent, some brilliantly colored in various patterns like some tropical lizards and snakes! (Subjectively, creationists tend to prefer the modern/current view, since it better reflects the handiwork of the Master Artist and Engineer!)

Occasionally, skin impressions of dinosaurs are found, and these can help a little with external reconstruction. Vary rarely, fragile color molecules or pigments are preserved in some fossil shells, so the same might occur in scales. Fossil dinosaur footprints, with or without "tail drags," can give the paleontologist clues to gait and stance.

For paleontologists willing to use them, dinosaur descriptions in the Bible, the writings of various cultures, and pictographs and petroglyphs (paintings and etchings, respectively, on stone) would be helpful, but not a lot of detail is included.

Where is the evidence?

No doubt children and curious people had been finding, digging up, and wondering about dinosaur bones for centuries. There are so many dinosaur bones, teeth, and claws at the surface that Plains Indians (Native Americans) in Wyoming and Alberta may have used them for benches, toys, and decorations. But scientists didn't get seriously interested in such fossils until the early 1800s. Some impressive specimens in England were brought to the attention of the famous anatomist and founder of the British Museum of Natural History, Sir Richard Owen (who was, by the way, a Christian and a creationist). Sir Richard's vast knowledge and experience enabled him to recognize the bones as reptilian, but of a kind and size unlike any reptiles then known to science. He called them "dinosaurs," meaning terrible lizards or terrible reptiles. The root word, -saur, means reptilian, or lizard-like; the prefix, dino-, means terrible or fearsome or awesome, and was used because the dinosaurs first named scientifically were much larger and fiercer looking than familiar reptiles like lizards and turtles.

Form your foundation.

Darwin's followers believe no humans ever saw dinosaurs, so they must ask artists to give dinosaur bones color and flesh — and artists, unlike CSI forensic scientists, only have the changing opinions of evolutionists to guide them. Creationists can use descriptions in the Bible and other historical records and art.

Building Inspection

1. _____Most evolutionists believe that (a) dinosaurs developed from struggle and death among early reptile groups about 220 million years ago; (b) dinosaurs were killed off when an asteroid hit the earth 65 million years ago; (c) no person ever saw a live dinosaur; (d) there are no rock printings or etchings of dinosaurs; (e) only evolutionary beliefs about dinosaurs should be taught in public schools, or (f) all of the above.

2. Do dinosaur fossils exist in the past or present? _____ Why is this question important?

   _____

   _____

   _____

3. Evidence can be empirical (repeatably observable) or circumstantial (consistant with a story, but subject to other interpretations). Mark the following evidences about dinosaurs as empirical (E) or circumstantial (C).

   _____ a. identifying a fossil as a dinosaur femur (thigh bone)

   _____ b. concluding a dinosaur fossilized in the wake of an asteroid impact 65 mya (million years ago)

   _____ c. some dinosaurs used sounds to coordinate pack hunts

   _____ d. evidence for a "dinosaur age" is strongly influenced by world view

   _____ e. the Bible and writings of other cultures include descriptions of dinosaurs seen by people.

4. Concerning dinosaur reconstruction from fossil bones, mark the following true (T) or false (F):

   _____ a. Reconstruction requires lots of training, knowledge, and skill.

   _____ b. Mistakes can be made, like putting the wrong head and body together ("Brontosaurus") or putting a thumb spike in the nose.

   _____ c. Opinions about the same evidence can change, such as changing dinosaur legs from out to the side to under the body, and the tail from dragging to held out as a counterbalance.

   _____ d. Dinosaur trackway impressions can give scientists ideas about stance, gait, and speed.

   _____ e. Although skin impression and color molecules are occasionally found, it's artists, not scientists, who give us color and "facial expressions."

5. A CSI forensic scientist examining a single human bone at a crime scene can reach conclusions about a person's skin color, eye shape, lip thickness, etc. Why can't paleontologists do that with dinosaur bones?

   _____

   _____

   _____

6. Who gave us the name "dinosaur" in 1841? _____ What does that name mean?

   _____

Chapter

9

"Terrible Lizards" or "Terrible Reptiles"

Although they are not called dinosaurs, some living reptiles do seem to qualify as "terrible lizards." The komodo dragon, or monitor lizard, is a monstrous scaly animal over 10 feet (3 m) long that has a huge forked tongue it flashes in and out like a snake's does. A popular attraction at larger zoos, it is native to the Komodo Island in the Indonesian Archipelago. There it attacks pigs and goats, working its poisonous saliva into its victim as it bites, and then feasts on the carcass after the poison does its work. Iguanas, a common pet store reptile, have a ferocious appearance with many sharp teeth and a frill down their backs. Before computer graphics, enlargements of iguanas were used as dinosaurs in the movies. In real life, they're strict vegetarians and friendly pets (but watch the sharp claws!). Australians at cookouts occasionally have to deal with goannas, six-foot (two m), tongue-flicking lizards with huge claws; fortunately, they are vegetarian, but can swallow a head of lettuce in one gulp and beg for more (and Americans complain about ants as picnic pests!). If scared, goannas try to climb the highest thing in sight — and in Australia's flat outback, that may be you!

Billboards for tourists in Florida often advertise alligators and crocodiles as "live dinosaurs." They certainly qualify as "terrible reptiles." Modern Florida gators nearly 20 feet (6 m) long have been seen, and the much more aggressive Australian crocodile is bigger and meaner and hunts its prey even in saltwater. Basking in the sun with its jaw flat on the ground and legs sticking out sideways, a crocodile may look slow and stupid, but its jaw is picking up ground-borne vibrations, and its legs are designed for incredibly fast takeoff! Several Aussies are killed each year by these "terrible reptiles."

A fossil crocodile about 50 feet (16 m) long has been found; when alive, it would have weighed more than *T. rex!* Besides that, crocodiles are found deeper in the rock layers (see geologic column diagram, p. 82–83) than dinosaurs. Their fossils are found with traditional dinosaurs, and crocodiles are surviving very well today. From a crocodile's point of view (if it had one), dinosaurs are second-rate reptiles that got off to a slow start and couldn't make it when the going got tough! Despite their ferocity and tenacity, however, even crocodiles have been brought to extinction or near extinction in some environments because of the hunting skills of the planet's top predator: man.

New Zealand is home to the tuatara, or beak-head lizard (scientific name *Sphenodon*). On the basis of some early attempts to define "dinosaur" by bone structure, the tuatara could have been called a "living dinosaur." But the definition of dinosaur was changed to exclude them, just as the definition of dinosaur was designed to exclude crocodilians. Note: the observable, measurable features used to describe a creature represent empirical scientific knowledge; decisions regarding what name should be given to a creature or group, and what features should be used to distinguish it from others, are subjective, not objective, and "semi-scientific" at best.

Scientific names and the features used to define them are decided at scientific conventions. Names and criteria change when subjective opinions change, even though the features scientifically described do not change. Too often, creatures are defined and named to support a particular view (or to honor self, spouse, or friend), and names change as views lose or gain popularity. (Science is really much in need of a more objective system of naming.)

Dinosaurs As Reptiles

Although an exact definition is still being debated, dinosaurs are almost always considered a subgroup of reptiles. Reptiles are vertebrates (animals with backbones) that have dry, scaly skin and lay eggs. Fossilized skin impressions show at least some recognized dinosaurs had a scaly body covering. The appearance of dinosaur bone under the microscope (microanatomy or histology) also resembles reptilian bone much more than it resembles the bone of vertebrates with body coverings other than scales (i.e., the hair or fur of mammals, feathers of birds, and moist, slimy skin of most amphibians).

From Montana and Alberta to China and Argentina, paleontologists have discovered hundreds of eggs belonging to several different types of dinosaurs. Rarely, the "baby dinosaur" is fossilized inside its egg; in other cases, presumptive identification of the egg is based on fossils of adults found nearby. Modern reptiles lay eggs, usually eggs with "leathery" shells that are more flexible than the more brittle shells of bird eggs.

Eggs of both reptiles and birds are called amniotes, and both are fabulously designed to retain moisture while allowing exchange of oxygen and carbon dioxide and providing the baby with sufficient nourishment to grow to hatching — a dramatic event programmed into the tiny animal's brain. By contrast, amphibians (frogs, toads, and salamanders) lay shell-less jelly-coated eggs in the water, and the young hatch into a free-swimming tadpole stage with gills that later undergo

What, then, is a dinosaur?

Figure 10.1: Vertebrate Classification

Class Reptilia (reptiles): egg layers with scaly skins.

Class Aves (birds): egg layers with feathers and flow-through lungs.

Class Mammalia (mammals): animals with hair or fur that nourish young on milk.

Class Amphibia (frogs, toads, etc.): animals with a tadpole stage and metamorphosis.

a fantastically complex change (metamorphosis) which transforms it into an air-breathing adult with lungs!

Reptiles, even sea turtles, usually lay their eggs on land (the oviparous condition), but in some reptiles, the eggs (shells and all) are retained in the mother's body and the young are hatched inside her and "born alive" (the ovoviviparous condition). "Live birth" in reptiles, however, is quite different from live birth in most mammals and in human beings, where there is no shell and the baby before birth is nourished through exchange with the mother's circulatory system, using her lungs and digestive systems (the viviparous condition).

Egg laying, bone structure, and scaly body covering all mean, to most scientists, that dinosaurs belong in the vertebrate Class Reptilia, as contrasted with Class Aves, Class Mammalia, and Class Amphibia (Figure 10.1).

Dinosaurs and Reptilian Subgroups

Defined as bony, air-breathing animals with scaly skins that lay shelled eggs, the reptile group certainly seems to include dinosaurs. But dinosaurs are also clearly different from reptiles such as turtles and snakes, and are considered a different subgroup than lizards and crocodilians. What makes dinosaurs a subgroup different from other reptilian subgroups?

The answer is not time! People often think of dinosaurs as ancient reptiles that lived long, long ago. But turtles, lizards, and other reptiles are found buried in fossil-rock layers *below* the layers that contain dinosaurs. So dinosaurs are not the oldest reptiles, and they are not the most "successful." Judged by evolutionary standards of "survival of the fittest" and position in the fossil-rock layers (geologic column diagram, p. 82–83), dinosaurs are *not* as old and *not* as fit to survive as turtles, lizards, or crocodiles!

Figure 10.2: Based on passages along the skull behind the eye socket, skulls can be classified as anapsid, synapsid, diapsid, or euryapsid. Dinosaurs are generally diapsid, with two large passages along the skull behind the eyes.

Rhamphorhyncus

Pteranodon

Mosasaurs

Ichthyosaurs

What, then, separates the dinosaurs from these other reptilian subgroups? Since paleontologists have scant knowledge of the soft parts, function, behavior, reproduction, and genetics of dinosaurs, they have looked to features of fossil bones to define the dinosaur subgroup. The currently popular definition is based on the pattern of passages in the skull (or, loosely, on "holes in the head"), shown in Figure 10.2. This may not be a well-chosen definition for dinosaurs, however, for two reasons: (1) skulls are among the least frequent dinosaur bones found, and they are often partial, crushed, or otherwise difficult to reconstruct; (2) skull openings (or holes in the head) are not a special feature with a known special function that makes dinosaurs a special group, so it is somewhat like grouping human beings on the size of their feet.

Most writers define dinosaurs to exclude two reptilian subgroups popularly associated with dinosaurs: (1) swimming marine reptiles such as plesiosaurs (the "Loch Ness" type), ichthyosaurs, and mosasaurs, and (2) the flying reptiles, the pterodactyls like *Pteranodon* and *Rhamphorhyncus*. Mode of locomotion (walking, swimming, flying) is a criterion used fairly often to break animals up into subgroups, and each mode is a "lifestyle" that requires a coordinated set of design features (adaptations). Most birds are flyers, of course, so swimming birds like penguins are put in one special subgroup and runners like ostriches, emus, and rheas are put in another (the ratites). But flyers, swimmers,

71

and walkers/runners are also lumped together in a larger group: the birds (Class Aves). It is not reasonable, then, to lump swimming and flying reptiles along with walking dinosaurs ("true dinosaurs," some would say) to form a group loosely and non-technically called "dinos."

From serious paleontologist to playful child, anyone who is interested in the origin, history, and fate of walking dinosaurs is inevitably interested in the flying pterodactyls and swimming plesiosaurs, and books and theories about one of these groups invariably include discussions of the others. So, in our discussion of the origin, features, fossils, and fate of reptiles, we will use "dinos," as most people do, to refer to all reptiles (walkers, swimmers, and flyers) except those still common today (turtles, snakes, lizards, and crocodiles).

But even our broad, non-technical definition of dinos faces two additional challenges. Stand-ins for the fossil "sail lizard," *Dimetrodon*, were used in early dinosaur movies, and plastic models are sometimes included in dinosaur kits (above). But fossils of *Dimetrodon* come before (are buried lower in the fossil-rock sequence than) "true dinosaurs," and some scientists — including some creationists — think that bones of "sail lizards" are more mammal-like than reptile-like. Let's examine right now, however, the bizarre but highly publicized suggestion that dinosaurs are more like birds than reptiles!

Form your foundation.

Because they laid eggs and had scaly skins, dinosaurs belong in the reptile group. But lizards, turtles, and crocodiles might call dinosaurs "reptile wimps," since fossils of those "modern" reptiles are found with and "before" dinosaurs, and some fossil crocodiles weighed more than *T. rex*!

Building Inspection

1. Match the descriptions below with the proper non-dinosaur "terrible lizard":

   ____ Komodo dragon   a. friendly, six ft. (two m), Australian vegetarian lizard

   ____ goanna   b. kill people every year in Australia; called "live dinosaurs" on some Florida billboards

   ____ crocodile   c. ten ft. (three m) monitor lizard that kills and eats goats and pigs

   ____ 50 ft. fossil croc   d. weighed more than *T. rex*

   ____ tuatara   e. the very dinosaur-like "beakhead lizard" of New Zealand

2. If they had a point of view, why might lizards, crocodiles, and turtles think of dinosaurs as the "wimpy reptiles"?

   _____

   _____

   _____

3. Available evidence suggests dinosaurs had dry scaly skins and laid eggs, so they are included in the vertebrate class called _____. Dinosaurs are separated from other reptiles on the basis of (choose one):

   a. belief they lived millions of years ago

   b. their huge size

   c. their fierceness

   d. certain large bony passages on the outside of the skull behind the eye sockets

   e. all of the above

4. What reasons might a scientist give for considering the current definition of "dinosaur" a bad one?

   _____

   _____

   _____

5. Although the current (poor?) definition of "dinosaur" excludes swimmers and flyers, most discussions and popular conversations about dinosaurs include extinct swimming reptiles such as _____, and extinct flying reptiles such as _____.

6. Can you think of a term that includes swimmers and flyers along with land dinosaurs in a single group of rare or extinct reptiles? _____

Dinosaurs and Birds?

The vast majority of scientists (both evolutionists and creationists) regard dinosaurs as distinctive kinds of reptiles that are nearly or entirely extinct. A vocal minority, who have attracted a lot of media publicity, believe instead that dinosaurs are still with us — flying around as birds!

Viewed at the Cincinnati Zoo bird exhibit in March 1997 was this intriguing sign:

Dinosaurs went extinct millions of years ago — or did they? No — birds are essentially modern short-tailed feathered dinosaurs.

According to this bizarre view, people have certainly seen live dinosaurs; indeed, they see them every day, and frequently enjoy some dinosaurs for dinner (e.g., chicken and turkey)! "Discovering Dinosaurs in the Museum of Natural History" makes this astonishing assertion: *The smallest dinosaur is the bee hummingbird,* Mellisuga helenae, *found only in Cuba.*

hummysaurus

Check the reaction you get the next time you spot a hummingbird and, proudly pointing, say, "Oh, look at the little dinosaur!"

The incredible belief that hummingbirds are really tiny dinosaurs might achieve a degree of scientific respectability if only some sort of missing link between dinosaurs and birds could be found — perhaps one like the "hummysaurus" pictured. You might think it's unfair and insulting to picture a proposed "dinosaur-bird" evolutionary link as partly bird and partly theropod dinosaur, the group that includes *T. rex.* But that's exactly what the popularized evolutionists are suggesting!

Those evolutionists who believe in a dino-bird link do not believe birds evolved from the flying "dino" reptiles, the pterodactyls. They do not believe they evolved from the dinosaurs with pelvic bones shaped like those of birds, the ornithiscian ("bird-hipped") sauropods (which include *Triceratops* and *Stegosaurus*). Instead, they believe birds evolved from theropod dinosaurs, bipedal dinosaurs with thick tails, heavy hind legs, and small forelimbs, such as the small *Compsognathus* and large *T. rex*, which are "lizard-hipped" (saurischian) dinosaurs.

"Feathers for *T. rex*" was the title of an article in *National Geographic* in November of 1999, an article that seemed intended to convince the public that evolutionists had finally found a long-sought link between major groups. With all the artistic (not scientific) skill for which *National Geographic* is famous, the public was treated to the picture of a baby "*T. rex*-bird" covered with down feathers like a newly hatched chick. Detailed artwork showed a close-up of the presumed "dinosaur feather." In three months, over 100,000 young people saw the "proof" for dinosaur-bird evolution on display at *National Geographic's* headquarters in Washington, D.C.

But it was all fake! The supposed fossil was fake. The artwork and article in *National Geographic* described a fake. What influenced so many students touring the *National Geographic* exhibit in Washington was the display of a fake.

Scientists with expert knowledge of birds, such as Storrs Olson at the prestigious Smithsonian Institute, also in Washington, D.C., recognized the scientific problems with *National Geographic's* story almost immediately. In an open letter published in the *Smithsonian* magazine (Nov. 1, 1999), Storrs Olson sternly rebuked *National Geographic* for "*. . . unsubstantiated, sensationalistic, tabloid journalism . . .*" putting the *Geographic* article in the same class as those about alien abductions and creatures part human/part animal.

Storrs Olson

The fake was not particularly clever or subtle, and is only the most notable (to date) of a long string of exaggerated claims that have been made since paleontologists first began reporting on dinosaur eggs and fossils being found in northeastern China (especially the Liaoning province). In a way that bolsters the myth that evolution is making scientific progress, a fawning and uncritical media publish splashy stories of hyperbolic claims, only to publish an obscure retraction or "different interpretation" a few weeks later.

The "feathers for *T. rex*" turned out to be fossils of bird parts cemented together with fossils of dinosaur parts. Locals were making a little extra income selling fossils to paleontologists. Apparently learning they were looking for a fossil of something partly dinosaur and partly bird, a local with fossils of both put them together to satisfy this yen.

As of this writing, *National Geographic* has not published an adequate retraction for their colossal blunder — one that would help erase the misinformation palmed off as science on so many unsuspecting school children. They did publish a short letter of apology from the scientist who — completely contrary to scientific protocol and international law — smuggled the fake fossil composite out of China. The "open letter" from Storrs Olson details many other examples of "scientific malpractice" in the *National Geographic*[1] article.

At least this time the evolutionist's error was so huge and obvious that it did get national media attention. The article detailing the fake in *USA Today*[2], for example, was headlined: *The Missing Link That Wasn't.*

What made it so easy to fool expert paleontologists with a specimen so obviously fake? One possible answer takes us back to 1860. Darwin's *Origin of Species* had just come out the previous year (1859). Although Darwin's book stimulated a fulmination of faith in evolution, Darwin freely admitted — completely contrary to the prevailing propaganda — that the fossil evidence available was quite **contrary** to his theory:

> *. . . intermediate links? Geology most assuredly does not reveal any such finely graduated organic chain,*

1. This article from the November 1999 issue of *National Geographic* was retracted after the purported type fossil for *Archaeoraptor liaoningensis* was shown to be fraudulent.
2. Tim Friend, "The Missing Link That Wasn't" (Feb. 1, 2000)

and this is perhaps the most obvious and serious objection that can be argued against the theory.

Perhaps because he knew how difficult it would be to defend evolutionary theory scientifically, Thomas Henry Huxley, "Darwin's Bulldog," attempted to attract support for evolution by using it to attack the Church and the standards of Christian morality he was well known to violate.

But in 1860, things changed. It seemed to many that the first of evolution's countless thousands of missing links had been found: *Archaeopteryx* (ARR key OP ter iks), a fossil found in the Solnhofen Limestone in Germany, was believed to "prove" that dinosaurs really did evolve into birds. Evolutionists have only ever claimed to have found a handful of "missing links," and *Archaeopteryx*, the first discovered, still ranks (along with "cave men" and the "horse series") among the top three used to seduce the public into acceptance of evolution.

Thomas Henry Huxley

Virtually every textbook and museum that treats fossils has a picture or model like those shown in Figure 11.1. If it weren't for the detailed impressions of feathers on the forelimbs and tail, the evolutionary story goes, the skeleton would probably be taken for that of a small dinosaur like *Compsognathus* (COMP so NAY thus). (In the opening scene of *The Lost World,* a little girl walking along a beach encounters a group of small "compies." In a real tribute to the success of evolutionary propaganda and the failure of science teaching, the little girl watches the scaly, featherless creature with a thick tail, huge legs, small forearms, and a long snout full of sharp teeth and asks, "What are you — some kind of bird?")

It must be admitted, however, that the two nearly complete *Archaeopteryx* fossils known (the Berlin and London specimens) do share several features with theropod dinosaurs and/or other reptiles: long bony tail; unfused backbones; claws on the wings; and socketed teeth in the bill. Yet the specimens also show detailed impressions of feathers on the wings and tail. "Aha," said the evolutionist of 1860, "an excellent combination of reptilian and avian (bird) features — a perfect example of a missing link that has been found!"

The "dino-bird" *Archaeopteryx* has been used effectively to promote belief in evolution for well over a century, but once again science has not been kind to the evolutionist's hope. The feather impressions were not some sort of "sceather," a transitional mixture of features that might suggest how the scales of reptiles might have evolved into the feathers of birds. Instead they were complete and complex avian feathers of several different types, including features of the primary flight feathers of a strong flyer.

Nor did the supposed "dino-bird" link show any evidence of evolution from leg to wing. The *Archaeopteryx* wing bone pattern was 100 percent like that

Figure 11.1

wing-feather

Missing

of birds today — and totally different from the pattern in any dinosaur or even a flying pterodactyl. Furthermore, *Archaeopteryx* had the extremely robust furcula (the fused clavicles or wishbone) of a strong flying bird.

What about the other features once thought to make *Archaeopteryx* reptilian? The penguin, a highly specialized bird, has a bony tail and unfused backbones. Birds like the ostrich, hoatzin, and turaco have claws on their wings. Living birds do not have socketed teeth, but several fossil birds had teeth. Besides that, some reptiles have teeth (e.g., crocodiles) and some don't (e.g., turtles), so that trait is not important for distinguishing or relating reptiles and birds.

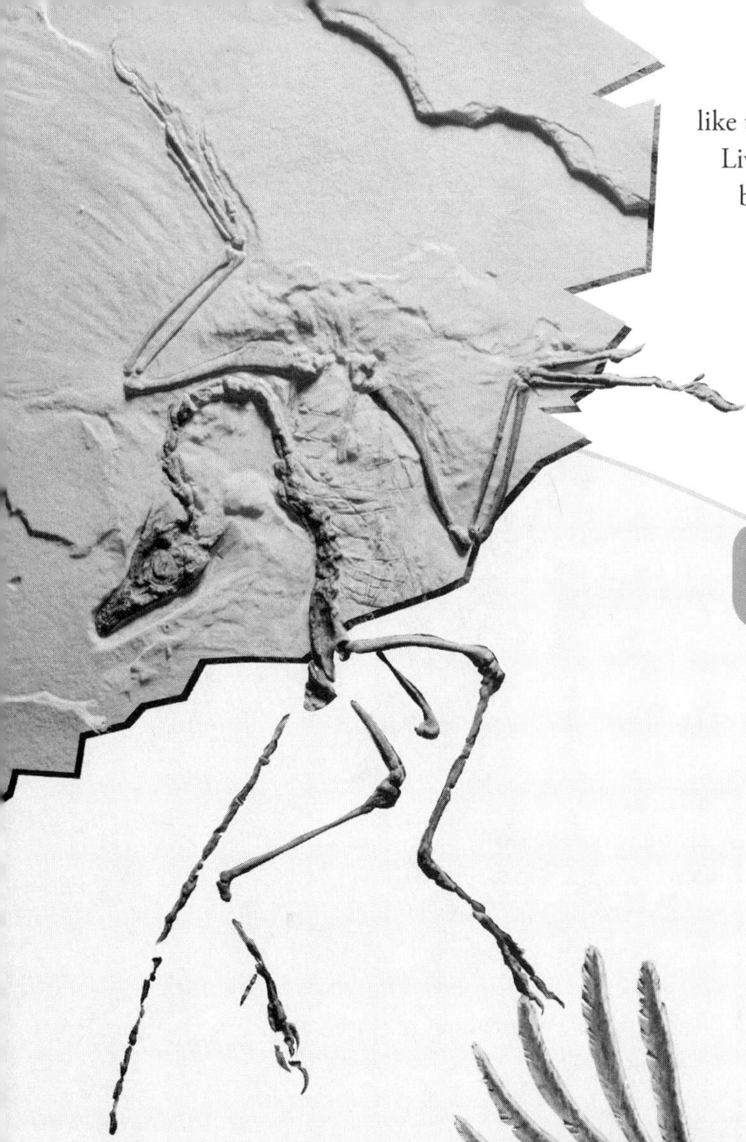

In short, scientists have concluded that *Archaeopteryx* is 100 percent bird, not a dino-bird missing link at all. All its features are shared by other birds, and its wings, feathers, and furcula are those of a strong flying bird. *Archaeopteryx* is different from other birds only in ways eagles are different from hummingbirds, not in the ways eagles

Dino-bird?

are different from lizards.

When I first visited the British Museum of Natural History in London, I was anxious to photograph the museum's *Archaeopteryx* specimen. The museum had paid a scandalously high price for the second complete Solnhofen specimen discovered in 1861. I found the impressive statues of Darwin and T.H. Huxley, but no *Archaeopteryx*. On my second visit, I finally found the *Archaeopteryx* display. It was not highlighted in a great room with major discoveries. It was not highlighted in a side room. It was simply one bird among many in a glass case in a room mostly full of stuffed birds, and the description referred to it not as a dino-bird link but, unpretentiously, as the "first bird."

Actually, *Archaeopteryx* does not even qualify scientifically as the first bird! Its fossils are found preserved in the middle (Jurassic) of three fossil rock systems evolutionists call the "Age of Dinosaurs" (Mesozoic). Fossils

[*Archaeopteryx*]

Link?

[*Compsaghatus*]

77

of ordinary birds are found in the fossil-rock system (Triassic) below the level where *Archaeopteryx* fossils are found. The *Archaeopteryx* fossils found, then, could not be the ancestors of birds, because birds were flying around, killed, buried, and fossilized before *Archaeopteryx* was. A person could believe, of course, the *Archaeopteryx* fossils will someday be found at the deeper level, but that would be an article of faith, not evidence from science. The evidence actually found by paleontologists suggests that several different kinds of birds and dinosaurs existed fully formed, separate, complete, and complex, before their first appearance in the fossil sequence.

So, the next time you hear a "dinosaur-bird missing link" has been found — and you will hear such stories — remember to ask two kinds of questions. First, ask about its level in the fossil-rock sequence: is the proposed "missing link" found deep enough to be a link between supposed ancestor-descendant groups? None of the Chinese fossils of birds and reptiles found in the area where *National Geographic* got its fake dino-bird could be a link from dinosaurs to birds, for example, simply because birds are already found fossilized in deeper layers.

Second, ask about the traits in the proposed missing link. Are there any in-between or transitional traits, something partly leg/partly wing, or partly scale/partly feather? Odd combinations of complete and complex traits, such as the wings and feathers of *Archaeopteryx,* only tell us at most about weaknesses in our human systems of classification. Any specimen claimed to be a missing link must show traits in transition, and evolutionists have only claimed a few of such transitional forms, and science has disproved them all.

The lesson of dino-birds for Christians is clear: When evolutionists claim they have found a missing link, just wait: science will catch up and show that the Bible has been right all along. The Bible suggests (1) that dinosaurs and birds were each created, complete and complex in several different kinds, separate right from the moment of their creation; (2) man's sin corrupted God's perfect creation and brought on disease, death, and the global destruction of Noah's flood. That's why we find fossils of dead birds and dead dinosaurs. What we see in God's world agrees with what we read in God's Word about the past, and that encourages us to believe God's Word about the future — rich and abundant life eternal and paradise restored at Christ's return!

Form your foundation.

Darwin's followers have claimed more than once to find a missing link between dinosaurs and birds, but scientists proved them wrong each time. *Archaeopteryx* (1860) turned out to be a strong flying bird. The Chinese specimen featured in *National Geographic* (1999) was a fake. When science and Scripture disagree, just wait until science catches up and shows the Bible has been right all along!

Building Inspection

1. According to a highly publicized group of evolutionists, dinosaurs did not become extinct; instead they sprouted _____ and became _____.

2. According to a nature encyclopedia, the bee hummingbird is the smallest _____. In its November 1999 issue, *National Geographic* published an illustrated article entitled "Feathers for _____."

3. "Archaeoraptor" was the name given to a Chinese fossil widely touted as a missing link between dinosaurs and birds. What did it turn out to be? _____

   a. What did Storrs Olson, bird expert and evolutionist at the Smithsonian, have to say about *National Geographic's* "feathered dinosaur"?

   _____

   b. What did *USA Today* call the Chinese fake fossil supposed to link dinosaurs to birds?

   _____

4. *Archaeopteryx*, the first fossil proposed to link dinosaurs and birds, has been used to "preach evolution" from 1860 to the "modern" museum or classroom.

   a. What features of *Archaeopteryx* were considered reptile-like?

   _____

   b. Are there "regular" birds with these supposedly reptilian feature?

   _____

   c. What features does *Archaeopteryx* have that are found in living birds but no living reptiles?

   _____

   d. Are any of the features of *Archaeopteryx* "traits in transition" (e.g., half scale/half feather)? Does this support creation or evolution?

   _____

   e. Compared to fossils of regular birds, where is *Archaeopteryx* found in the sequence of fossil-bearing rock layers? Does that support creation or evolution?

   _____

5. Thinking as a scientist, what should you do the next time you hear a news report or read a *National Geographic* article claiming a missing link between dinosaurs and birds has been found?

   _____

   _____

What about Dino Extinction and an "Age of Dinosaurs"?

Only a handful of evolutionists, promoted by media publicity and not by their scientific discoveries, tout the belief that dinosaurs survive disguised as birds. Most evolutionists believe dinosaurs became extinct, leaving no descendants.

But why did dinos become extinct? According to evolution, dinos were superbly "fit to survive" and were the dominant (most conspicuous and most successful) form of animal for about 150 million evolutionary years, the so-called "Age of Dinosaurs." (By contrast, according to evolution, modern man or *Homo sapiens*, has yet to prove he is fit to survive even one million years.)

It is popular today for evolutionists to claim the so-called "Age of Dinosaurs" ended with a mass extinction when an asteroid hit the earth and caused a worldwide catastrophe. Creationists/Flood geologists already believed, of course, that the worldwide catastrophe of Noah's flood killed all the land dinos except those aboard the ark.

Actually, the biblical flood concept does a much better job of explaining dinosaur decline than the evolutionists' asteroid hypothesis. Noah's flood would affect all dinosaurs living in all environments on earth all at the same time. The asteroid impact would have affected only those dinosaurs living at the end of the so-called "Dinosaur Age." If there really were a "Dinosaur Age," then evolutionists could not use a worldwide asteroid catastrophe to explain the demise of so many dinosaurs they believe became extinct long before the asteroid hit.

Asteroid 951 Gaspra as seen by the Galileo spacecraft in 1991. Asteroids vary greatly in size. The largest and first-known asteroid, Ceres, was discovered in 1801. It is 580 miles (933 kilometers) in diameter. Ceres is believed to contain about 1/3 the total mass of all the asteroids. One of the smallest, discovered in 1991 and named 1991 BA, is only about 20 feet (6 meters) across. NASA

But was there ever really a "Dinosaur Age"? Evolutionists love to talk about an "Age of Dinosaurs," an "Age of Fish," a "Coal Age," and various "Ages" of this or that. However, the concept of "Age of . . ." is based on an incorrect interpretation of fossil-bearing rock units.

Rock units can be named for the minerals they contain (e.g., limestone or sandstone), but they can also be named for the fossils found in them. Regardless of the minerals found in it, a rock unit that contains mostly certain kinds of trilobite and lampshell fossils, for example, is called "Cambrian." Based on the fossils found in them, scientists have named 12 major "fossil-rock" units, called geologic systems.

Age of Dinosaurs?

The 12 fossil-rich geologic systems are usually diagrammed in a certain vertical order called the geologic column diagram — GCD for short (Figure 12.1, p. 82–83). Much of the pioneering work identifying geologic systems and suggesting the geologic column diagram was done in the 1800s by creationists/Flood geologists who believed they were describing groups of plants and animals buried in sequence by water during the year of Noah's flood. First buried in abundance were bottom-dwelling sea creatures, then near shore, lowland and upland life zones were buried, with sea creatures going all the way to the top as finally, "all the high hills that were under the whole heaven, were covered" in the worldwide flood (Gen. 7:19).

Most early geologists accepted fossil deposits as the evidence of God's just judgment for the violence, struggle, and death by which man's sin had corrupted God's originally perfect creation. But then evolutionists came along with a new interpretation. Instead of seeing fossil groups as the buried remains of plants and animals living in different pre-Flood environments, evolutionists treated them as different stages in the presumed evolution of life on earth. For evolutionists, the geologic column diagram no longer represented stages in the burial of different life zones in the rising waters of Noah's flood; it represented instead stages in the evolution of new forms of life. "First" and "last" meant first and last buried for creationists/Flood geologists; for evolutionists, "first" meant first evolving on earth and "last" meant last surviving before extinction. Instead of seeing geological systems as environmental zones, evolutionists believed they were time zones.

Almost all dinosaur fossils are found in one of three geologic systems: the Triassic, Jurassic, and Cretaceous (GCD 8, 9, and 10 in the geologic column diagram). Taken together, these three systems are called the Mesozoic. Creationists/Flood geologists think the Mesozoic fossil-rock grouping includes the places where dinosaurs lived in the pre-Flood world, about 5,000 years ago; evolutionists believe it is the time during which dinosaurs lived on earth, about 220–65 million years ago. Creationists/Flood geologists might call a rock deposit rich in dinosaur fossils a "Dinosaur Zone" (place or environment); evolutionists call Mesozoic rock a "Dinosaur Age."

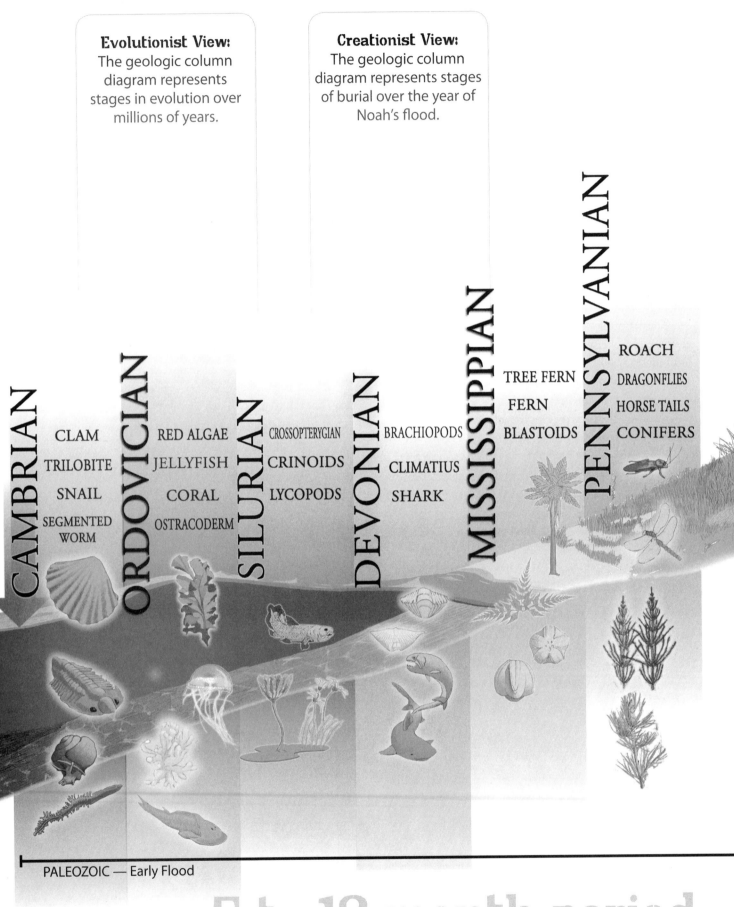

CAMBRIAN

CLAM
TRILOBITE
SNAIL
SEGMENTED WORM

ORDOVICIAN

RED ALGAE
JELLYFISH
CORAL
OSTRACODERM

SILURIAN

CROSSOPTERYGIAN
CRINOIDS
LYCOPODS

DEVONIAN

BRACHIOPODS
CLIMATIUS
SHARK

MISSISSIPPIAN

TREE FERN
FERN
BLASTOIDS

PENNSYLVANIAN

ROACH
DRAGONFLIES
HORSE TAILS
CONIFERS

PALEOZOIC — Early Flood

5 to 12 month period

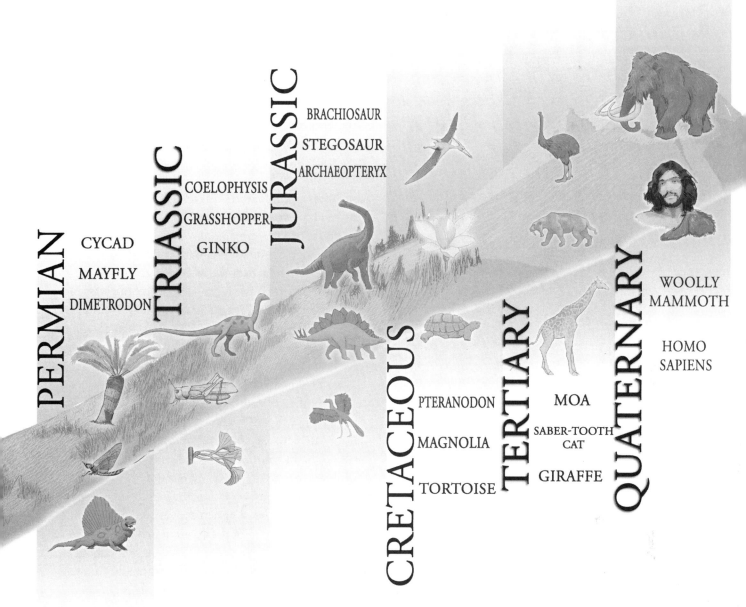

PERMIAN

CYCAD
MAYFLY
DIMETRODON

TRIASSIC

COELOPHYSIS
GRASSHOPPER
GINKO

JURASSIC

BRACHIOSAUR
STEGOSAUR
ARCHAEOPTERYX

CRETACEOUS

PTERANODON
MAGNOLIA
TORTOISE

TERTIARY

MOA
SABER-TOOTH
CAT
GIRAFFE

QUATERNARY

WOOLLY
MAMMOTH

HOMO
SAPIENS

On the basis of the fossils it contains, a rock layer or unit can be assigned to a geologic system or paleosystem. Twelve system names are used worldwide, and these are usually displayed in a certain vertical order called the geologic column or geologic column diagram (GCD).

Most early geologists thought fossils were largely remains of plants and animals buried in the worldwide flood at Noah's time. Groups of fossils (geologic systems) would represent plants and animals living together in certain environments in the pre-Flood world, and the geologic column diagram (GCD) would represent stages in the burial of pre-Flood environmental zones in the rising waters of the year-long flood.

Later on, evolutionists claimed fossil systems showed stages in evolution over millions of years, but science contradicted that view. The first abundant fossils show complex beginnings for all major animal groups (Cambrian Explosion); and links that show how one kind of life changed into others are still missing. Mount St. Helens, the Grand Canyon, etc., show layers were stacked up by a lot of water, not a lot of time.

MESOZOIC — Mid Flood

CENOZOIC — Late & Post Flood

following 40 days of rain!

First, if a dinosaur was not on the ark, then it drowned in the flood.

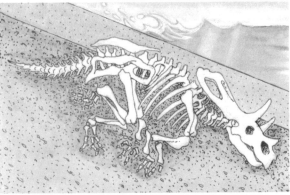

Next, the animal was buried rapidly as the flood deposited soft layers of material that later hardened into stone.

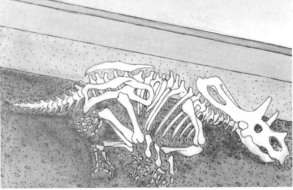

Then, a process of fossilization occurred, such as the bones being replaced by dissolved minerals in the ground water.

Finally, the fossils became exposed as the ground around the animal eroded away.

Note: scientists never have, never will, and never could dig up the "Age of Dinosaurs." Scientists can and do dig up the fossilized bones of dead dinosaurs, and they can and do describe the place where these fossils are found. But belief in a "Dinosaur Age" is not, was not, will not be, and could not be a discovery of science. The so-called "Age of Dinosaurs" is a belief about the past, a belief made up by people who were not there, who do not claim to have a historical record left by reliable observers, people who do not want to accept the biblical record as reliable history, people who want to believe fossils represent progressive development caused by time, chance, struggle, and death, people who do not want to believe fossils are the just judgment on a sin-cursed world by the God who created the original paradise with plan and purpose.

Dinosaur fossils are facts — facts that can be scientifically described, measured, and repeatedly studied by many qualified observers. But fossil facts do not, will not, and cannot speak for themselves. Two scientists can agree completely on a fossil's description and its location, then they can tell two radically different stories about where and when the dinosaur lived and what it was doing just before it died. Scholars who accept the Bible as "The History Book of the Universe" find it easy to relate design features in dinosaur fossils to God's creation, their defects and disease to the corruption of creation by man's sin, their worldwide burial and fossilization to the catastrophe of Noah's flood, and their persistence into modern times as a tribute to the ark of preservation provided by Christ.

Evolutionists tell a radically different story about the same dinosaur fossils. They believe the first dinosaur evolved by chance mutations from a more generalized reptilian ancestor about 220 million years ago (mya), leaving fossils in lower Triassic rock (GCD 8). Chance mutations among the first dinosaurs produced a variety of new traits, the story continues, and Darwin's

The glyptodont, an extinct animal known only from fossil remains, is believed to be an ancient relative of the armadillo.

84

variety of new traits, the story continues, and Darwin's "war of nature" (struggle and death) changed these varieties into new species of dinosaurs during the presumed 150 or so million years of Mesozoic time, the so-called "Age of Dinosaurs." According to evolutionists, many dinosaurs lost the "struggle for survival" and became extinct in lower (Triassic, GCD 8) and middle (Jurassic, GCD 9) Mesozoic time, but those most "fit to survive" were earth's ruling reptiles into upper (Cretaceous, GCD10) Mesozoic "time" — until, near the peak of dinosaur diversity and dominance, an asteroid impact 65 mya brought a sudden and horrific end to the "Age of Dinosaurs."

The evolutionist's story of a "Dinosaur Age" is overwhelmingly popular — and, as detailed in later chapters, overwhelmingly contradicted by scientific facts from paleontology, geology, biology, radiology, physics, and other sciences. Belief in a "Dinosaur Age" is based on faith in evolution, not on the facts of science.

We will examine the multitudinous scientific errors of evolution throughout this *Creation Foundations* series, but let us look at one right now — the evolutionist's misconception about mass extinction. Ever since the extinction of so many "fit" dinosaurs was blamed on an asteroid impact, the concept of worldwide mass extinction has become increasingly popular with evolutionists and with the media. There is one major mass extinction, or mass near-extinction, recorded in Scripture, of course, the record of the worldwide catastrophe at Noah's flood. Indeed, before they accepted the asteroid impact idea, evolutionists had ridiculed the concept of worldwide mass extinction, apparently fearing that it might lend credibility to the biblical record.

There are many differences, however, between the real worldwide near-extinction recorded in biblical history and the hypothetical concept of long ago mass extinctions proposed by evolutionists.

Imagine you are on a scuba diving trip to the Florida Keys. Just as you exit the boat and are ready to dive, the dive master says you have special dive gear that will take you back into the past. As you descend through the lifeless water out at sea, you think, *This must be the earth's primordial ocean, before life evolved.* As you reach the sandy, muddy bottom, you spot some worms and a few clams and snails, and exclaim, "Aha! Evolution has at last produced a few simple life forms!" As you swim toward shallower water, it seems some of the worms and shellfish you first saw became extinct, but some, you think, must have evolved into the rich diversity of corals and brightly colored fish you now see before your eyes. As you swim farther, however, the corals disappear, leaving only a few sand dollars, dull-colored fish, and crabs. You wonder, "What caused the mass extinction that wiped out all those beautiful corals?"

Farther on, the water becomes too shallow for swimming, and you notice some animals spend their lives partly in water and partly on land. "Aha," you speculate, "perhaps these are like the fish that evolved into the first land animals (amphibians), and those are like the land animals that evolved back into the sea (e.g., whales)." But then you reach the sandy, windswept beach and begin to wonder, "What catastrophic mass extinction reduced life on earth to a few insects, lizards, and blades of grass?" As you walk across the beach into a hammock of trees, you breathe a sigh of relief. "At least the few living things that did survive the mass extinction evolved into a new and even more complex variety of plants and animals. In the long struggle that leads ultimately to death, at least there are cases where life finds a way."

Creationist View
- 12 major geological systems are viewed as 12 broad-based ecological systems
- Exisiting at the same time in different places

Evolutionist View
- 12 major planet-wide geological systems
- Each lasting millions of years

Creationist	Evolutionist
Quaternary	Quaternary
Tertiary	Tertiary
Cretaceous	Cretaceous
Jurassic	Jurassic
Triassic	Triassic
Permian	Permian
Pennsylvanian	Pennsylvanian
Mississippian	Mississippian
Devonian	Devonian
Silurian	Silurian
Ordovician	Ordovician
Cambrian	Cambrian

Each layer/level contains fossils of what lived in different ecological zones. All creatures found in all layers/levels existed at the same time, and fossilized over a period of about a year.

Each layer/level contains fossils of only what lived during that time period (lasting millions of years), thus formed over millions of years.

Since we can see the earth today has ecological zones of different creatures living in different places at the same time, no one would take seriously the "scuba time machine" story above. But evolutionists believe that fossil-rock groupings represent different time zones, not different ecological zones, so when they see rocks full of fossil mammals on top of rocks full of fossil dinosaurs, they say, "See, some mass extinction ended the Age of Dinosaurs, and the few survivors evolved (through missing links we haven't found yet) into the 'Age of Mammals' that followed." A creationist/Flood geologist would say, "No, you just dug up the fossil remains of mammals in one environment that got buried on top of the remains of dinosaurs washed in from another environment."

In a thought experiment, imagine the whole earth suddenly entombed in extraterrestrial dust and ash that fossilized its creatures. An evolutionist digging in the ash might claim to find the "Age of Fishes" buried off Florida, the "Age of Coal Swamps" in the Everglades, the "Age of Elephants" in East Africa, etc. A creationist would simply claim to have found a place, or ecological zone, where fish, swamp plants, and elephants once lived on earth.

Evolutionists do concede that fossil-rock groupings are at least partly ecological. Indeed, "paleoecology" is the study of the possible ecological relationships among those plants and animals now buried together as fossils. Such studies have shown, for example, that Cretaceous dinosaurs are buried with flowering plants, Jurassic dinosaurs with lots of cycads (cone-bearing seed plants with palm-like leaves), and Triassic dinosaurs with other conifers and with many ferns and fern allies. Dietary preferences, not survival of the fittest, many have determined which dinosaurs lived where. Furthermore, rock layers with dinosaurs grade laterally into rock layers full of sea creatures, including the awesome "shelled squids" called ammonites. A vertebrate paleontologist may call Mesozoic rock the "Age of Dinosaurs," but invertebrate paleontologists call it the "Age of Ammonites," and plant paleontologists (paleobotanists) call part of the Mesozoic (the Jurassic) the "Age of Cycads." All that really means is that earth had many ecological zones in the past just as it has many ecological zones in the present — and many ecological zones can exist on earth at the same time.

The creationist/Flood geologist thinks that the 12 major geologic systems represent 12 broad-based ecological zones all existing at the same time in different places in the pre-Flood world. There was just one major mass extinction (near-extinction) about 5,000 years ago, when many plants and animals from all these ecological zones were rapidly buried in sequence from sea bottom to near shore to lowland to upland (with sea creatures going all the way to the top) in the rising waters of Noah's flood. Radioactive decay (e.g., uranium and carbon-14) plus lots of geological evidence support this view.

Dinosaurs did not, therefore, live and die in a "Dinosaur Age" long before man appeared. Dinosaurs were created when mankind was, and they lived in various environments on earth in the pre-Flood world just as mankind lived in other environments. Many dinosaurs died and were fossilized in some Flood deposits while human beings were fossilized in other deposits. But eight people, and two of each kind of dinosaur, survived aboard the ark. That means man and dinosaur got off the ark together and began to multiply and refill the post-Flood earth.

Earth's single, global, mass extinction — Noah's flood — did severely reduce the numbers of dinosaurs living in all three Mesozoic pre-Flood ecological zones, including the parts of the Triassic, Jurassic, and Cretaceous where dinosaurs lived. But that worldwide catastrophe did not bring dinosaurs to complete extinction, because two of every kind of land dinosaur were on the ark and got off the ark to repopulate the earth (see p. 55–56).

So, if neither Noah's flood nor an asteroid impact brought dinosaurs to total extinction, what did?

Unfortunately, extinction is far too easy for scientists to explain. Even today, climate changes are major contributors to extinction, and the aftermath of Noah's flood brought severe climate changes, including the continuing Ice Age that at its peak covered 30 percent of earth's continental surface with ice. Climate shifts affect rainfall, vegetation, soil fertility, and all the animals that depend on those factors. Subsurface imagery shows the Sahara Desert, now a vast, nearly lifeless wasteland, was once crisscrossed with flowing streams and covered with vegetation. Historical records show Indians (Native Americans) in the Southwest enjoyed excellent farming conditions until perhaps A.D. 1000, when some climate change dried up their farms and their cultures.

Fungi causing chestnut blight and Dutch elm disease (Figure 12.3) wiped out huge areas once home to these majestic trees, and also wiped out the homes for many creatures that depended on them for shelter and sustenance. Because it makes them unsuitable for food, the flowering of bamboo forests every 50 years or so threatens the survival of the fragile panda. Fires, floods, droughts, and earthquakes can bring an end to specialized plants and animals living in narrowly restrictive habitats. (See Figure 12.2.)

Small, isolated populations can even be brought to extinction by evolution. Evolutionists like to call mutations the raw material for evolutionary progress, but scientists know mutations usually cause defects and diseases (Figure 12.1).

Before the asteroid impact idea became popular, evolutionists used a variety of factors like those above to explain dinosaur extinction: it got too hot, it got too cold, egg temperatures produced some dinosaurs with only one sex, a dinosaur virus plague got them, small mammals ate the eggs, etc. Those who wanted to make dinosaurs more bird-like claimed they were "warm-blooded" (endothermic), and such creatures required much more food than "cold-blooded" ones (ectothermal) just to maintain body temperature. The late great evolutionist Carl Sagan, at a lecture in San Diego, mentioned the idea that a laxative plant required in the dinosaur diet became extinct, and dinosaurs died of constipation!

Florida Panther

Figure 12.1: The Florida panther was nearly brought to extinction by evolution, (i.e., mutations that damaged its reproductive and circulatory systems so badly that no cubs could survive to reproduce). They were "saved" by crossing with Western panthers, which had non-matching mutations.

Brown Pelican

Figure 12.2: The brown pelican was listed as endangered in 1970 because of widespread pollutant-related reproductive failures. They are extremely sensitive to bioaccumulation of the pesticide DDT, which causes reproductive failure by altering calcium metabolism and thinning eggshells.

In 1985, brown pelicans on the Atlantic Coast had recovered enough that they could be removed from the endangered species list.

Pelicans are dependent on northern anchovies and Pacific sardines, which have declined due to over-fishing by humans. Breeding populations and nesting productivity vary dramatically from year to year depending on El Niño events and other climatic changes.

Dutch Elm Disease

Figure 12.3: Fungi causing chestnut blight and Dutch elm disease wiped out huge areas once home to these majestic trees, and also wiped out the homes for many creatures that depended on them for shelter and sustenance.

87

Many species have been driven to extinction by human beings. Passenger pigeons whose flocks once darkened the sky were killed off completely by settlers arriving in America, and the millions of buffalo on America's plains were nearly brought to extinction. The great blue whale, whose volume could hold two of the largest land dinosaurs, would have been hunted to extinction if not protected. Florida was once home to elephants (mammoths and mastodons), camels, llamas, giant bison, rhinos, and the giant ground sloth, which was bigger than *T. rex*, but, according to Florida's State Museum, the last of these large land mammals were killed off by the Native Americans about 4,000 years ago.

If man in certain areas killed off large mammals far bigger than the average dinosaur, perhaps man also killed off some of the dinosaurs that had begun to multiply and fill the earth after the Flood. Indeed, cultures from around the world tell of "heroes" who slew large, scaly animals, some matching the descriptions of known kinds of dinosaurs. Archaeologists easily recognize rock paintings and etchings (pictographs and petroglyphs, respectively) of people hunting varieties of elephants, like the woolly mammoth, thought to be extinct. Although you won't see them in textbooks or television programs, other pictographs and petroglyphs seem just as clearly to show various types of dinosaurs!

A few scientists believe some dinosaurs might still be living in remote habitats on earth. An evolutionist at the University of Chicago, Dr. Roy Mackal, founded the science of cryptozoology, the search of hidden (rare and/or reclusive) animals. Without yet finding the elusive creatures, Dr. Mackal and others have followed up reports of natives in the African Congo who say they have seen a creature ("mokele mbembe") closely resembling long-necked sauropods with forelimbs shorter than hind limbs (e.g., *Diplodocus* or *Apatosaurus* types) perhaps 30 feet (9 m) long.

Evolutionists define the "Dinosaur Age" as the time when dinosaurs lived in certain environments on earth. If the numerous sightings of live dinosaurs are really true, that means the "Dinosaur Age" was not long, long ago; the "Dinosaur Age" is now, and we're in it! (Of course, parts of the earth are also in the "Age of Fish," "Ice Age," and "Stone Age," too — all at the same time.)

Belief in a "Dinosaur Age" that began and ended millions of years ago turns out to be a myth; belief in dinosaur extinction may turn out to be a myth as well — a product of evolutionary faith, not scientific fact.

Regardless of whether any dinosaurs remain alive today, however, there is abundant historical evidence that dinosaurs have lived on earth in the recent past. Most evolutionists restrict themselves to only the fossil evidence as a source of information about dinosaurs. Scientists with minds open to all the evidence are free to search historical records as well.

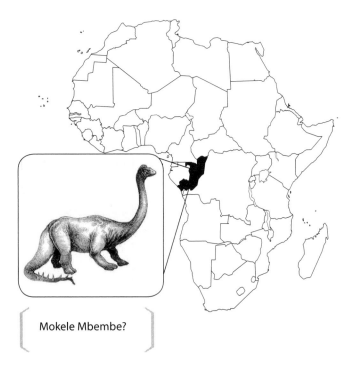

Mokele Mbembe?

Form your foundation.

The geologic column diagram shows burial of different environmental zones during the year of Noah's flood, from complex sea life to near shore, lowland, then upland life. Three systems called the "Dinosaur Age" are really "Dinosaur Zones," or places where dinosaurs lived in the pre-Flood world — while most people lived at the same time in different places.

1. A rock layer identified by the fossils it contains is called a _____. Twelve geologic systems arranged in a certain vertical order are called the _____ diagram. Creationists/Flood geologists think the systems in the geologic column represent stages in the burial of different environmental zones by _____. Darwin's followers believe geologic systems represent stages in _____,

2. Most dinosaur fossils are found in three systems of the geologic column diagram (GCD), the Mesozoic (GCD 8, 9, 10). Those three systems are the buried remains of life zones where dinosaurs lived about 5,000 years ago according to (Flood geologists/Darwin's followers) _____, but they represent changes from one species of dinosaur to others from 220–65 million years ago according to _____. (1) Initial complexity of each group, (2) links missing between kinds, and (3) evidence for lots of water vs. lots of time are three lines of evidence that favor the view of _____.

3. A dinosaur fossil is a (fact of science/belief about the past) _____, but a "Dinosaur Age" is a _____. An eyewitness account of past events that can be checked by scientific tests is provided by (the Bible/Darwin's book) _____.

4. A rock layer with lots of dinosaur fossils would be called the Dinosaur "_____" by Darwin's followers, but a Dinosaur "_____" by Flood geologists.

5. An event that kills a great many life forms all over the world is called a _____ extinction. What mass extinction is recorded in Scripture? _____. What do Darwin's followers believe eliminated the dinosaurs? _____. Which of these two could explain the near extinction of all dinosaurs, not just those living at the end of the so-called "Dinosaur Age"? _____

6. Climate changes and overhunting by people may have caused the final extinction of _____ that got off the ark, but reports like those of mokele mbembe suggest some _____ may still be alive.

7. Cite three environmental changes after the Flood that may have made dinosaur survival difficult:

   _____

   _____

   _____

8. Cite three evidences that suggest some dinosaurs may have been killed off by people:

   _____

   _____

   _____

Chapter

12

Dinosaurs in Recorded History

In *The Great Dinosaur Mystery and the Bible*,[1] Paul Taylor did pioneering work documenting historical encounters between mankind and dinosaurs. Bill Cooper includes many more such encounters in his recent book, *After the Flood*.[2] Writings, pictographs, petroglyphs, and art objects record "regular" land dinosaurs and other "dinos" (dinosaur-associated reptiles) that evolutionists assign to a "Dinosaur Age," such as the flying pterodactyls (e.g., *Pteranodon*) and the swimming marine reptiles (e.g., plesiosaurs, ichthyosaurs, and mosasaurs). For these striking and often fearsome dino-reptiles now nearly or completely extinct, cultures around the world use a term equivalent to the old English word *dragon*.

1. Paul Taylor, *The Great Dinosaur Mystery and the Bible* (Denver, CO: Accent Books, 1998).
2. Bill Cooper, *After the Flood* (West Sussex, UK: New Wine Ministries, 1995).

The dragon (*Draco*) is one of the constellations recognized worldwide. The dragon is the symbol on the Welsh flag. Chinese art and literature abounds with references to dragons; dragons appear in parades and celebrations, and there are records of dragon eggs and dragons being bred in captivity by Chinese emperors. A dragon was kept as an object of reverence by King Nebuchadnezzar in Babylon, and by a tribe in India visited by Alexander the Great. By slaying menacing dragons, men like Gilgamesh in Sumer and St. George in England became cultural heroes. Just as cave art and other art objects show "prehistoric" mammals like the woolly mammoth, they also show various kinds of quadrupedal and bipedal dinosaurs (Figure 13.1).

Quadrupedal — four footed

Bipedal — two footed

Figure 13.1

Human beings have a tendency to exaggerate, however, and as the numbers of dragons became smaller, stories about them tended to grow larger (finally reaching Godzilla proportions in Japan!). Furthermore, it seems that stories about one kind of dragon got mixed up with stories about others, so that some dragon artwork came to look like composites of several different animals, e.g., one that might show the head of a vicious carnivore on the body of a herbivore with the wings of a pterodactyl and the tail of a plesiosaur (Figure 13.2)! Unfortunately, this tendency to exaggerate and to put parts of different dragons together has made it easy for some to ridicule the existence of dragons without even looking at the solid historical evidence that lies beneath the legends and really fits with the fossil evidence.

The notion of a "fire-breathing dragon" is regularly held up to ridicule any relationship between dinosaurs and dragons. Actually, scientists would find it very easy to explain an animal that could literally breathe out flames. Many animals generate methane in their digestive tracts. Methane, or natural gas, is quite flammable, and there's a college prank (which I will not describe) based on setting human methane on fire! Some scientists think that dinosaurs belched so

much methane that a "greenhouse gas" may have helped keep the polar regions of earth warm! Scientists also know of dinosaurs that had cavities in their skulls with tubular passages leading to the fronts of their mouths. Imagine such chambers contained an enzyme that would accelerate the chemical reaction between methane and oxygen. If the enzyme were injected just as the belching dinosaur opened its mouth, the methane blast would burst into a fiery stream of flame as the methane hit the oxygen in the air.

Figure 13.2: Dinosaur art by Native Americans (Petroglyphs)

That may sound far-fetched, but matches can produce streams of flaming methane from the rear end of the digestive tract in human beings with a real "talent" for controlled gas release! More to the point, scientists have already described in detail an analogous system in a half-inch (10 mm) insect, the bombardier beetle (Figure 13.3). The beetle stores explosive chemicals and enzymes in separate chambers at its rear. When the enzymes and explosive chemicals are mixed in the beetle's combustion chamber, the rapid reaction enables the bombardier to fire off machine-gun bursts of hot, noxious gas at the boiling point of water (100°C or 212°F) into the mouth of a would-be beetle-eater. In a similar way (but from the other end), injecting an enzyme into methane in the "combustion chamber" (mouth) of a dinosaur would let it belch flame into the face of a would-be predator (although it's possible the flame could also be used to cook vegetables or to light a path on a dark night!).

There are no "living flamethrowers," and the historical evidence is only suggestive, not conclusive. However, many cultures have stories of fire-breathing dragons, and one may be implied in the Bible (Job 41:18–21). One

Figure 13.3: Bombardier Beetle

thing is for sure, the existence of such creatures would be very easy for scientists to explain (and those ridiculing the possibility are really only revealing their ignorance of simple science).

Unlike the restricted term "dinosaur," the term "dragon" extends to flyers and swimmers. The Greek historian Herodotus, whose writings are considered very reliable, recorded live pterodactyls and their skeletons so well that we know he was describing a *Ramphorhynchus* type (small, bill with teeth, long tail) rather than a *Pteranodon* type (large, toothless bill, stubby tail). Some think the stylized Thunderbird symbol of the Sioux Indians is based on sightings of *Pteranodon*. A live pterodactyl was found, controversially, in a French coal mine in the 1800s, and reports still circulate of pterodactyls living in the dense rain forests of large equatorial islands like Papua-New Guinea, Borneo, and parts of the Indonesian archipelago.

Waters off Madagascar and Indonesia are now known to be home to huge fish, the coelacanths, reaching over 6 feet (2 m) in length. Evolutionists once thought they became extinct in the "Dinosaur Age." Fishermen on the Comoro Islands in the Indian Ocean had been catching and eating the big coelacanths for centuries, but these "dinosaur-age fish" remained undetected by scientists until the mid 1900s, and the Indonesian ones weren't discovered (by scientists) until the 1990s. If such big "dinosaur-age fish" escaped scientific detection for so long, maybe the oceans are also home to "dinosaur age" swimming reptiles, such as the plesiosaurs.

Scotland's "Nessie" is certainly the best known of the possible plesiosaur sightings. Skeptics might argue at first that if there is a swimming "dino" in a Scottish lake, drain the lake and haul it out! But Loch Ness is really an inlet from the North Sea, a gash in the earth filled with murky water up to a mile (1.6 km) deep, bordered by rocky sides pockmarked with caves and subterranean entrances to air-filled chambers. A breeding colony of plesiosaurs could survive there for centuries, only occasionally sighted by locals while avoiding repeatedly verifiable (i.e., scientific) detection.

The person who took the most famous "Nessie" photo claimed on his deathbed that it was fake. That proves the man was a liar and a publicity seeker — but we really don't know whether he was lying the first time or the second! Reports of plesiosaur carcasses washing ashore have been reported from several continents — but the evidence was allowed to rot away.

Many large animals shy away from human contact. Thousands of travelers and hikers traverse the Rocky Mountains without ever seeing a grizzly bear, and some local stories are dismissed as exaggerations, but that certainly would not "prove" grizzly bears do not exist! If pandas weren't repeatedly photographed and found in zoos, who would believe the reports that cute and cuddly, slow-moving black and white "teddy bears" live in remote Chinese forests, using their "carnivorous teeth" only to eat bamboo? The okapi, an animal much bigger than a horse, was unknown to science until 1901. The graptolite, a sea creature which evolutionists thought had been extinct five times longer than *T. rex*, was found alive and well in the Indian Ocean off West Australia. One of the reasons given for protecting rain forests is belief that many new species, known only to natives, remain yet to be discovered by scientists.

Not long ago a grove of Woolemi pines, thought long extinct, was found in Australia, prompting one scientist to exclaim that it was like finding a live dinosaur! The cycad plants that were abundant in Jurassic dinosaur environments (the "Age of Cycads") survive in reduced numbers in restricted environments today, and are called "living fossils." It's possible scientists will one day discover what natives somewhere already know, that there are still a few "living fossil-dinosaur animals" just like there are "dinosaur plants."

Although some evidences are better documented than others, the sheer abundance of historical evidence makes it clear to all but the closed-minded that dinosaurs and other "dinosaur-associated reptiles" have shared the planet with mankind in the recent past.

What about fossil deposits — do they also show that mankind and dinosaurs lived at the same time?

Mankind and Dinosaurs: The Fossil Evidence

To say that mankind and dinosaurs have lived at the same time in the recent and remote past is not to say that they lived in the same place (environment). Very few people today, for example, live where there are herds of elephants or caribou, an abundance of desert Gila monsters or kangaroo rats, and none live where starfish and corals are the dominant life forms. Most fossils are found buried somewhat near the place they once lived in abundance, and few if any environments would likely be home to both an abundance of dinosaurs and an abundance of people. Nevertheless, human beings live in at least small numbers in practically every environment, so we might expect to find at least a few human fossils or artifacts in almost any geologic system including terrestrial remains — and we do.

As we'll see in the next section, human fossils and/or artifacts have been found in geologic systems evolutionists call the "Coal Age," "Trilobite Age," "Age of Giant Mammals," and the "Dinosaur Age." For

∧ Fossilized dinosaur tracks (above)
< Paluxy River bottom (left)
> Paluxy River bottom footprint (right)

creationists, this is not surprising, since these so-called "ages" are really just the remains of different environments buried in Noah's flood.

In Utah, the Morrison Formation, world famous for its dinosaur deposits, has yielded fossil human bones, sometimes called "Malachite Man" because of the greenish mineral stain they absorbed. Two human skeletons deeply buried in the Morrison dinosaur formation were found during a mining project. Contrary to the spirit of free scientific inquiry (and perhaps fearing the results?), Utah universities have so far not allowed qualified creationist scientists to examine the bones.

Interest and controversy continue to surround reports of dinosaur and human tracks found together in Cretaceous limestone in the Paluxy River bottom near Glen Rose, Texas. In the early 1970s, Films for Christ produced a captivating and controversial film, "Footprints in Stone," which documented trails of human tracks of various sizes crisscrossing trails of various dinosaur tracks. Stunned evolutionists could only try to claim the human-like tracks were carvings or erosion marks. They could not explain why erosion marks should come in a left-right stride, or why so many should have heel, arch, and toe impressions! They could not explain why supposed carvings did not cut through fine laminations in the limestone. Finally, they could not begin to explain why either carvings or erosion

marks could be formed between limestone layers unreached by erosion or carving.

Things got complicated, however, when severe drought left the tracks high and dry for an extended period in the mid-1980s. An investigator noticed a peculiar red stain around *some* of the larger human-like tracks. The stain could be seen but not felt, since it had no relief (depression plus "mud" push-up) like the man-like tracks. The red stain had a peculiar shape, unlike any known dinosaur or any other creature. In spite of these problems, evolutionists immediately dropped their claims the human-like tracks were erosion marks or carvings and instantly insisted they were real tracks — dinosaur tracks!

The dinosaur track assertion really did not make any sense. There is certainly no known dinosaur (or any other creature!) with a lump in the middle of its foot, a

to ridicule creationists, as many creationists had feared — possibly either because creationists had already capitulated or because they knew the argument was flawed.

A few creationists — but not those originally involved in the research — think the human-like tracks have been re-authenticated. Suppose the red stains really were the tracks of some kind of large creature, dinosaur or not, made while it walked across a ledge covered with a thin layer of limey mud. Later, a human being, wondering if the mud were too deep to walk through, noticed the trail of shallow imprints left by some animal. Knowing those spots at least were safe, the person stepped from one track into the next — somewhat like the author remembers as a boy literally walking in his father's footsteps as they hiked to fishing spots across swampy ground (which occasionally turned into water holes!). Remember also that many human-like tracks were found in the dinosaur rock with no red stain around them.

The historical evidence for mankind and dinosaurs living together is abundant and increasing, but still con-

lump shaped like the mold of a human footprint, that is surrounded by a lightweight flap of skin shaped like an elongated, three-fingered mitten that's able to leave a red stain in lime mud without making an impression in it. Nevertheless, not wanting to continue using discredited evidence as evolutionists had so often done, creationist leaders immediately withdrew the popular film about the prints (at great personal expense) and published warnings to creationist laymen to quit citing the Paluxy tracks as evidence for the coexistence of humans and dinosaurs.

Some think the creationists may have surrendered too quickly. The red-stain dinosaur-track hypothesis was never published in a major scientific journal, perhaps because evolutionists felt defending it would be too difficult. Popular evolution writers did not even use the red stain

troversial. Perhaps more evidence of their paleontological association will be discovered in museums, in boxes in the back rooms. The fresh Alaskan dinosaur bones were actually discovered long ago, but were left with unidentified specimens by scientists whose expertise was in mammalian bone. Because of specialization in the sciences, many fossils remain in storage, unidentified and unreported, until a scientist with a different expertise — or a different point of view — takes a fresh look at them. Evolution itself often acts as a set of blinders, preventing evolutionists from recognizing fossils in rocks considered "before" they evolved or "after" they became extinct. Maybe some young people reading these pages will become the Christian paleontologists so desperately needed to take a new look at the old evidence!

There are problems with the theory of heat and pressure over long periods of time when explaining large areas of metamorphic rock. Variations in minerals, the need for heat, and other problems can be explained by a catastrophic event, such as a worldwide flood.

Evolution
(lots of time)

– VERSUS –

Catastrophe
(lots of water)

The Good News

Christians and creationists certainly have ample reason to be optimistic about dinosaur studies. The widely popular evolutionary belief that dinosaurs lived and died millions of years before man appeared is being buried under an avalanche of contradictory historical and scientific evidence. It's the Bible that makes sense of the dinosaur evidence.

(1) **Creation:** Design features in dinosaur bones, distinct differences between dinosaur kinds, and dinosaur eggs with baby dinosaurs (not birds) inside tell us about dinosaur *creation*: well designed to multiply after kind. Swimming and flying dino-reptiles were created on day 5, land dinosaurs on day 6 with mankind.

(2) **Corruption:** Bite marks, diseased bones, and death evident in dinosaur fossils tell us about the *corruption* of God's perfect creation by man's sin, which brought time, chance, struggle, and death — Darwin's "war of nature" making things worse.

(3) **Catastrophe:** Mass graveyards of dinosaur bones, bones turned to stone, and dramatic decline in reptile size and variety testify to the worldwide *catastrophe* of Noah's flood, and to the dramatic climate change, violent storms and "Ice Age" that followed the flood. DNA, protein, and carbon-14 suggest that most dinosaur fossils are not millions of years old but only thousands. The biblical record suggests the Flood occurred 4,500–5,000 years ago.

(4) **Christ:** God provided the ark, a type of *Christ*, to save faithful human beings and two of every kind of air-breathing land animal — including dinosaurs. Fresh Alaskan dinosaur bones and numerous historical records, art objects, pictographs, and petroglyphs show that dinosaurs did begin to multiply and fill the earth after the Flood, but the climate change and over-hunting by people brought their severe decline and possible extinction (in all but perhaps the most remote areas).

Remember, when human opinion dressed up in scientific lingo seems to contradict what the Bible says, just hang on. Science, the study of God's world, will catch up and show the Bible, God's Word, has been right all along!

Form your foundation.

Like many "living fossils" once thought extinct for millions of years, dinosaurs are part of human history, included with dragons in the Bible and writings and art of cultures around the world.

Building Inspection

1. What name is used in the Bible and cultures around the world for dinosaurs and reptilian swimmers and flyers? _____

2. Some dragons that seem obviously mythical may actually be composites made of parts from different kinds of real _____.

3. Would scientists find it hard to explain how a dragon could breathe fire? Explain in detail.

   _____

   _____

   _____

4. Match the creatures below with descriptions that relate them to discussions of dinosaurs/dragons in history:

   _____ a. dragon on flag   A. China

   _____ b. dinosaur eggs raised for emperor   B. Wales

   _____ c. live dinosaur kept for worship   C. Nebuchadnezzar of Babylon

   _____ d. shoots out hot gases   D. St. George

   _____ e. huge fish thought extinct with dinosaurs   E. coelacanth

   _____ f. slew dragon in England matching dinosaur   F. bombardier beetle
           fossils there

   _____ g. grove of "dinosaur trees" thought extinct   G. graptolite

   _____ h. thought extinct five times longer than dino-   H. Woolemi
           saurs, alive off Australia

   _____ i. swimming reptile, possibly plesiosaur   I. Malachite Man

   _____ j. human fossils reported from Morrison   J. Paluxy Man
           "dinosaur formation"

   _____ k. controversial tracks of dinosaurs and man   K. Loch Ness monster
           (?) together

   _____ l. flying reptile seen by Greek historian,   L. pterodactyl
           Herodotus

   _____ m. pictograpts and petroglyphs   M. dinosaur rock art

5. Use something about dinosaurs to illustrate the four Cs of biblical earth history:
   a. Creation
   b. Corruption
   c. Catastrophe
   d. Christ (restoration)

6. What should you do when you hear some new claim that seems to contradict the Bible?

   _____

   _____

Chapter

13

97

Unit 3: Human Origins

For its *Man Alive* series, the Canadian Broadcasting Company (CBC) once did a half-hour creation/evolution program called "Puzzle of the Ancient Wing," which featured the author as the principal creationist spokesman.

To capture the audience's attention, the opening scene revealed a medieval princess in a long, flowing gown wandering in a castle garden. She seemed to be looking for something. Then came the sound, "Ribbit, ribbit." The camera panned over to the edge of a garden pond. There sat a big green frog with bulging eyes. "Ribbit, ribbit." As a feeling of unbelief swept through the audience, the princess bent over and kissed the frog. Sparkling stars exploded across the screen! As the starry burst subsided, it revealed the princess, now in the embrace of her tall, handsome prince.

Into this idyllic scene stepped the program's popular narrator, saying words like these: "If you believe a frog turns into a prince instantly, that's a fairy tale. If you believe a frog turned into a prince in 300 million years, that's evolution." Most evolutionists would not choose, of course, to describe evolution that way. But the narrator's words really do express the essence of evolution in graphic language. For Darwin's followers, the only difference between amphibians, like the frog, and human beings, like the prince, is time, chance, struggle, and death. Time is the hero of evolution's drama, and chance, struggle, and death (Darwin's "war of nature") are its principal players and driving force.

The producer of the CBC public television program was Tom Kelly, whose kindness and thoughtfulness stand out strikingly among the numerous TV personnel with whom the author has worked. After the program aired, Tom Kelly wrote a letter to the author "for the record." Two sentences are especially worth sharing. First, Tom wrote, "For the record, I went into the program as an evolutionist, without knowing why or quite what that meant." Many could say the same thing. Asked if they believe in evolution, many people would say something like this: "Sure, I guess so. Doesn't everyone? Hasn't science proven evolution?" Pressed for what they mean by evolution, many might say, "It's the belief that apes changed into people in lots of little steps over a long time. Some say God used evolution; some say evolution disproves God. I'm not sure. I don't really think about it much. It's an answer you put on a test, or something you say you believe so people won't think you're stupid or some sort of religious fanatic."

But then Tom wrote, "By the time I had done the research, of one thing I was sure, that if evolution is true, the chance-and-time process just does not work." But evolution is all about "chance-and-time" (and struggle and death) as a substitute for God. If it's not time, chance, struggle, and death, could it be plan, purpose, and special acts of creation? As you read this section on human origins, think about which of these choices you prefer — and which produces predictions most consistent with the scientific evidence. Learn to express what you believe — and why you believe it.

"Cave Men" and "Human Evolution"

It's unusual for public television to compare human evolution with belief in the fairy tale change from frog to prince (previous page), but the chief differences between the fairy tale and the evolutionary scenario is the amount of time involved and the Darwinian processes of chance, struggle, and death.

According to evolution, once upon a time long, long ago (about 300 million years), the only four-legged vertebrates (tetrapods) on earth were amphibians, the group that includes frogs and sal-amanders with a tadpole stage in their reproductive development. As millions of years of time rolled by, more and more random, accidental changes (chance mutations) occurred in amphibian DNA, producing more and more genetic variation, includ-ing some that produced new and improved traits. Darwin's ceaseless struggle for survival (struggle and death) eliminated many of

the mutants but gradually changed others into new forms of life — the reptiles: animals with dry, scaly skins that replaced the tadpole stage with shelled eggs laid on land.

As more (mythical) millions of years passed, Darwin's followers assert chance mutations produced new variet-ies of reptiles (including dinosaurs); struggle and death eliminated many of these, but gradually transformed others into animals with hair instead of scales, that nursed their young on milk — the mammals. Then time, chance, struggle, and death produced more specialized groups of mammals, such as the primate group with flat fingernails and stereoscopic vision, including various monkeys and apes.

Finally, chance mutations among members of one primate group, the "anthropoid" apes, including chimpan-zees and gorillas, produced some forms that could walk upright, which freed their "hands" to use tools, which paved the way for increased brain size and intelligence.

Those forms that were best at walking upright, using tools, and outsmarting others killed off or reproduced faster than their competi-tion, say evolutionists, gradually transforming themselves through *hominoid* and *hominid* stages into full-fledged human beings — *Homo sapiens*.

Note several things about this story of the evolutionary emergence of mankind:

(1) Nothing supernatural was involved, but only the ordinary evolutionary processes presumed to produce all non-human life forms as well: time, chance, struggle, and death.

(2) There are no goals, purposes, or planning ahead in the evolutionary process. New traits for evolutionary "progress" are a matter of chance, and their survival a matter of beating out the competition in a ceaseless struggle to the death. If human beings have any purpose, it is only one made up in their own imaginations.

(3) Human beings are neither the pinnacle nor the final stage of evolution. They have been on earth only a short time, and have not yet proved themselves as fit to survive as either dinosaurs or cockroaches. Man's knowledge of medicine and genetics has allowed him to interfere with evolution, but the evolutionary process is continuous, and many evolutionists believe mankind will someday lose its dominant position to another species.

(4) Evolution ("Mother Nature") is no more interested in human life than she is in any other life form. If human beings are wiped out by some viral plague, bacterial epidemic, or their own war-like nature, that merely means human beings were not the "fittest to survive." Like all other life forms, human beings are only temporary winners in the struggle for survival that began in the primordial ooze and ends when the sun burns out and all life ceases.

(5) Individuals and societies may struggle with the competitive animal instincts that brought mankind into being, say Darwin's followers, but there is no such thing as "sin" or "guilt" as a consequence of violating the absolute standards of some mythical god who created the first of all human life. "Right" and "wrong" are relative terms created by societies to promote the survival of their particular groups, and one standard for all peoples will evolve only when all people see themselves as one society, earthlings, dedicated to the preservation of the planet that gave them birth.

One can be a "three-, four-, or five-point" evolutionist, but there can be little doubt that evolution is the dominant cultural myth of the 21st century. From the Dark Ages to Darwin, the intellectual giants and leaders in science, art, music, literature, politics, and philosophy expressed their messages on morals and mission on the biblical backdrop of belief that God's perfect world, which was ruined by man's sin and destroyed by Noah's flood, would be restored to new life in Christ. Now metaphors of human morals and mission are expressed in terms of Darwin's "war of nature," time, chance, struggle, and death. Freed at last from the Word of God, man's words reign supreme, and every person is free to do what is right in his own eyes — except as he is controlled by other people.

In the CBC "frog-to-prince" production described in the introduction to this unit on human origins (p. 99), a famous evolutionist, Swinton, captured the essence of this creation/evolution "war of the world views." Speaking slowly, even wistfully, he told the television audience that he had grown up in a religious household. It would be nice to believe that God created man, he said, and put in him the Garden of Eden to care for and superintend the earth. But it isn't so, he asserted. The whole of his scientific training, indeed the whole of scientific discovery since Darwin, he continued, had convinced him the Bible was myth and evolution was true.

Then Swinton's eyes and voice saddened as he explained how mankind was nothing special in the evolutionary process, and that evolution would continue long after mankind's extinction. It was not yet obvious, he concluded, what animal — or plant — would replace us.

Contrary to the sad commentary by the expert evolutionist above, most laymen and social engineers see themselves as the pinnacle of evolutionary progress. But, as the late great evolutionist S. J. Gould once put it, the fate of every species is extinction, including man. Too

many people jump at the chance to set their own rules while ignoring the laws of God, forgetting both that other people can set different rules and that evolution knows only one rule: The life form with the best survival skills wins, and there are no rules of fair play. Evolution is a winner-take-all struggle for survival to the death among different members of the same species. Then the winning mutants must compete ecologically with winners from other species for a place in the world biosphere.

Before we just accept the evolutionary propaganda that is preached by textbooks, television, museums, and magazines, perhaps we should ask just one question about the concept of human evolution: Is it true? The overwhelming preponderance of scientific, historical, and paleontological evidence collected in the last 150 years gives us an unmistakable answer: As a scientific-historical model, the concept of human evolution has been falsified!

Ever mindful of evolutionists' propaganda putting a positive spin on negative evidence, let's now examine the enormous errors of evolution regarding human origin.

Chance? Time? Struggle?

Neanderthal "Cave Men"

The first fossils used as "proof" for human evolution were fossils found in caves in the Neander Valley in Germany in the 1860s. The cave art and cultural artifacts suggested the bones belonged to intelligent human beings, but the first reconstructions of the skeletons portrayed Neanderthals as "beetle-browed, barrel-chested, bow-legged brutes." Artists (not scientists) depicted the missing flesh and hair to make the individuals look "apish" to conform to evolutionary belief (not science). Some of these early models are shown below.

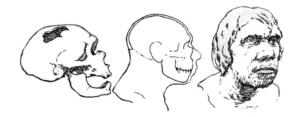

To make matters worse, the first bones put together belonged to older individuals with bone diseases and various health problems. Doctors can still see the evidence of rheumatism and arthritis and severe disease affecting the jaws and teeth. Like American Indians living in the northern Great Plains, some Neanderthals from central Europe had skeletal abnormalities  related to vitamin D and iodine deficiencies. Before the time of vitamin D-enriched milk and iodized salt, people got iodine from seafood and vitamin D from fish oils or sunshine acting on ergosterol in the skin — and all those things were in short supply in central Europe where the first Neanderthals were found. Neanderthals later found in Mediterranean environments, like those from the Mt. Carmel region in Israel, did not show these deficiency diseases.

Vitamin D is required for calcium absorption to produce proper bone growth. Children with insufficient vitamin D have a condition called rickets, which means they produce weak bones. Weakened leg bones often bow, and the bow-legged condition can persist through adulthood. Iodine is an essential part of the thyroid hormone, thyroxine, which plays a crucial role in metabolism and growth. Stunted growth, both physical and mental, occurs in children with insufficient iodine (cretinism). Adults with iodine deficiency may experience overgrowth of some bones relative to others, making hands, feet, and the lower jaw look too big for the body (acromegaly).

Aging and age-related conditions such as osteoporosis can cause loss of calcium from bones, producing weakened, pitted, or spongy bone and consequent changes in body shape and posture, including a hump-backed, forward slumping appearance. In his book *Buried Alive*, Dr. Jack Cuozzo, a dentist with an avid research interest in Neanderthals, claims to have found symptoms of highly advanced age in the bones and teeth of some Neanderthals he had studied. Neanderthals may be post-Flood peoples, but the Bible, which records pre-Flood ages in the 900s, tells us that ages into the 600–800s persisted for several centuries after the Flood, gradually declining exponentially to averages of 70–80.

Although some Neanderthals, especially those first reported, show symptoms of various diseases, deficiencies, and/or great age, fossils of many younger, healthier adults found later suggest that Neanderthals were just ordinary people. The brain volume of the average Neanderthal (about 1650 cc) was actually considerably larger than the brain size of the average person living today (1450 cc). Casts of Neanderthal brain cases show all the parts of the human brain were well developed, including the Broca's area responsible for the control of human speech. Many animals communicate by sound, but the "topics of conversation" are basically just food, sex, safety, and dominance. Human speech (except for certain degenerate TV sitcoms, "talk shows," and dating games) can operate in a totally different dimension, enabling human beings to verbalize philosophic concepts and communicate goals, dreams, ethics, and world views through both space and time from one individual and culture to others. Chimpanzees can be pictured in pensive poses, but "a penny for their thoughts" would be far too high a price to

pay for their musings on the meaning of life! It's not just talk that helps distinguish human beings from animals; it's what people talk about.

Cave art depicting their perceptions and activities, the cultural artifacts they crafted, and burial of their dead in a way suggesting belief in an afterlife — all these things,

103

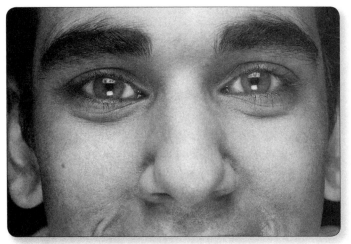

in addition to Broca's area for speech, imply Neanderthals were verbalizing at a fully human level. Fossil bones of healthy individuals show their skeletal features lie completely within the range of variability seen among different peoples living today (i.e., Neanderthals were no different from the "average" modern man than an American Indian is different from an Oriental, European, African, or Australian aboriginal). Neanderthals had a stocky build, but many people today have a stocky build without being considered more ape-like than tall, thin people!

Another group of "cave men," the Cro-Magnon (Crow-man-yon), stood taller and had higher foreheads than Neanderthals, and evolutionists have always classified them as *Homo sapiens*, the scientific name given to modern man. It is now apparent that Cro-Magnon and Neanderthal peoples lived side-by-side and intermarried, just as people from different cultures do today. For these reasons and those cited above, most scientists, even evolutionists, now classify Neanderthals as 100 percent human, *Homo sapiens*.

A museum in Germany once literally dressed up its Neanderthal model in a business suit to emphasize his humanity, asserting it was wrong to continue deceiving the public into thinking "cave men" were somehow "missing links" between apes and people. Who were "cave people"?

The scientific answer is simple: Cave people were/are people who live in caves!

There are cave people in the Bible. David lived in a cave for years while he fled from Saul. The Witch of Endor was a "cave woman." There are still cave people — people living in caves — today, and in some environments (and at today's housing prices!) there is nothing unintelligent or sub-human about living in a cave!

Although the vast majority of both scientists and evolutionists accept the clear evidence that Neanderthals are 100 percent human (*Homo sapiens*), a few evolutionists are still fighting a rear guard action in support of the old belief that Neanderthals are somehow subhumans or pre-humans, more ape-like than modern man.

It has been asserted that the thick brow ridges and sloping forehead mean Neanderthals cannot be fully human, but some human beings living today have those features without sacrificing their humanity. It was even proposed that Neanderthals couldn't be human, since the Neanderthal nose had an extra bony shelf (turbinate). Besides being astonishingly trivial, the claim ignores any knowledge that environment can influence bone development. A child growing up at high altitude, for example, will have a larger chest cavity than a twin with the same genes growing up at low altitude. The extra nasal shelf could have been a physiological/developmental adaptation for additional warming of the cold air breathed by Neanderthals in "Ice Age" environments. (There are surely many people who would object to the belief that having a big nose somehow makes an individual less than human!)

The least scientific of all attempts to make Neanderthals something less than *Homo sapiens* involves DNA taken from the cell's major energy organelles, the mitochondria. Each mitochondrion has a loop of DNA with thousands of bases in its sequence, but a series of 322 bases presumably extracted from the

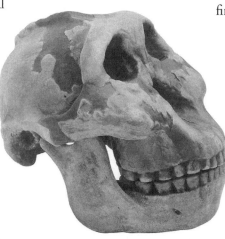

Proof?

mitochondria of a long-dead Neanderthal was chosen to compare with what was presumed to be the corresponding sequence in mitochondria taken from people in different ethnic groups living today. No scientist could possibly be surprised that differences in base sequences were found, and that the differences between the one long-dead Neanderthal and the human "average" today was greater than the differences found between different ethnic groups now living. Scientists should be surprised to hear the claim that such differences "proved" Neanderthals were not fully human, and they should be shocked to find such a claim published in otherwise respectable scientific literature!

Since DNA in dead bodies decomposes, finding no differences between modern and Neanderthal DNA would have required a miracle! The differences found may tell more about time of death than about similarity of life. Furthermore, scientists usually expect proper statistical procedures to be employed. There is no statistical justification whatsoever for drawing scientific conclusions about the Neanderthal/human relationship on the basis of a small sample of part of the DNA from a small organelle retrieved

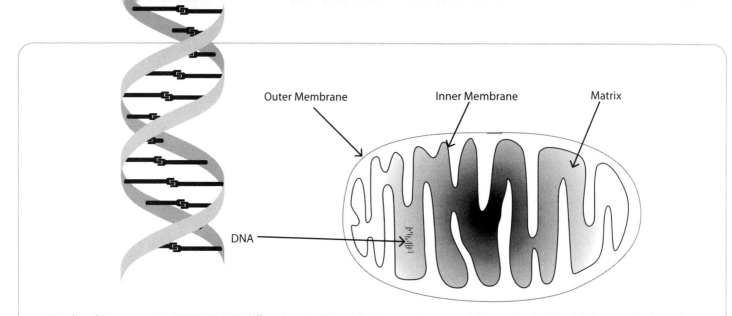

Outer Membrane   Inner Membrane   Matrix

DNA

Mitochondria are very tiny ORGANELLES (different parts of the cell). There can be several thousand mitochondria in one cell, depending on what the cell's job is. If a cell needs a lot of energy, it will have more mitochondria. The actual structure has two membranes. The OUTER MEMBRANE covers the mitochondria and the INNER MEMBRANE folds many times. There is a purpose in the folding. That folding of the membrane increases the SURFACE AREA. The surface area inside the mitochondria is like the table top where the reactions to break down food can take place. The more tabletop space you have, the more energy you can create. All around inside the mitochondria is a fluid called MATRIX.

from a statistically insignificant sample of one long-dead Neanderthal individual! A freshman biology student turning in such a research report might well be given an "F" and encouraged to major in something besides science!

The Neanderthal DNA studies (and there's another one to be discussed later!) may prove the power of evolutionary propaganda, but it also shows how far evolutionists can stray from the proper practice of scientific principles and procedures. It may be no mere coincidence that the scores of American students on tests of science knowledge and process skills declined precipitously with the rising use of government-sponsored science textbooks that made adherence to evolution, not scientific procedures or principles, the chief integrating concept in science classes. Countries where science teaching remained centered on science concepts and science skills, not belief in evolution, did not experience America's decline.

Fortunately, few have fallen for attempts to separate Neanderthals from *Homo sapiens*, and most modern evolutionists accept Neanderthal "cave men" as 100 percent human. Unfortunately, Neanderthals are not the only people once considered subhuman "missing links" between apes and man.

Form your foundation.

Darwin's followers tried to use "cave men" as a link in their "frog-to-prince" evolutionary chain, but scientists disproved them, showing that, healthy Neanderthals were fully *Homo sapiens*, just people living in caves!

1. A creation/evolution program on secular TV in Canada (CBC) started by comparing a princess's kiss turning a frog into a prince with evolution turning amphibians into people. What similarities and differences are there between these two stories? Put an "x" in front of each statement below that expresses a classic evolutionist's belief about human origins:

_____ a. Human origins required nothing supernatural, but only time, chance, struggle, and death.

_____ b. Features of human beings were brought into being by winning Darwin's struggle for survival, not from plan and purpose working toward a goal.

_____ c. Human beings are not the end point of evolution, and mankind will probably eventually lose the struggle for survival to some other animal or even plant.

_____ d. If it's not extinct or replaced first, mankind will eventually be destroyed when the sun expands and burns up all life on earth.

_____ e. People do things that harm others because of their competitive animal instincts, not "sin," and only "enlightened self-interest," not "god," can save us from the consequences of our animal urges.

2. Concerning the Neanderthal fossils often called "cave men," mark the following true (T) or false (F):

_____ a. Neanderthals were once considered "ape-men" because the first fossils found had bone diseases and abnormalities.

_____ b. Scientists have linked Neanderthal bone diseases to such things as vitamin D and iodine deficiencies and very old age.

_____ c. The brain volume of Neanderthals was larger than that of the average American's.

_____ d. Brain casts showing Broca's area for speech, their superb cave art, and ceremonial burial suggesting belief in an afterlife all indicate the Neanderthals had a fully human level of intelligence.

_____ e. Neanderthals intermarried with Cro-Magnon "cave men," who are readily accepted as *Homo sapiens* by all leading evolutionists.

_____ f. Most scientists today, even evolutionists, classify Neanderthals as *Homo sapiens*, indicating they are no different from one people group to another today.

3. If Scripture and ideas popular in science at a given time disagree, what should a Christian do?
   a. Quickly come up with a new interpretation of the Bible to show how it could agree with the popular ideas, so people won't laugh at us or Jesus.
   b. Trust the clear meaning of God's Word and hang in there until science catches up and shows the Bible was right all along.

Chapter 14

Enormous Errors in the Evolutionist's Evidence

Evolutionary Racism

Groups of people have been mistreating each other at various times and places throughout history, but in the 1800s and early 1900s, many people used evolution to justify their belief that some "races" were more evolved and superior to others. Hitler believed evolution had established the Aryans as the superior race, and that gave him the right, even the responsibility, to eradicate or subjugate inferior races, with his success virtually guaranteed by natural law ("survival of the fittest"). He even had social and laboratory experiments conducted to perfect and propagate the superior Aryan traits.

The full title of Darwin's first evolutionist book (1859) was *On the Origin of Species by Means of Natural Selection, or the Preservation of Favoured Races in the Struggle for Life*. In that book, he used "race" primarily to describe "subspecies," i.e., distinctive varieties within a large species of plant or animal. In his second evolutionist book, *The Descent of Man* (1871), which is now somewhat scientifically embarrassing and largely ignored, Darwin used "race" to refer to different groups of people, treating some as if they were less evolved than others. He considered African blacks to be substantially inferior intellectually and artistically to European whites, for example, but he also thought they were similar enough to "modern man" to be treated paternalistically as in Rudyard Kipling's words, the "white man's burden."

Ernst Haeckel

Ernst Haeckel, a very influential early evolutionist sometimes called "Germany's Darwin," carried evolutionary racism to the extreme. Taken from his book on the evolutionary history of the natural world, these citations enshrine forever his unfathomable ignorance and/or prejudice and/or dishonesty:

At the lowest stage of human mental development are the Australians [Aboriginals], some tribes of the Polynesians, and the Bushmen, Hottentots, and some of the Negro tribes. In many of these languages there are numerals only for one, two, and three: no

Australian language counts beyond four. Very many wild tribes can count no further than ten or twenty, whereas some very clever dogs have been made to count up to forty and even beyond sixty.

Thus, for example, a great English traveler, who lived for a considerable time on the west coast of Africa, says: "I consider the Negro to be a lower species of man, and cannot make up my mind to look upon him as 'a man and brother,' for the gorilla would then also have to be admitted into the family."

Henry Fairfield Osborne

The famous American evolutionist Henry Fairfield Osborne wrote an article, "The Evolution of Human Races," for the January 1926 issue of the popular science journal *Natural History*. It was selected for inclusion in the April 1980 issue of *Natural History*, an issue dedicated to reprinting articles important in the history of evolutionary thought. In that memorable article Osborne wrote:

If an unbiased zoologist were to descend upon the earth from Mars . . . he would undoubtedly divide the existing races of man into several genera. . . .

Note that Osborne considered different human races not just different *species* but different *genera* — a larger

difference, implying to him an even greater evolutionary distance and separation! He went on to proclaim:

The standard of intelligence of the average adult Negro is similar to that of the eleven-year-old youth of the species Homo sapiens.

Osborne considered Negroes a different *species*, intellectually too inferior to be put into species *Homo sapiens* with himself and other "whites" of European descent.

It's hard to imagine (and evolutionists today repudiate) the abuse of science that went into such evolutionary claims. Every American who has at least one African-American friend or acquaintance knows how ridiculously false are the claims of both Haeckel and Osborne, but these claims were publicly supported by science — or at least "science falsely so-called." In spite of the evidence that human intelligence does not correlate with brain size, eager evolutionists measured (or mismeasured) brain volumes to "document" racial inferiority "scientifically." In his work; the leading evolutionist (and vitriolic anti-creationist) S. J. Gould exposes the early evolutionists' deception of rejecting large Negro skulls as diseased so that they would not have to be counted in the racial average!

Australian Aboriginals suffered even more from evolutionary racism than the African blacks. In the 1874 edition of Ernst Haeckel's book on human evolution (*Anthropogenie*), Aboriginal peoples were considered Australian animals, and pictured sitting in a tree with other animals from other parts of the world, the chimpanzee, orangutan, and gorilla. Bones and skins of Aboriginals were prized as specimens for "scientific" study. As dramatized in the fictional movie *Quigley Down Under*, Aboriginals were occasionally hunted and killed as "farm pests." The European settlers of the Australian state of Tasmania deliberately

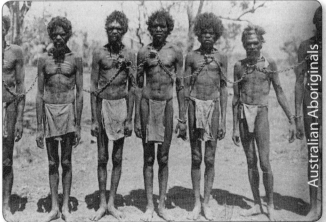

Australian Aboriginals

"cleared" the island of Aboriginals, like western ranchers once killed off wolves and bears. The dying wish of the last surviving Tasmanian native, a woman named Truganini, was that she be buried with her "people," not embalmed and shipped off to a museum as a display specimen. She died and was shipped off to a museum as part of a display on human evolution.

History itself would provide vital and vivid reasons for rejecting evolutionary racism. Osborne's article on "The Evolution of Human Races" came out in 1926, just in time to fuel Hitler's claims for Aryan racial superiority. But the triumphal performance and demeanor of an American black athlete at the 1936 Olympics in Berlin exposed the lie for all to see — if only enough people had been looking. Unfortunately, the Jesse Owens triumph also showed us that too many people were willing to let evolutionary belief overrule the facts of science.

Fortunately, science has once again caught up and shown that what is true is what the Bible has been saying all along. In a sermon based on creation preached on Mars Hill in Athens, the apostle Paul put it this way:

[God] hath made of one blood all nations of men for to dwell on all the face of the earth, and hath determined the times before appointed, and the bounds of their habitation (Acts 17:26).

There's just "one blood" — one race, the human race — and we are all part of it. There are different cultures and customs (tribes), different languages (tongues), and different political systems (nations), but only one people, who are all descendants of the one couple who were specially created by God. All people have the same first parents, Adam and Eve; all people have the same problem, sin and death; all people need the same solution to the problem of sin and death, salvation in Jesus Christ, the only begotten Son of God, the God of all people at all times in all places.

The creation of all mankind in God's image is the basis for human unity and compassion, and the basis for total repudiation of racism. The Bible doesn't even use the word race — except for a contest to see who or what can run the fastest or farthest!

The only thing sadder than the history of evolutionary racism is the number of Christians who bought into the lie! There are many Christian leaders today who claim Christianity can earn scientific respectability by accepting evolution, and there were Christian leaders in the past who accepted evolutionary racism, and most unfortunately, Christian laymen who practiced it!

Christians who try to fit "evolutionary progress" into the Bible have to bend the biblical text, and it took a real twist to try — unsuccessfully — to get evolutionary racism into Scripture. You may have heard of the "curse on Ham," but you never read it in the Bible. Ham is in the Bible, but the "curse on Ham" is not. Ham was the son of Noah who became the ancestor of many peoples, including (among many others) groups we think of today as African Blacks.

Unlike the writings of human religions that often make their leaders god-like, the Bible never covers up the sins and shortcomings of heroes of the faith. After the Flood, Noah got drunk, and his son, Ham, found him unclothed. Instead of trying to help, Ham (possibly accompanied by his son Canaan?)

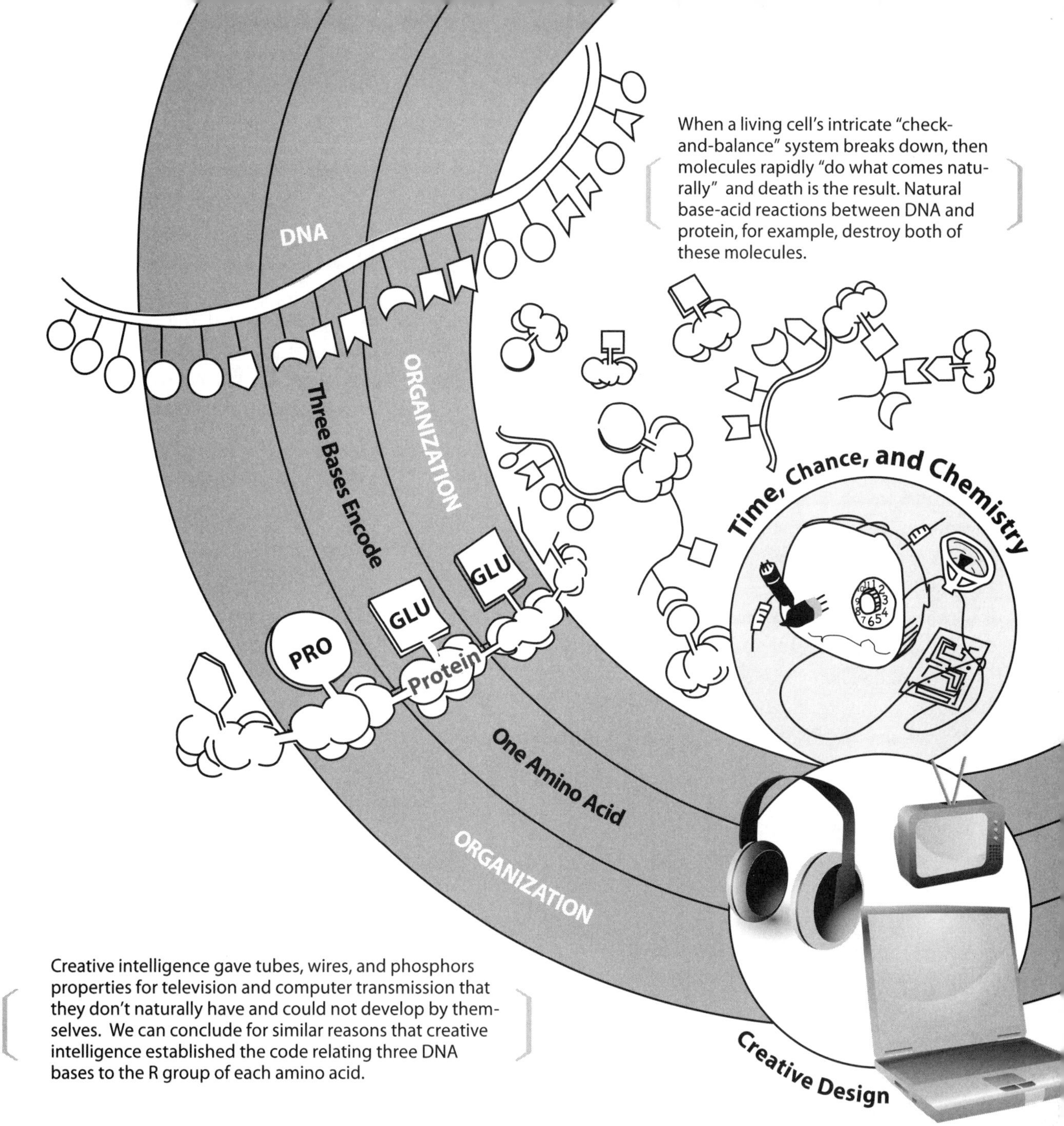

When a living cell's intricate "check-and-balance" system breaks down, then molecules rapidly "do what comes naturally" and death is the result. Natural base-acid reactions between DNA and protein, for example, destroy both of these molecules.

DNA

ORGANIZATION

Three Bases Encode

Time, Chance, and Chemistry

GLU

GLU

PRO

Protein

One Amino Acid

ORGANIZATION

Creative Design

Creative intelligence gave tubes, wires, and phosphors properties for television and computer transmission that they don't naturally have and could not develop by themselves. We can conclude for similar reasons that creative intelligence established the code relating three DNA bases to the R group of each amino acid.

further embarrassed his father. Noah later pronounced judgment, *not on Ham but on Ham's son Canaan*, saying that the sons of Canaan (not Ham) would be the slaves of their brothers' descendants (Gen. 9:21–27). Reference to slaves apparently made shallow-thinking Americans in the 1700s and 1800s think of blacks, but the Canaanites weren't black, and their slavery to their brothers occurred when the Israelites conquered the land of Canaan many centuries ago!

Despite all these obvious facts, some compassionate Christians in the segregated South into the 1950s felt that blacks should be treated well — but separately. The Bible exposes all sorts of human sins and man's inhumanity to man, but never once mentions abuse based on skin color alone. They had been duped into accepting racial inferiority based on evolutionary racism — and, thanks in part to our failure in both science education and Bible training, some held on to that belief even after evolutionists abandoned it! Mixing "science falsely so-called" with the Bible is a recipe for disaster.

Evolutionary racism has produced tragic social consequences; it has also produced misunderstanding of the science of skin color. Many are still surprised to learn that everyone on earth (except albinos) has the same skin color pigment. This one, universal skin color pigment found in all people (and many animals) is the protein called melanin. A person can have a little melanin and a light skin shade, a lot of melanin and a dark shade, or something between.

Using A, a, and B, b to represent the two major pairs of genes controlling the amount of melanin a person produces, we can describe different melanin skin variations thus:

Very light	0 "capital" genes	(aabb)
Light	1 capital	(Aabb or aaBb)
Medium	2 capitals	(AaBb, AAbb, aaBB)
Dark	3 capitals	(AABb or AaBB)
Very dark	4 capitals	(AABB)

Perhaps because miseducation has made them think it's a tough question, evolutionists sometimes try to embarrass creationists by asking where all the different skin colors came from if God created just two people a few thousand years ago. The simple, scientific answer can be given in one genetic chart with 16 squares (Figure 15.2).

The Bible does not tell us what skin shade or amount of melanin our first parents had, but Adam and Eve were designed to be the parents of all people. If Adam and Eve had genes AaBb and a medium amount of melanin, their children in the first generation would show every skin shade from the very lightest (aabb) to the very darkest (AABB). It would be no problem, of course, to repopulate earth with the full variation in melanin amounts from the eight people who got off the ark 4,500–5,000 years ago.

We can say now that evolutionary racism has been completely falsified. Science and Scripture emphatically agree that all human beings share one skin color protein (melanin), and that variations in amount do *NOT* make one more or less human! In the words of a once-popular song for children's church, "Red and yellow, black and white, they are precious in His sight; Jesus loves the little children of the world."

Figure 15.2: Maximum Variation

AaBb x AaBb:

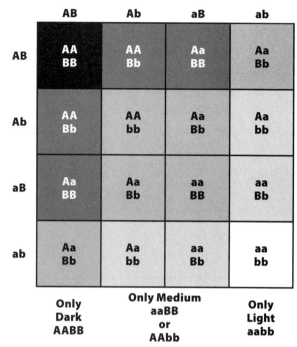

All human beings have the same basic skin-color agent (melanin), just different amounts of it. From parents created with medium skin color as diagrammed, all the variation we see today could be produced in one generation. In the same way, plants and animals created with a mixture of genes could have filled all of the earth's ecologic and geographic variety. As people break up into groups, however, some groups would develop limited variability — only dark, only medium, or only light as indicated.

Piltdown Man ("Eoanthropus dawsoni")

Even while they still considered Neanderthals, blacks, and Aboriginals as subhuman "missing links," evolutionists in 1912 shifted their focus to fossils found outside the English village of Piltdown. The skullcap looked human, but the jaws looked ape-like, and the teeth seemed between those of apes and man. First reported by a man named Dawson, "Piltdown Man" was given the scientific name *Eoanthropus dawsoni*, "dawn man of Dawson."

Almost everyone knows now that Piltdown Man was a deliberate hoax. But it wasn't shown to be a hoax for over 40 years! From 1912 into the 1950s, the message in the textbooks and museums was something like this: "You can believe in creation if you want to, but the facts are all on the side of evolution." The "facts" in this case turned out to be an ape jaw with the teeth filed and a human skullcap with distinctive parts missing, both pieces stained to make them look older.

Piltdown was not a particularly clever hoax. The fossils buried with it in the English countryside were brought in from Africa. The parts needed to distinguish ape from human bones were the very parts not present. One scientist exclaimed that the file marks on the teeth sprang immediately to the eye — but that was over 40 years after Piltdown's "discovery," and only after tests showed the minerals in the bones did not match minerals in the rock that presumably had fossilized them. It was also after numerous "scientific" reports on the Piltdown "finds" had been published.

The real mystery is not who committed the hoax, but why any scientist believed it. People may wonder, "Is it really possible that the world's experts could be completely wrong about human evolution?" This answer is a resounding yes! The world's most famous experts on human evolution were wrong about Neanderthals, wrong about African Blacks, wrong about Australian Aboriginals, and wrong about Piltdown Man, *Eoanthropus dawsoni* — and they were continuously wrong for 40–100 years (over several generations of students!) in these cases.

The Piltdown Skull Fragments

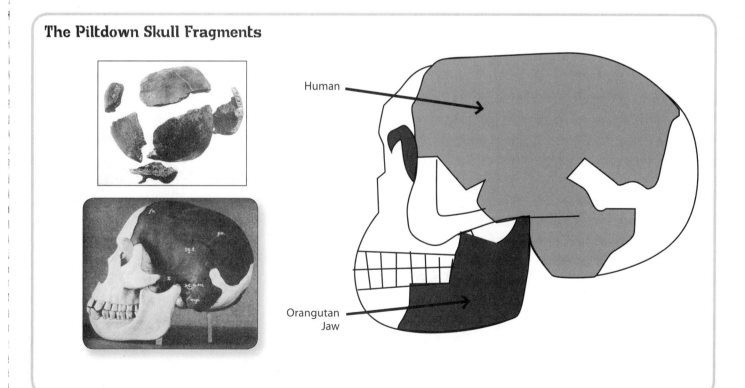

Human

Orangutan Jaw

Java Man
("Pithecanthropus")

Although it is still presented in some textbooks, nature programs, and museum displays, evolutionists were certainly wrong about "Java Man."

The famous discovery was never anything more than an ape-like skullcap and a human-like femur (thigh bone), and these two bones were discovered about 50 feet (15 m) apart in a gravel layer. Since gravel consists of pieces of rock broken off, transported some distance, and redeposited, there was never any scientific reason to assume the skullcap and leg bone belonged to the same individual or even the same species.

The only reason for making anything out of the two bones was a blinding belief in evolution and eager desire to find a "missing link" that far outstripped critical judgment. The discoverer, Eugene Dubois, seemed to have an ample supply of both. Dubois was a student of Ernst Haeckel, "Germany's Darwin," who convinced so many that African blacks and Australian Aboriginals were subhuman products of evolution. It seems that Dubois learned from the master how to make the most out of propaganda and the least out of science.

Dubois had set sail for Java in 1887 with the stated intent of finding the missing link, which he announced in 1891. The popular press published the propaganda, but serious scientists were more skeptical. A group from the Berlin Academy of Science mounted an expedition to the Java site in 1907, but found no evidence to support

Dubois's claim. In the 1920s, Dubois himself finally admitted he had found fully human skulls in the same layer. He had kept that evidence secret for decades, knowing the discovery of fully human bones would rule out his claim that bones from the same layer could be mankind's ancestor. Once again, science finally triumphed over evolution.

The so-called "Java Man" fossils are meaningless, but the name given to them is not. "Pithecanthropus" literally means "ape-man" (*pithecus*, "ape"; *anthropus*, "man"). Many modern evolutionists (but not some famous ones) want to avoid the "ape-man" stigma and say that man and apes are cousins that evolved from a common ancestor. What they fail to note, however, is that every common ancestor ever proposed would look like an ape and be classified as an ape. We can understand why evolutionists would want to separate themselves from the enormous errors of the past, but they really are still hoping to find an "ape-man."

Although of no scientific value, Java Man is included by evolutionists in a group called *Homo erectus*, a hodgepodge of highly variable fossils ranging from meaningless disassociated fragments like Java Man to the well-preserved remains of a 12-year-old boy (discussed later) that should be called *Homo sapiens*.

Form your foundation.

Early evolutionists (Darwin, Haeckel, Osborne) taught that some "races" (e.g., African Blacks, Australian Aboriginals) were inferior, even sub-human. The Bible teaches there is only one race, the human race. Disproving evolutionary racism, science showed all people have different amounts of the same skin color protein, melanin.

1. Evolutionary theory in the late 1800s and early 1900s was used as "scientific support" for a new and deadly kind of racism based primarily on skin color. Put an "X" in front of each example below of "science falsely so-called," a "fact of evolution" from the past now rejected by modern evolutionists:

_____ a. In his *Descent of Man* (1871), Darwin argued that African blacks were not fully human, but close enough to deserve care and protection from European whites.

_____ b. "Germany's Darwin," Ernst Haeckel, wrote that the dark-skinned Australian aboriginals could not count as high as some dogs could.

_____ c. Aboriginals were once pictured in evolutionist "science" books as Australian animals and their skins and skeletons were collected for evolutionary "scientific" study.

_____ d. In the decade before Hitler made evolutionary racism the basis for his slaughter of Jews and "science" experiments on people during World War II (1939–45), a leading evolutionist claimed the intelligence of adult blacks was about that of an "eleven-year-old youth of species *Homo sapiens* [i.e., whites]."

2. According to the Bible from Genesis through Paul's sermon on Mars Hill (Acts 17:26), there is only one race, the human race: all people have the same first parents, _____ and _____, and all who believe are delivered from sin and death by the same Savior _____. Science adds that all people have only varying amounts of the same skin color substance, a protein called _____.

3. Use the skin color chart on page 112 to help complete the following: Using Aa and Bb to represent genes controlling the amount of skin coloring melanin the body makes, the most melanin and darkest skin tone would result from (AABB/AaBb/aabb) _____ genes and the least melanin and lightest tone from _____ genes. Two parents with AaBb genes (Adam and Eve's condition???) would have a (dark/medium/light) _____ melanin skin tone, but their children (could/couldn't) _____ include those with the most melanin/very darkest tone (and also/but not) _____ a brother or sister with the least melanin/lightest tone. Evolutionists once taught that it would take (thousands or millions of years/one generation) _____ for people with one skin color to produce descendants with a different color, whereas science and Scripture show that certain people could produce children with all the different amounts of skin color in (thousands or millions of years/one generation) _____.

4. Mark the following true (T) or false (F). "Piltdown Man"

_____ a. was made up from modified parts of a human skull cap and an ape jaw.

_____ b. was a deliberate hoax that fooled nearly all the world's leading evolutionists for over 40 years.

_____ c. is a warning that science classes may teach fake evolutionary ideas to students for many decades before science proves evolution wrong!

5. Mark these true (T) or false (F). "Java Man"

_____ a. was given the name "Pithecanthropus," literally meaning "ape-man."

_____ b. consisted of a skull and leg bone found 50 ft. (1m) apart in a gravel deposit.

_____ c. was later rejected by its "discoverer" ("inventor"?), DuBois, who finally admitted finding a fully human skull in the same deposit.

_____ d. was accepted as "proof for evolution" by many Christians, which should warn Christians today not to compromise the never-changing, infallible Word of the infinite God with the ever-changing, fallible words of finite man.

Nebraska Man and the Scopes "Monkey" Trial

Nebraska Man epitomizes extremes, representing both human evolutionists'

BIGGEST SCIENTIFIC BLUNDER

and

GREATEST PROPAGANDA VICTORY!

In 1922, a single tooth found in western Nebraska by Harold Cook was presented to the leading American evolutionist Henry Fairfield Osborne, the same man who wrote the famous 1926 article on "The Evolution of Human Races" described earlier. Osborne declared that the tooth exhibited a combination of chimpanzee and human traits, making it a candidate for an "ape-man" link, which he dignified with the scientific name *Hesperopithecus haroldcookii*.

Although only a single tooth was found, the tooth was imagined to belong to a skull, the skull was imagined to belong to a skeleton, and the skeleton was imagined to have flesh, hair, a family, and a culture! Mark Twain once commented that what he admired most about "science" [or "science falsely so-called"] was that one could get such wholesale returns from such a trifling investment of fact.

Pictures of Nebraska Man and his wife appeared in the *Illustrated London News* on June 24, 1922, shortly before the famous Scopes "monkey" trial in 1925. Two years after that trial was over, the single tooth that had "evolved" into Nebraska Man was found to be identical to the tooth of a fossil pig! The kind of pig, once thought extinct, was found alive and well in South America in

Megalodon and *Carcharodontosaurus* teeth. The *Charcharodontosaurus* tooth was found in the Sahara Desert.

Figure 16.1–Scenes from the Scopes Monkey Trial

Darrow examines Bryan.

Anti-Evolution League stand in Dayton, Tennessee.

William Jennings Bryan giving speech during trial.

Photo taken of Clarence Darrow and William Jennings Bryan during the Scopes trial in 1925.

1972. What was a horribly embarrassing moment for science and for evolution was part of a propaganda coup, whose effects are still being felt across America and around the world.

The Scopes "Monkey" Trial — Riding the wave of ever-illusive evidence for evolution, social Darwinism was running rampant through Europe and America, justifying "robber baron" capitalism, loosening moral restraints, nurturing evolutionary racism, and building a "wall of separation," not between church and state, but between

John T. Scopes

God and mankind, between faith and life. Apparently realizing the weakness of the evidence, T.H. Huxley, "Darwin's Bulldog," did not try to convince scientists to accept evolution; instead he used belief in evolution to attack the Church.

The Church was teaching that God created mankind, and that God's Word was superior to mankind's words. Evolution promised to reverse that, claiming that man created "God" in man's image when he reached a certain stage in evolution, which meant "god" was only a figment of the human imagination, making man's opinion supreme. In our post-Edenic world, it was fairly easy to convince those who considered themselves intellectuals to put man's words above God's Word. The only thing impeding the rising tide of evolutionary humanism were those Christians who accepted the Bible as God's absolute, authoritative, infallible Word presenting the true history and destiny of the universe from before the beginning to after the end. For evolutionists to win the "war of the world views," Bible-believing

Christians had to be stopped. Apparently knowing they could not win on the evidence, evolutionists opted, consciously or not, for the tactic prophesied in 2 Peter 3: scoffing or ridicule.

John T. Scopes was the man chosen; Dayton, Tennessee, the place; and 1925 the time. Tennessee had a law forbidding the teaching of evolution. The ACLU, an anti-Christian lawyer's union then as it is now, wanted a test case to challenge that law. They hired a substitute teacher, John Scopes, to say he taught evolution in a Dayton public school, promising to pay his fine (they planned to lose) and to pay for his graduate schooling.

The lawyer chosen to present the evolutionist's case was Clarence Darrow. Darrow was famous for defending a delivery boy who committed murder; Darrow said it was chance over eons of time ("evolution") that deprived the murderer of a conscience. (The "evolution made me do it" defense was used in Australia years later to exonerate a murderer with the XYY chromosome condition.) Darrow's fame may have been used to lure William Jennings Bryan to speak for creation. Bryan, called the "Silver-Tongued Orator," was a three-time presidential candidate and well known as a Bible-believing Christian.

Dayton took on a carnival atmosphere. Major media figures, most notably H.L. Mencken, covered the contrived trial. The friendly towns-folk seemed to enjoy the attention. In a dramatic violation of normal court procedure, whose significance continues to ripple around the world, Darrow asked

Clarence Darrow

117

Bryan to take the stand to defend biblical creation, and Bryan agreed.

Bryan was a fine Christian and eloquent speaker, but his responses to Darrow "let the team down." To a question about where Cain got his wife, Bryan cleverly responded that he was not concerned about other men's wives. The media made sure, however, that the world understood that the biblical story of Adam and Eve could not give solid answers to even simple questions about human origins. To Darrow's question about how long the days of creation were, Bryan said he did not know, and then, under prodding, was willing to concede they might have been millions of years. The media made sure the world knew that meant the Bible could not be trusted to present any scientific, or even logical, information.

Apparently accepting Bryan's response as a greater victory than they had dared hope, Darrow conceded the guilt of his client (the almost-forgotten Scopes) and halted the trial before Bryan had a chance to make his counterpoints and to present his closing arguments. Bryan died within a few days of the trial's end.

As evolutionists hoped, the media version of the trial had a devastating effect on Christianity that has continued

Scopes, Neal, and Rappalyea beneath "Read Your Bible" banner (Bryan College Archives)

into the present, more than 75 years later. Christians at first just enjoying the carnival came to realize their hero didn't know what the Bible meant by "day" nor how people multiplied to fill the earth. We shall see later those questions are easy to answer biblically, and the answers from God's Word are strongly supported by the scientific and historical evidence in God's world. At the time of the Scopes trial, however, Bible-believing Christians were portrayed as backward bigots, ignorant of science, history, and even the Bible itself.

Before the monkey trial, "fundamentalist" meant a Christian who believed in the fundamentals of the Christian faith, God's literal-historical plan of salvation through Christ, summarized in the "Fundamentals of the Faith," which echoed the ancient Apostle's Creed and God's revelation of himself in history as Creator, Sustainer, Judge, and Redeemer through creation, corruption, and catastrophe to the final victory of life on the Cross and the return in glory of Jesus Christ! After the monkey trial, "fundamentalist" came to mean an ignorant religious fanatic. In the past decade or so, the media has started using "fundamentalist" as "hate speech," branding any fanatic who uses religion to justify killing as a fundamentalist: from abortion clinic

Silenced?

bomber, to gay basher, to serial killer, to (most especially) "fundamentalist" Muslim terrorists!

Ridicule and hate speech are powerful tools of propaganda, and they have nearly achieved their goal: silencing Christians and censoring Christian thought right out of public thinking. Threats of lawsuits and godless judicial whim (not the merits of logic or constitutional law) are used to ban the free speech of Christians who would speak for God and the Bible, while they promote the free speech of those who hate God and His Word. It is still okay to speak up for God while looking in the mirror or talking within isolated groups (e.g., churches) of those who already believe, but speaking up for God in public can cost you your job, career, recognition, family — even time in jail.

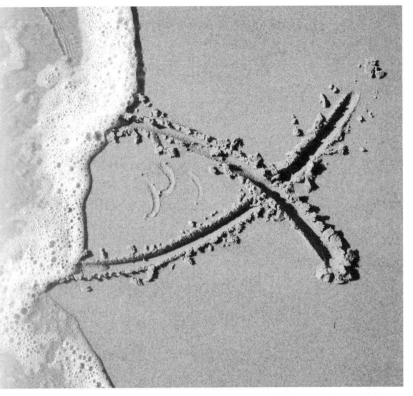

"Apologetics" is the name given to a tough intellectual discipline; giving reasons for your hope in God (1 Pet. 3:15) and defending God's Word against critics. Too many Christians now seem to think it means apologizing for your faith, and making sure your beliefs don't offend anyone. (It's okay if their beliefs offend you.) Next to a soul in hell, Satan's favorite is a Christian who keeps his or her faith bottled up inside; Satan regrets that such a Christian is going to heaven — but rejoices that he or she won't be taking any family or friends along!

The Christian faith that conquered the Roman Empire, fostered science and democracy, freed women and slaves, and brought new and eternal life in Christ to peoples around the world stumbled hard at the monkey trial. Atheists and agnostics loudly proclaimed that science had proved evolution, and evolution meant that the idea of "god," too, was just a product of evolution, and that one culture's concept of god was just as good (or bad) as the god imagined by any other culture. Since gods were only the figments of human imagination, that meant human opinion, not God's Word, was the basis for right and wrong, good and bad, and the ultimate court of appeal. The easiest people to convince were self-styled intellectuals, of course, since they already placed a high value on their own opinions. What powerful scientific evidence for human evolution in 1925 convinced the world's intelligentsia that human opinion was superior to God's Word?

Errors of Evolution

1. Neanderthal "cave men," which were then regarded as apes on the way up, not old men on the way down.

2. Evolutionary racism, which taught and treated African blacks and Australian Aboriginals as subhuman, inferior "races" not fit to be considered *Homo sapiens*.

3. Piltdown Man, "*Eoanthropus dawsoni*," a deliberate but not very clever hoax that fooled the world's leading evolutionists for over 40 years.

4. Java Man, "the *Pithecanthropus* ape-man" that persisted in textbooks and museums long after scientists and its discoverer discredited it.

5. Nebraska Man, "*Hesperopithecus haroldcookii*," the fossil tooth, whose skull, skeleton, flesh, hair, family, and culture were pictured by the media during the time of the "monkey trial," was quietly abandoned by the media when it was discovered, two years after the trial was over, that the fossil tooth was a pig's tooth.

How could so many Christians be embarrassed to silence by such incredibly shoddy evidence? Perhaps the answer is found in 2 Timothy 2:15:

Study to show thyself approved unto God, a workman that needeth not to be ashamed, rightly dividing the word of truth.

Study and *workman* are not favorite words for easy-believism Christians who think that Jesus is primarily a warm, fuzzy feeling, or icing on the cake of life. When T. H. Huxley used Darwin's beliefs to attack the Church in 1860, the Church responded emotionally, surrendering both God's Word and God's world. They shouted belief in the Bible and/or offered hasty "reinterpretations" to accommodate evolution. They did not even check the facts of what turned out to be "science falsely so-called," or they would have discovered much earlier what we now know — the evidence in God's world agrees with what we read in God's Word about God's perfect creation, mankind's corruption, the Flood catastrophe, and new life in Christ!

It falls to your generation to study, to become the workman who will tear down the powerful but mythical "wall of separation" between church and state, and raise up instead the ultimate healing power of the cross of Christ, restoring the "bridge of communion" between God and mankind, and loving fellowship among peoples all made in His image!

You can do it — "Not by might, nor by power, but by my spirit, saith the LORD of hosts" (Zech. 4:6).

"Inherit the Wind," and "Reap the Whirlwind" — At the real "monkey trial" in 1925, Christians were defeated by evidence for human evolution now known to be 100 percent false. The damage was continued into future generations, however, by a popular film, *Inherit the Wind*, which produced a lasting false impression of the trial that has outlasted the false evidence. Although the fictional film did not claim to accurately represent the real trial, key features made the association inevitable: the evolutionist lawyer put the creationist lawyer on the stand, and the case involved a teacher presenting evolution in violation of state law.

In the film, the teacher who dares to bring evolution into his classroom is an idealistic young man who believes his students must be made aware of advances in modern "science." In the real trial, the teacher was a substitute hired by the ACLU who promised to pay his fine and pay his way through graduate school.

In the film, the daughter of a local pastor was in love with the idealistic teacher, and her pastor/father was portrayed as an ignorant, judgmental fanatic, full of hate and opposed to any change. In the real trial, the Christian community in Dayton, Tennessee, was so friendly and open that they even earned compliments for their cordiality from the evolutionist's attorney, Clarence Darrow.

In the film, the creationist lawyer was put on the stand to demonstrate his unthinking, anti-intellectual, blind faith and bigotry and his opposition to advancements in science and human thought. In the real trial, the creationist lawyer did fail to properly handle two questions (the ones about creation days and Cain's wife mentioned previously), but William Jennings Bryan was otherwise an eloquent speaker and an admired intellectual. Notes show that Bryan had prepared a carefully reasoned and challenging closing argument, but Darrow — well aware of his opponent's true stature — chose wisely to concede defeat, forfeit the $100 fine, and deny the jury and the world the chance to hear the creationist

defense that might well have changed the course of American education and even world politics!

Knowing how woefully weak the evidence for evolution really is, the evolutionists' chief tactic from T. H. Huxley ("Darwin's Bulldog") through Darrow at the monkey trial, right into today's science classroom has been the same — ridicule the Bible and fanatical Christians and don't give creationists a chance to present their evidence! Unfortunately, the tactic has worked all too well. For fear of ridicule, many Christians keep to themselves and don't even try to influence society. And many people, including most Christians, don't even know there is an overwhelming amount of evidence — scientific and historical — that strongly favors creation over evolution.

A mission for your generation, should you choose to accept it, is to change that — to help restore Christ's dominion to the dominion of Christ!

In addition to the power of God's Spirit, you have help from faithful creationists, like the scientists at ICR (the Institute for Creation Research), who have looked at God's world through God's Word and have exposed the enormous errors of evolution. From the mid-1970s through the 1980s, at major universities throughout the world, creation scientists, led by Dr. Henry Morris and Dr. Duane Gish ("Creation's Bulldog"), debated the scientific merits of creation vs. evolution with evolutionists from every

scientific specialty bearing on origins: biology, geology, paleontology, biochemistry, genetics, anthropology, physics, astronomy, etc. Even the evolution-friendly media acknowledged that creationists usually won the debates. One famous evolutionist lost so badly in a nationally televised debate that he said he was ashamed to go home to his wife. Admitting that the scientific debates only seemed to make creationists look good, evolutionist groups and leaders urged an end to the scientific debates; it is now very difficult to find an evolutionist scientist willing to defend evolution in a public scientific debate.

Debates about the evidence introduced students and the public to the depth and breadth of evidence strongly supporting creation. Evolutionists, therefore, retreated to their previously successful tactic — censoring evidence of creation from the public arena and banning criticism of evolution in the classroom. But they left an opening. So far, it is not illegal for students to raise their

Dr. Henry Morris

Dr. Duane Gish

hands to ask questions, including questions that present challenging information. Most teachers are pleased to see student involvement, and student questions and comments can really stimulate interest from other students. Many teachers are more than happy to have students do reports on creation/evolution, and some are pleased to

WARNING!

sponsor classroom debates to get students involved and thinking. Questions, reports, and discussions or debates that include real scientific data and concepts are great ways to teach science process skills, critical thinking, and true tolerance for diverse views. Studies show students learn more about evolution when it's contrasted with creation than when evolution is taught as boring, dusty "facts" to memorize.

WARNING: A few teachers are so insecure, and a few school censors are so intimidating, that they will throw out or give failing grades to students or reports that challenge evolution, especially if creation is mentioned. Such a position obviously violates the First Amendment, which both guarantees free speech and makes it illegal for Congress (or judges!) to make any law that prohibits the free exercise of religion.

In the face of vein-popping evolutionist emotionalism, however, being right can be very hard. As Christian students at Columbine demonstrated, however, the new generation can stand as firmly for Christ as the persecuted Christians in the first century!

Form your foundation.

By ridiculing the Bible, the ACLU's lawyer won a great propaganda victory at the Scopes trial, but science disproved all their evidence for human evolution: Neanderthals (people who lived in caves), racism, Piltdown hoax, Java fake, and Nebraska Man (pig's tooth).

What will it take for the new generation to reverse the Christian defeat at the monkey trial and reestablish Christ as King of conscience, classroom, and culture? The answer has always been right there in 1 Peter 3:15:

But sanctify the Lord God in your hearts: and be ready always to give an answer to every man that asketh you a reason of the hope that is in you with meekness and fear.

Darwin turned the world upside-down; to turn it right side up again, Christ will use informed Christians ready to share reasons for their hope in God. But don't forget the second part of that verse, "in meekness and fear" (KJV) or "in gentleness and meekness" (RSV). The truth is *not* a club to be used to win an argument; it's to be used to win hearts, minds, souls, society, and the world to Christ!

CHURCH ST SE 100

STATE ST SE 500

1. What makes "Nebraska Man" both the "biggest scientific blunder" and "greatest propaganda victory" for evolutionists?

   _____

   _____

   _____

2. Following are pairs of statements (a-A, b-B, etc.) about the famous Scopes monkey trial. Mark one true (T) and one false (F) for each pair:

   _____ a. The trial concerned an idealistic young teacher (John Scopes) whose conscience led him to teach evolution in spite of Tennessee's state law.

   _____ A. The ACLU staged the trial, paying part-time teacher (John Scopes) to teach evolution, using a famous lawyer to defend him and to embarrass Christians.

   _____ b. Evolutionist lawyer Darrow put creationist lawyer Bryan on the stand to expose him as an ignorant, bigoted, hate-mongering, fundamentalist fanatic.

   _____ B. Catching his usually eloquent opponent on two Bible questions, Darrow forfeited the case before anyone could hear Bryan's carefully reasoned and persuasive closing.

   _____ c. Media reports and movie reports on the evolutionists' trickery and the creationists' legal victory slowed the impact of evolution on schools for over 50 years.

   _____ C. Media reports and a movie so ridiculed them that many Christians withdrew from the "war of the world views" and let evolution spread like wildfire.

   _____ d. Losing the case, evolutionists won the "Scopes war" by ignoring scientific evidence and ridiculing Scripture.

   _____ D. Winning the case, creationists lost the "Scopes war" by ignoring scientific evidence and retreating from Scripture.

3. All the "scientific evidence" the media "preached" as proof for human evolution at the time of the Scopes trial proved false. Match the false claims for evolution below with what they turned out to be:

   _____ a. Neanderthal "cave man"   A. fossil pig's tooth
   _____ b. Blacks and Aboriginals   B. human and ape bones in a gravel deposit
   _____ c. Piltdown Man   C. a hoax that fooled experts over 40 years
   _____ d. Java Man   D. fossils of people
   _____ e. Nebraska Man   E. living people in the one human race

4. Apparently feeling they can't win by using scientific evidences, what tactics do evolutionists use to try to defeat creationists?

   _____

   _____

5. What "tactics" should Christians use to "win" creation/evolution debates — and to "win" people to Christ?

   _____

   _____

6. Write a report on the difference between apologizing and apologetics, and how that relates to God's commands in 1 Peter 3:15 ("be ready always to give an answer") and 2 Timothy 2:15 ("study to show thyself approved").

Chapter
16

Australopithecines

In the last generation, creationists won the scientific battle over Neanderthal "cave men," African Blacks, Australian Aboriginals, Piltdown Man, Java Man, and Nebraska Man. The battle over human evolution in this generation centers on a group called australopithecines (aus-trall-oh-PITH-ee-seens).

Raymond Dart reported the first australopithecines in 1924 from ape-like fossils described in South Africa. The scientific genus name, *Australopithecus* means "southern ape" (*australo-*, "southern"; *-pithecus*, "ape"). Finding fossils of apes in Africa did not seem at first to be an astonishing discovery, of course. But the situation changed in 1959 when, working in Olduvai Gorge in Kenya, East Africa, Louis and Mary Leakey found australopithicine bones in rock layers that also seemed to contain simple stone tools.

For evolutionists, the Leakey find had this obvious formula: *ape-like bones + tools = tool-using ape = ape-man!*

That was enough to earn support from *National Geographic,* and the Leakeys have been famous human evolution researchers (paleoanthropologists) through two generations, right into the present.

Actually, the crushed skull originally reconstructed by the Leakeys was totally ape-like. It had a small brain cavity, a huge lower jaw, and a large bony crest at the top of the skull to anchor the massive jaw muscles required

to move the massive jaw (Figure 17.1). It was first given the scientific genus name *Zinjanthropus,* but its common name was "Nutcracker Man." It looked like a gorilla that could crack coconuts!

No one would have thought the skull belonged to anything other than an ape similar to a gorilla — except for the tools found with the skull. The tools took on a totally different meaning in 1973, however, when son Richard Leakey found what he called "bones virtually indistinguishable from those of modern man" in a rock layer at Olduvai Gorge *below* the level of his father's find. The Nutcracker specimen found could not be man's ancestor, therefore, since people were living, dying, and being fossilized before Nutcracker was.

The Nutcracker finds were renamed genus

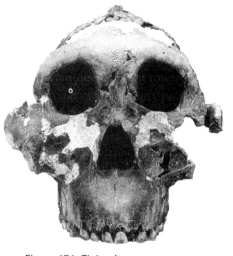

Figure 17.1: *Zinjanthropus,* "Nutcraker Man." Crushed skull originally reconstructed by the Leakeys.

Mary Leakey on site at Laetoll, Tanzania.

Palaeontologists Louis and Mary Leaky

Palaeontologist Donald Johanson

Australopithecus and species either *robustus* or *bosei¸* and they are now considered extinct varieties of apes "full of sound and fury, signifying nothing."

Perhaps the tools found with the original Nutcracker skull were used *on* the owner of that skull rather than *by* the owner of that skull. That would make the Nutcracker specimen man's meal, not man's ancestor!

The same may be true of *Homo erectus* fossils once called "Peking Man" (Figure 17.2). Although casts were made, all these Chinese fossils disappeared during World War II and the records are unclear, so it's doubtful anyone will ever be sure just what the fossils were. Several skulls were found in a cave near Peking (now Beijing), along with evidence of fire use and tools. Again, the tools (and fire) may have been used on the ape-like skulls, rather than by the possessors of those skulls. The skulls were all bashed in at the rear, which made the skull (which may have been cooked) into a bowl for holding the delicious ape brains. Monkey meat is very tough and sinewy, but monkey brains in a skull cup are still a delicacy in parts of the world today. That would make Peking Man, like Nutcracker Man, man's meal, not man's ancestor.

Still touted today as the perfect common ancestor for apes and mankind are the fossil fragments assembled by Donald Johanson's 1974 team to form the specimen called "Lucy" (Figure 17.3). Lucy's fame is based on the claim that her knee joint and pelvic (hip bone) structure "proved" Lucy walked upright. Lucy's height (about 3½ feet or 105 cm) and other bone features were very chimpanzee-like, and estimates of her brain volume fall within the chimpanzee range. To an evolutionist, that means Lucy took the

Figure 17.2: *Homo erectus,* " Peking Man"

first upright steps away from being an ape and toward being a human being — the perfect ape-to-man (or woman) link! According to the evolutionary scenario most popular today, Lucy's upright posture freed her hands for tool use, and tool use favored the evolution of larger brains until… here we are talking about our origin!

That evolutionary story above is told and retold in textbooks, classrooms, museums, TV nature programs, zoos, and conversations with friends who wonder why you are a Christian in the face of such convincing evidence of human evolution. Scientists, however, have several serious scientific objections to accepting Lucy as a link.

(1) The knee. The angle made by the upper and lower leg bones where they meet at the knee is different for apes and human beings. With lots of individual variation, apes are usually more "bow-legged" and humans more "knock-kneed." Johanson found fragments of Lucy's knee joint scattered over a fairly broad area, and he put them together in a way that made Lucy look "half-way" between apes and humans, suggesting that, even if she was clumsy, Lucy walked somewhat upright.

Charles Oxnard, an evolutionist and internationally respected anatomist, wrote an article for the *American Biology Teacher* stating that the evidence "cautions against a too-ready acceptance of this view." Johanson just lined up the bones at the knee in line with his subjective opinion, which meant he failed to use the objective measurements and techniques employed by scientists. There are "bumps and grooves" on bone surfaces where ligaments and tendons attach, and these can be analyzed objectively and scientifically by computers that give data on the real knee joint

Figure 17.3: "Lucy"

Australopithecus

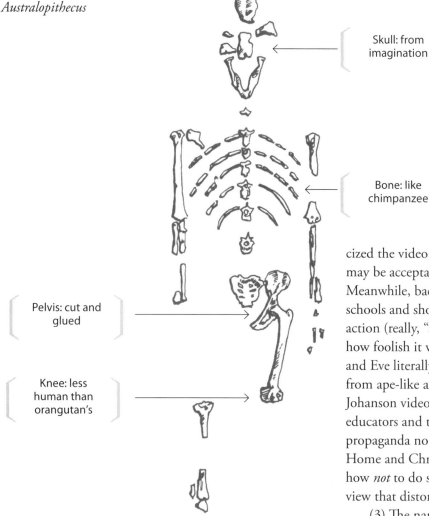

Skull: from imagination

Bone: like chimpanzee

Pelvis: cut and glued

Knee: less human than orangutan's

alignment. Analyzing knee joints from australopithecines like Lucy, both Oxnard and British anatomist Lord Zuckerman concluded that Lucy did not walk upright, at least not in the human manner. In fact, the evidence suggested orangutans would walk more like humans than Lucy, and no one regards them as human ancestors.

(2) The pelvis. When Lucy was first discovered, Johanson stated his firm belief that her pelvis (hip bone) also "proved" Lucy walked upright. In his own video production about Lucy done over 20 years later, however, Johanson finally admitted that Lucy's pelvis really did not fit with the idea that Lucy walked upright! Then, he told the viewing audience, he finally spotted the problem: the bones of the pelvis (a fusion of three bones) fit together "too perfectly."

Normally, of course, a perfect fit between bones is not a problem; it is a scientist's dream come true! You don't have to guess subjectively how the bones fit together; you can see objectively how they really fit together! But the scientific evidence did not fit Johanson's evolutionary view. So, right on his own video, he shows an anatomist

sawing a replica of Lucy's pelvis into several pieces and then gluing the pieces back together. Incredibly, Johanson announces to his video audience that the cut-and-glued pelvis finally really does prove Lucy walked upright!

I was in New Zealand on a creation science lecture tour when Johanson's video was first aired. Citing the cut-and-glued pelvis and a number of other scientific blunders, a major New Zealand newspaper review severely criticized the video, saying the standard of evidence presented may be acceptable in America, but not in New Zealand! Meanwhile, back in America, the video was bought by schools and shown to students, both to show "science" in action (really, "science falsely so-called") and to suggest how foolish it would be to take the Bible's story of Adam and Eve literally when Lucy proved mankind evolved from ape-like ancestors. The uncritical acceptance of the Johanson video really demonstrated how easily American educators and the media would swallow evolutionary propaganda no matter how bad the "science" behind it! Home and Christian schools can use the video to show how *not* to do science and how to guard against a world view that distorts observable evidence.

(3) The name game. Australopithecines had long been believed to exist in two forms: robust and gracile. The first, bigger form had heavy-duty bones, the second form had much smaller and more delicate bones. Some thought they might be male and female of one species, but most evolutionists classified them into two species, *Australopithecus robustus* (or *bosei*) (e.g., the "Nutcracker" form), and *A. gracilis,* the group to which Lucy was originally assigned.

Just as I was getting ready for my back-to-back first and second creation-evolution debates — the second with an anthropologist — newspapers flashed the story of new support for human evolution discovered in the Afar region of Africa! With understandable apprehension, I awaited the announcement made at Donald Johanson's press conference. The announcement came. It was not a new discovery. It was just Lucy, who was already part of my presentation. The "new" was only a new species name. Johanson wanted to call Lucy *A. afarensis* instead of *A. gracilis.* Even the name wasn't new; it was also already part of my presentation. *Time* magazine actually exposed

Johanson's news conference as just a cheap publicity stunt, and chided the press for being so easily taken in.

(4) Scientific peer review. Remember, even when a prestigious scientist calls a news conference to announce a major discovery, it is not really science until other qualified scientists have examined the same evidence and come to the same conclusion. The requirement for peer review by other scientists is a major reason science can remain more objective than other disciplines, even in the face of competing hypotheses.

Johanson announced the discovery of Lucy in 1974, but he didn't let scientists outside his team look at the evidence for over seven years. Meanwhile, Johanson and Lucy — without objective scientific peer review — became more and more famous and more and more a part of textbook teaching and talk shows. When scientists, even Johanson's fellow evolutionists, finally got their first objective look at the "evidence," they were dismayed. Most just kept silent (perhaps not wanting to encourage creationists), but some spoke out publicly. Leading paleoanthropologists Adrienne Zihlman and Vincent Sarich published a scathing scientific criticism. (Sarich had frequently engaged Duane Gish in cordial but pointed creation-evolution debates.)

In their article, Zihlman and Sarich pointed out the curved finger bones that suggested life swinging in the trees, not standing upright scanning the African plains. They pointed out numerous other chimpanzee-like features in Lucy, and even showed a picture of Lucy's skeleton superimposed on the skeleton of the living rain forest or *pygmy chimpanzee, Pan paniscus,* also called the bonobo. A troop of these chimps lives in a fabulous habitat in the San Diego Zoo, and they can occasionally be seen walking upright, just as well as Lucy ever could. But they are obviously chimpanzees, and not ape-to-man links. No one would become famous, of course, by claiming to find fossil chimpanzee bones in Africa — and Lucy appears to be nothing more.

(5) Wrong place; wrong time. Lucy could not be a human ancestor, of course, if human beings were living, dying, and being fossilized before Lucy was. When Richard Leakey found bones like those of modern man below the fossil-rock layer where his father had found Nutcracker Man, for example, evolutionists quit calling the Nutcracker fossils human ancestors. Specimens found below others in the fossil-rock sequence (geologic column diagram) must have lived and been fossilized before those found above (often only

minutes or months before for creationists vs. millions of years before for evolutionists). In the late 1970s, Mary Leakey found evidence that should have made evolutionists quit calling Lucy a human ancestor.

It often takes several experts taking many measurements to tell whether a fragment of leg bone is ape or human or something else. But anyone can tell the difference between ape and human footprints. An ape's foot looks somewhat like a hand, since it has an opposable big toe; both ape and human hands have an opposable thumb used in grasping. No animal known, living or fossil, has a footprint like a human being's, with its distinctive heel, arch, and angled row of toes with short, flat nails. Tracks are highly prized as fossils, both because they often can be clearly identified and because they provide information on behavior that a bone fragment can't.

In an East African volcanic ash deposit near Laetoli in Tanzania, Mary Leakey found a series of tracks that looked very human. The footprints were found in a layer deposited before the fossils of Lucy or any other proposed human ancestor. As a well-known evolutionist (wife of Louis and mother of Richard), she was at first reluctant to call the trackways human, since that would rule out all the evidence (including Lucy) previously used to support belief in human evolution. However, in a superb demonstration of true scientific spirit, Mary Leakey was also unwilling to

Pygmy chimpanzee

ignore or distort (or cut-and-glue) the observable, measurable evidence actually found. In a television special she did later, she simply called them human tracks. Mary Leakey continued to believe in human evolution, but she also believed the evidence to support that belief would have to be found among fossils below the level where the Laetoli tracks were found.

Evolutionist Russell Tuttle also recognized the significance of the Laetoli tracks. Since a bear's track is more like a human footprint than an ape's is, Tuttle studied tracks of a circus bear made in mud. He announced his conclusion as "shocking, disturbing, and upsetting," because he couldn't tell the difference between human and Laetoli tracks. The evidence is not upsetting to creationists, of course.

Evo-logical!

Richard Leakey maintains his faith in human evolution but, like his mother, believes the scientific-historical evidence is yet to be found. A major article in *Life* magazine contrasted the views of Donald Johanson and Richard Leakey. Johanson's view pictured human evolution as a "Y" with apes at one tip, humans at the other, and Lucy at the split as the perfect common ancestor. Knowing that the scientific evidence showed both advanced ape and human fossils below Lucy's level, Leakey's diagram showed lines for ape and human evolution coming closer together (his faith in evolution) but not meeting (his scientific knowledge). It is easy for creationists to respect Leakey's belief in evolution because we can admire his respect for science.

(6) Evolution vs. science. *National Geographic*, the St. Louis Zoo, and many evolutionists seem to have taken a far less scientific approach than the Leakeys have. *National Geographic* reported Mary Leakey's discovery of the Laetoli tracks in its April 1979 issue. Its close-up drawing showed human feet making the human tracks. Its double-page panorama of the African savanna showed the usual creatures: elephants, giraffes, gazelles, zebras, guinea fowl, etc. A strip of cool, damp, recently deposited Laetoli volcanic ash runs across the scene. Guinea fowl are shown having made guinea fowl tracks in the ash, but — without any scientific basis at all — they put Lucy carrying a baby and Mr. Lucy in the human tracks! The Laetoli tracks are smaller than the average adult

human tracks, but they could be older children or smaller adults. (The Pygmies live near Laetoli today.)

Take a look again at the fossil remains of Lucy — and notice the feet are missing (Figure 17.3)! The known features of Lucy are like those of the living bonobo chimpanzees, and those animals have a foot with an opposable big toe that, like those of other apes, resembles a hand. Finally, the fossils of Lucy (*A. afarensis*) are found hundreds of miles north in a layer of fossil-rock higher (and, for an evolutionist, thousands or millions of years later) than the Laetoli tracks. Only a blind faith in human evolution, contrary to the fossil evidence presently at hand, is the basis for putting Lucy in human tracks. Evolutionists could have had artists draw the same picture without finding any evidence at all, never ever looking for it.

It's no wonder some believe evolution is giving science a bad name. Remember, however, that evolutionists can be very smart. Their problem is not intelligence. They have simply chosen a world view that is at odds with the evidence in God's world.

The evolutionist's science may be incredibly weak, but his/her faith is incredibly strong! A committed evolutionist cannot even consider that human beings made the human tracks at Laetoli. Their absolute, unswerving commitment to origins by means of millions of years of struggle and death will not allow them to even pretend there could be any human beings around to make the Laetoli tracks. Since the tracks are real and fossils of Lucy are real (even if "footless"), it's "evo-logical" for them to assume undiscovered specimens of Lucy's kind, living earlier in Laetoli, made those tracks. That's not strong evidence, but it is strong faith.

If the average Christian had faith as strong as the average evolutionist's, perhaps they could conquer the "evolution empire" like faithful first-century Christians conquered the Roman Empire!

Form your foundation.

Still touted by textbooks and TV, "Lucy" has been disproven as an "ape-woman link."
The pelvis had to be sawed and glued to fit evolutionary belief; the knee angle, curved finger bones, and brain volume are all ape-like; and the Laetoli tracks show humans were fossilized before "Lucy" was.

1. Creationists of the last generation won the "science wars" over "cave men," races, and Piltdown, Java, and Nebraska Man. This generation faces the African fossils called _____, which means "southern apes." They became famous in 1959 when the Leakey family found a (gorilla/human)_____-like skull in a rock layer with (legs/ribs/tools) _____. When Richard _____ later found human bones in a lower layer, it seemed the tools were used (on/by) _____the former "owner" of the skull. The fossil remains which were once called "Peking Man" may also have been man's (meal/ancestor) _____.

2. In 1974, the team of Donald_____ found scattered Ethiopian fossil fragments they put together to form a specimen popularly called "_____," given the scientific name _____ *afarensis*, and claimed to be a perfect link between _____ and _____.

3. Textbooks, television, magazines, and museums all hail "Lucy" as the perfect link between apes and mankind, but scientists who otherwise accept evolution find major flaws in the Lucy story (3a-3d):

3a. On the basis of his subjective look at the angle made where upper and lower leg bones met at the knee, Johanson claimed Lucy had a chimp-sized brain but walked upright. Using modern computer techniques, world-class anatomists Oxnard and Zuckerman (supported/disproved) _____ this view, and warned that Lucy's "walk" was (less/more) _____human than an orangutan's.

3b. After claiming for years that Lucy's pelvis supported belief in her upright walking, Johanson finally had another scientist (agree with/cut and glue the pelvis to make it fit) _____ his interpretation.

3c. Although a theory cannot properly be considered scientific until other scientists test it, Johanson kept others from examining Lucy for seven years. When leading evolutionists Sarich and Zihlman finally got to examine the fossils, they concluded Lucy was (a young human being/a nearly perfect ape-man link/little different from the living pygmy chimp or bonobo)_____.

3d. Footprints of humans and apes are quite (similar/different) _____. When Mary Leakey found fossil human footprints below the rock level where Lucy's fossils were found, the claim that Lucy was an ancestor of human beings was (supported/discredited) _____. Evolutionists claimed the human tracks found by Mary Leakey at Laetoli belonged to others of Lucy's kind, but (no/many) _____ foot bones of Lucy have been found and (no/many) _____ specimens of Lucy's kind are found near, so the evolutionist claim is based on (solid science/blind faith) _____.

4. Human evolution continues to be believed and taught in spite of abundant scientific evidence repeatedly refuting it. Can belief in human evolution be called "good science"? If not, why do so many people believe it?

    _____

    _____

    _____

5. When it comes to human origins, both creationists and evolutionists must build on faith. So what's the difference? And, when it comes to evidence presently available, which faith bests fits the facts?

    _____

    _____

    _____

Chapter

17

"Away from Evolution"

In university debates with creationists, evolutionists almost never cite any fossil evidence for human evolution. After a quarter century, Lucy is still considered the best fossil evidence for human evolution — and you can see why a knowledgeable evolutionist would not want to use that evidence in debate with a knowledgeable creationist!

Like other major news magazines, *Newsweek* normally promotes evolution; it is certainly not biased toward creation! Yet long after Lucy was discovered and became evolution's heroine, a review article by evolutionists in *Newsweek* made these astonishing admissions (Nov. 3, 1980: "Is Man a Subtle Accident?"):

> *The missing link between man and apes . . . is merely the most glamorous of a whole hierarchy of phantom creatures. In the fossil record, missing links are the rule. The more scientists [sic] have searched for the transitional forms between species, the more they have been frustrated.*

How refreshing it would be to have textbooks, teachers, television, museums, and the media admit that human evolution is based on "phantom creatures" — ghosts, or figments of the imagination! You may want to make *Newsweek's* summary quote into a plaque and donate it to your local high school biology classroom:

> *Evidence from fossils now points overwhelmingly away from the classical Darwinism, which most Americans learned in high school.*

Long after Lucy's discovery, the evidence still (as it always has) points overwhelmingly away from Darwinian evolution.

If the evidence points overwhelmingly away from belief in human evolution, what does it point toward? As we shall see, the evidence in God's world clearly points toward the truth of God's Word (Rom. 1:20).

> *In the beginning God created the heaven and the earth* (Gen. 1:1).
> *So God created man in his own image, in the image of God created he him; male and female created he them* (Gen. 1:27).

Science vs. Human Evolution

If human evolution were a concept based on science, it would have been discarded long ago as completely falsified by the scientific evidence. Despite continuing misrepresentation by media and museums, despite tall tales told by textbooks, teachers, and television, every single fossil ever claimed to show that mankind evolved from ape-like ancestors has been proven false. The claims have been proven false by the repeated and verified observations of scientists examining each fossil's structure, association, and location. To their credit, most of the scientists who have disproved the claims of fossil support for human evolution are evolutionists (for reasons other than human fossils!), but they have refused to let their belief in evolution overrule the clear scientific evidence.

The whole concept of missing links shows that human evolution began as a belief, not as a conclusion from evidence. Before they looked at any fossil evidence whatsoever, evolutionists (including Darwin) rejected the concept that mankind was a special creation of an all-loving, all-powerful Creator God; they believed instead that mankind evolved in small, gradual steps from ape-like ancestors through what Darwin called "intermediate links." Knowing (by faith in evolution) that no God created man as man, they believed with all their hearts, souls, minds, and strengths that such intermediate links, or stages in evolution, must exist as fossils, so they went looking for them. Since they found no such links, they labeled them "missing." You can't believe a link is missing unless you first believe (by faith) that it must have existed — which puts belief before evidence.

Think about this: What is the difference between a supposed ape-man link that is missing and one that never existed at all? If God created human beings as a distinct kind, just as different at the start from the various kinds of apes as we are today, we should just find human fossils and ape fossils, with nothing in between. According to creationists, nothing is missing. Just as we would predict from reading biblical history, we find fossils of men, apes, fakes and mistakes, but no ape-man links (Figure 18.1). The absence of fossil ape-men is not telling us the links are missing; it's telling us the links never existed at all!

At least creationists and evolutionists can agree on one point about missing links: they are missing!

The search for man's supposed evolutionary ancestry is full of examples of outrageous "scientific malpractice": sick and dark-skinned peoples treated as sub-human (Neanderthals, blacks, and Aboriginals), fakes and mistakes that fooled the experts for years (Piltdown, Java, and Nebraska Man), man's meal considered man's ancestor (Nutcracker and Peking Man), and the wrong bones in the wrong places (australopithecines). Most people think that scientists work by steadily accumulating evidence that points toward a new conclusion, but that is certainly not true of the search for human evolution's missing link.

The missing link search began with belief, not evidence — but, by itself, that was not the scientific malpractice. Science is based on the continuous give and take between ideas and evidence. Evidence may suggest new ideas, but a new idea may stimulate the search for evidence to support or refute the idea. Many scientific breakthroughs began with a flash of insight or brilliant idea. An idea or belief in advance qualifies as scientific, however, if and only if both evidence is found to support it and no compelling evidence is found against it. Before

Figure 18.1

Evolutionary "Ape-Man" Claim	→	Scientific Conclusion
Neanderthal "Cave People"	→	Man (*Homo sapiens*)
African Blacks	→	Man (*Homo sapiens*)
Austrailian Aboriginals	→	Man (*Homo sapiens*)
Piltdown (*Eoanthropus*)	→	Fake
Java Man	→	Mistake
Peking Man (*Homo erectus*)	→	Man's Meal
Nebraska Man (*Hesperopithecus*)	→	Pig's Tooth
Ramapithecus	→	Ape's Jaw
Leakey's "Zinj" (*A. robustus*)	→	Ape
Johanson's "Lucy" (*Arafarensis*)	→	Ape
Laetoli prints (M. Leakey)	→	Man
12-year-old boy (R. Leakey)	→	Man

the search for evidence got underway, Darwin and others could propose fossil ape-man links as a scientifically testable hypothesis. After 150 years of intensive searching turned up no links to support that view and many fossils to refute it, clinging to a falsified hypothesis out of blind faith contrary to the evidence at hand is unscientific and even anti-scientific.

It's no wonder some people think evolution is giving science a bad name, and, even worse, such "science falsely so-called" might discourage Christian students from following God's call into careers in science! Remember, God himself tells us that the evidence in God's world points toward the truth in God's Word (Rom. 1:18–20; Ps. 19:1–4)!

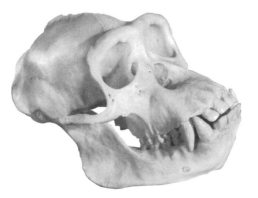

More Science vs. Human Evolution: Classification

If you've been to the zoo or seen nature films on jungle life, you have no doubt noticed similarities between man and the apes and monkeys. There's a God-given tendency for people, including scientists, to put animals, plants, and objects into groups on the basis of shared features that stand out in the classifier's mind. It's common for people, including scientists, to classify animals as birds, mammals, or reptiles, for example, on the basis of their body covering, such as feathers, fur, or scales.

When people, including scientists, look at apes, monkeys, and their fellow human beings, it's features of the face and hands that seem to stand out most. Like people, apes and monkeys have forward-looking eyes that give them stereoscopic or binocular vision and a face that looks somewhat like ours. Those animals also have four fingers and an opposable thumb like we do, and instead of long, sharp, pointed claws, they have blunt, flat fingernails like ours. Those

who believe flat fingernails and forward-looking eyes are important traits for classification have put man, apes, and monkeys into a "mid-level" grouping called order Primates. You have probably heard man, apes, and monkeys called primates.

Does putting mankind in the primate group mean or prove that man evolved from apes or monkeys, or that man, apes, and monkeys shared a common ancestor? Absolutely not, for several reasons:

(1) Calling people "primates" is merely a shorthand way of saying people have flat fingernails and forward-looking eyes. It describes human features, not their ancestry. Creationists and evolutionists could both use the term descriptively, yet they have radically opposite views of human origin.

(2) The term "primates" tells us more about the person doing the classifying than it does about the creatures being classified. Who's to say, for example, that flat fingernails and forward-looking eyes are more important than running upright on two legs with hands free, or speaking and singing with a very complex range of vocal tones? If running upright were considered more important, mankind might be grouped with ostriches instead of apes. On the very important basis of complex vocal tones, people have more in common with dolphins and whales than they do with apes. Do those alternate groupings sound strange only because we are "brainwashed" from pre-school to think in terms of other groups? Studies of classification (systematics and taxonomy) are "para-scientific" at best; the repeatable, verifiable observation of features in detail is certainly scientific and requires depth of knowledge and skill, but the criteria for grouping organisms on the basis of such observations is very subjective and strongly influenced by world view, prejudice, or even whimsy.

(Gen. 2), recognizing and classifying them on the basis of their distinctive features! The discipline of classification has always strongly favored creation over evolution.

As mentioned, primates are a "mid-level" grouping called an "order." On the basis of progressively more specific, narrowly defined traits, an order is subdivided into families (a classification rank here, not "mom, pop, and the kids"); families into genera (sing., genus); and genera into species (sing., also species). A common subdivision of order Primates is shown in Figure 18.2. Taken together and offset from regular print by italics or underlining (etc.), genus (first name with first letter capitalized) and species (second, lower case) comprise the scientific name, e.g., *Homo sapiens* for mankind.

The distinctive features of each primate subgroup are indicated in Figure 18.2. If evolution were true, the criteria used to distinguish those groups would blur more and more as fossils were found deeper and deeper in fossil-rock layers (geologic column diagram). That is, if evolution were true and you were digging deeper, at first the difference between fossils of man and ape would blur, and you would find "ape-men" that would share features of both. Further down, fossils would just look

(3) Evolutionists have "pirated" the biological classification scheme and "re-interpreted" it to mean common ancestry. The discipline of classification, however, was founded by a Christian creationist, Carolus Linnaeus, who based classification on biblical principles of multiplication after created kind and on trait categories reflecting creation according to a common plan. The first job given to the first man God created was to name the animals

Figure 18.2

Prosimians

Anthropoids

Platyrrhines

Catarrhines

Hominid

Old World monkeys

Gibbon

Orangutan

Gorilla

Chimpanzee

Human

Presumed millions of years ago

Modern prosimians

New World monkeys

Presumed millions of years ago	Epoch
0	Recent / Pleistocene / Pliocene
10	Miocene
20	
30	Oligocene
40	Eocene
50	Paleocene
60	

Early prosimians

like "apes in general," and the differences between gorillas, chimpanzees, and orangutans would disappear. Below that level, fossils might look vaguely "primate," but even the differences between apes and monkeys would become indistinct. Finally, it would be hard to tell a primate from an animal in a different order, like a bear (order Carnivora) or a sloth (order Edentata).

However, since evolution is *not* true, fossils of primates do *not* at all form a series from specialized down to generalized, as described above. Not only are there no links that blur the distinctions between apes and man, there aren't even links between chimps and gorillas, between apes and monkeys, or between primates and any other order. Because each kind was created to multiply after its kind, the differences between man and apes, between apes and monkeys, and between primates and other animals are the same in the past as they are in the present. Paleontologists distinguish among the fossils of man, apes, and monkeys using the same features that biologists use to classify those groups today.

There is, however, a major difference between primate groups recognized by fossil experts and those living today: there was a greater variety of primates living in the past than the present. The persistence of the criteria for classification points to creation, living things created to multiply after kind; the decline in variety points to the corruption of creation by man's sin, and the ecological deterioration that followed the catastrophe of Noah's flood. According to the evolution model, variety should generally increase with time as mutations produce more and more forms expanding into more and more environmental niches, the opposite of what we observe.

The biblical creation model explains both the persistence of criteria for classification and the decrease in variety; evolution explains neither.

Anatomy

Features of the face and hands can be used to put man and apes together — without evolutionary implications — in order Primates. But bone features (skeletal anatomy) used to distinguish man and apes today are the same features paleontologists find separating fossil apes and fossil humans.

Teeth make good fossils because their enamel coating is so hard, and they are small with distinctive shapes and markings. Apes generally have a U-shaped jaw with large canines (the pointed teeth) near the corners of the U. There are gaps (diastema) in the opposing jaws to make room for the canines when the jaws are shut. Humans have a parabolic (arch-shaped) jaw with shorter canines and no canine gap. Those traits distinguish apes and humans today, and the same traits separate fossil apes and humans.

Ramapithecus was considered the first ape to show emergence of human tendencies. Fossils of a few teeth and jaw fragments found in Africa were reconstructed so the jaw had a curve between the U-shape of the ape and the parabolic arch of the human. The jaw was claimed to be an ape-human link that was no longer missing. But then more fossil evidence of *Ramapithecus* was found. The new, more complete evidence showed the Rama jaw was 100 percent ape, and using the title of a review article in *Natural History, Ramapithecus* was dropped as a "False Start to the Human Parade."

Ramapithecus 1932–1977

Man

Ramapithecus 1977–present

Ape

Remember, when evidence is reported that seems to contradict biblical truth, just hang in there. Science will catch up and show that the Bible has been right all along.

As described earlier, Lucy has curved finger and toe bones, classic traits of an arboreal (tree-dwelling) chimpanzee with arms designed for swinging through the branches (brachiation). Her short, stocky hind limbs and long, powerful forelimbs also suggest brachiation ("tree swinging"). The ratio of lower arm to upper arm length is 80 percent in humans, 95 percent in living chimps. Even those believing Lucy is an ape-man link reported Lucy's value at 92.5 percent, very near the chimp average.

Apes have "four hands," in effect, each foot with a grasping, opposable big toe that acts like a thumb. Despite popularized misrepresentations of the facts (i.e., lies?), the human-like Laetoli tracks Mary Leakey found extend the clear distinction between man and apes into fossil-rock layers below those where Lucy was found. Ignoring scientific measurements of Lucy's knee, cutting and gluing her pelvis, and imagining foot bones not found for her all add up to mere wishful thinking, "science falsely so-called," which is contradicted by the current scientific evidence showing that both living and fossil apes and people walk in quite different manners.

Skulls of apes and people also have distinctive differences — and those were the features deliberately removed from the ape jaw and human skull used in the Piltdown hoax. Gorillas and apes with huge jaws have a bony ridge (sagittal crest) running the length of the skull, something never present in human skulls. Finding a large sagittal crest in "Nutcracker Man" should have encouraged Louis Leakey to consider the stone tools found with that skull were used on that skull, not by its owner.

Brain volumes for Lucy's group run 380–450 cc (cm³), extensively overlapping the range for living chimps of 330–400. The nearly complete skull of an adult male A. afarensis found in 1994 was completely ape-like. On the other hand, brain volume for the 12-year-old boy (improperly called *Homo erectus*) found by Richard Leakey's team is 880 cc, well within the large range of 750–2,000 found among intelligent people today. Since other features of that famous fossil boy are also within the human range, scientists unfettered by evolutionist bias would correctly call it *Homo sapiens,* the same scientific name given to you and me. Once again, the line between man and ape is clear and distinct.

Indeed, even diehard evolutionists admit that it is not the objectively repeatable and verifiable science of anatomy that causes them to give sub-human names to the 12 year old; it's the dating. Once again, evolutionists have let the findings of solid science be overruled by "science falsely so-called."

Form your foundation.

It took an act of faith to start the search for "missing links," and failure to find them exposed evolution as a faith the facts have failed. The evidence found in God's world agrees with God's Word: Man and apes have always been separate kinds!

AABB   **AABb**   **AaBb**   **Aabb**   **aabb**

The Bible has always taught that there is only one "race," the human race, and all people are part of it (Acts 17:26). But early evolutionists taught that different "races" were in different stages of evolution, some still sub-human.

A. Science disproved evolutionary racism, and Darwin's followers today agree that all "ethnic groups" are fully *Homo sapiens*, and all have various amounts of the same skin color protein, melanin. If God created Adam and Eve with two pairs of genes, AaBb, to control the amount of melanin produced, then all the variations from most to least melanin (darkest to lightest tone) would occur in one generation. Believing each gene (A,a,B, and b) were produced by chance and spread through the population by ceaseless struggle to the death, how would an evolutionist explain skin color variation? Can you see why Darwin's early followers were racist?

B. Too many Christians quickly compromised with Darwin's and Haeckel's beliefs on racial superiority/inferiority and accepted evolutionary racism. How would you counsel Christians who want to compromise with evolution today? Is our skin color part of God's image in us?

C. In the case of skin color genetics, did science prove to be the "friend" of the creationist or the evolutionist? What would you advise Christians to do when it seems that science and Scripture disagree? Why?

1. Complete this quote from *Newsweek*, a secular summary of the fossil evidence through Lucy related to human origins:

a. "The missing link between man and apes . . . is merely the most glamorous of a whole hierarchy of (links found to support evolution/phantom creatures) _____. In the fossil record, missing links are the (rule/exception) _____. The more [evolutionary] scientists have searched for the transitional forms between species, the more they have been (encouraged/ frustrated) _____. Evidence from fossils now [long after Lucy] points overwhelmingly (toward/ away from) _____the classical Darwinism, which most Americans learned in high school."

2. Explain how the concept of "missing links" shows that evolution is a faith-based belief system. Is it starting with faith or something else that suggests evolution is "science falsely so-called"?

   _____

   _____

   _____

   _____

3. Concerning ape and human classification, mark the following true (T) or false (F):

   _____ a. Humans and apes are both put in order Primates because both have flat fingernails and forward-looking eyes with 3-D vision.

   _____ b. It's common features, *not* common ancestry, that allow scientists to group people with primates.

   _____ c. Among deeper fossils boundaries between kinds should blur, say evolutionists, and stay the same, say creationists. The evidence supports creationists.

   _____ d. Our system of classification was made up by evolutionists, but "pirated" by creationists, beginning with Linnaeus.

4. Concerning ape and human anatomy, mark the following true (T) or false (F):

   _____ a. Fossil fragments called *Ramapithecus* were given a jaw shape between the U of ape and parabola of people, but finding a whole jaw that was U-shaped forced Rama to be dropped as a, "false start to the human parade."

   _____ b. When other evolutionists finally had a chance to look at Lucy's bones, they immediately saw the curved fingers and long arms with long forearms, suggesting Lucy was a tree swinger (brachiator), *not* walking upright.

   _____ c. The brain volume of Lucy's kind strongly overlaps that of chimps and gets nowhere near the human level.

   _____ d. Apes have a foot with an opposable big toe that makes it more like the human hand than foot, so the Laetoli tracks Mary Leakey found suggest scientifically that people were living and dying before Lucy was fossilized, eliminating her as a possible human ancestor.

5. Richard Leakey's team found the fossils of a 12-year-old boy, all of whose features were completely in the range for *Homo sapiens* — yet he was classified as "*Homo erectus*." Why? Is that good science, or merely evolutionary belief?

   _____

   What would a creationist say about the discovery?

   _____

Chapter 18

Dating Fossils of Apes and People

Even evolutionists admit that *Homo erectus* specimens like the 12-year-old boy could be called ordinary people, *Homo sapiens,* if only they weren't "too old." But how do evolutionists know how old the fossils are?

If you asked a scientist how old the fossils were, a scientist might answer something like this: "I don't know. I'm a scientist. As a scientist, I limit my study to processes and patterns of order other scientists and I can repeatedly, objectively observe and measure in the present. I can measure how fast something is wearing out, for example. If I know that it was wearing out at that same rate in the unobserved past, and if I know what condition it was in when it started wearing out, then I could give you an estimate (or guesstimate) of what its age might be. But, as a scientist, I don't know what the object was like in the past, and I don't know that it has always been wearing out at the same rate, so, as a scientist, I can't really tell you how old it is."

Radiometric "Dating"

Radioactive elements "wear out" as they decay from parent element into a daughter element. At rates presently measured, for example, half of the radioactive carbon-14 in a fossil would wear out and change into nitrogen-14 in 5,730 years.

Evolutionists would like people to believe scientists use radioactive elements to measure time. They do not measure time; they measure the amounts of certain elements (isotopes) in a fossil or in the surrounding rock. The isotopes can be measured very accurately, but it takes lots and lots of assumptions — some shaky, some highly unlikely, and a few probably false — to turn those real, scientific isotope measurements into hypothetical, evolutionary assertions about time. Always remember: radiometric dates are not measures of time; they are measurements of elements converted into ideas about time by numerous compounded assumptions.

Among the assumptions of radiometric are these: the original amounts of parent and daughter elements are known (almost always false; estimates must be based on further assumptions); no parent or daughter elements were added or subtracted from the specimen (nearly always false); rates of radioactive decay (which can be measured with fair accuracy today) were never different in the past. The last assumption (severely challenged by recent research) is the most reasonable, but a "clock" ticking regularly (the decay rate) will not give you accurate time if you don't know when it started and you do know that someone has tampered with the settings!

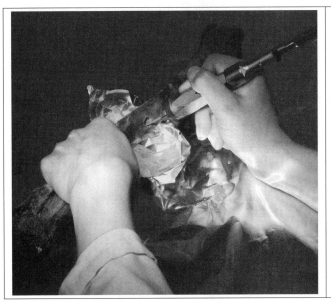

Radiometric "dating"

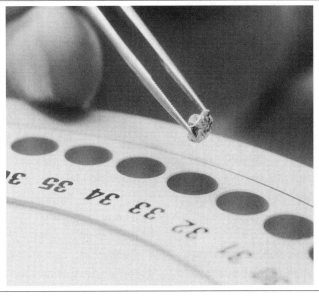

Carbon Dating

Because it has a decay rate that evolutionists think is appropriate for the time they believe is involved, human evolutionists stick themselves with the worst radiometric "clock," potassium/argon. Potassium-40 (K-40) changes into argon-40 (Ar-40) with a "half-life" of 1.25 billion years. If minerals in volcanic ash surrounding a fossil had equal amounts of K-40 and Ar-40 (half parent/half daughter), it would be considered 1.25 billion years old. But then the problems begin. (1) How much Ar-40 was already in the ash? Probes sent to the planet Venus show evolutionists were hugely wrong about the amounts of Ar-40 present in the atmosphere there, and they have no solid scientific basis for guessing the starting setting on the supposed K/Ar "clock" here. (2) Argon is an inert gas that moves freely through spaces between minerals, so it can be easily added or subtracted to a sample. Underground water flow can add and subtract K-40. Evolutionists sometimes cite these as reasons lava flows in Hawaii observed within the past 200 years give "ages" of 169 million and 3 billion years. (3) Potassium-40 also decays into Ca-40. Could elements with shorter half-lives have once decayed into Ar-40? Measurements of excess heat flow from rocks do suggest the prior existence of now "extinct" radiation, a problem more serious the longer the time presumed.

When Johanson's team first found Lucy, they were anxious for her to be older than anything the Leakeys had found, so she could be considered the "real" missing link and the ancestor of Leakey discoveries. The first date, checked three different ways, was a little less than

three million evolutionist years (3 my). That was not old enough, and Johanson reported how disappointed his team was. But then the dater offered a new date: 3½ million evolutionist years (3.5 my)! Johanson immediately accepted that date without even asking why that date should be any better than the three wrong dates previously done. Another scientist got involved, but his measurements of K-40 and Ar-40 isotopes in the volcanic ash above Lucy made Lucy even younger than the first dates reported. An editor for *Science News* reviewed the problems and inconsistencies under the title, "Lucy: The Trouble with Dating an Older Woman."

Actually, human evolutionists may benefit from the fact that the so-called K/Ar "clock" is so sloppy and flexible. If a "modern" (human-like) fossil is found at a lower level than a "primitive" (ape-like) specimen, they can rather easily be given new dates. Skull 1470, which Richard Leakey found below his father's once-considered "missing link," was originally dated at 2.8 my. Then paleoanthropologists learned how modern it was. Now it's dated at 1.8 my. At a meeting in San Diego, Mary Leakey once lamented that different dating labs kept giving her conflicting dates, making it hard for her to choose the best spot to look for human ancestors.

Why do evolutionist dates come out in millions or billions of years (thousands with carbon-14)? The answer is simple, and circular. To "date" a fossil or rock, evolutionists choose a radioactive element whose half-life matches the age they expect to find; e.g., uranium-238 for samples thought to be billions of years old, K/Ar for a few million, and carbon-14 for thousands. Multiplying a huge half-life by a measurable ratio of parent/daughter isotopes will usually give uranium "ages" in billions, K/Ar "ages" in millions, and carbon-14 "ages" in thousands.

Stratigraphic Dating

For the same reason you can't build a house from the roof down, people assume fossils on the bottom of a stack of rock layers are older than layers on the top. But how much older? Fossils found around the world can be pictured in a vertical series of layers called the geologic column diagram. Evolutionists believe the fossils at the bottom are over 500 million years older than those on top; creationists think they are about five months older, buried rapidly after one another in the rising waters of Noah's flood. Evolutionists believe human fossils can be found only near the top of the column, because they only evolved recently. Creationists believe they are usually found near the top because they lived largely in upland environments in the pre-Flood world.

For evolutionists, finding undisturbed (in situ) human fossils or artifacts in rock layers assigned to the middle or lower parts of the geologic column is totally impossible, since those rock layers were, according to evolution, laid down and hardened millions of years before mankind evolved. For creationists, such fossils or artifacts would be rare, because those layers are deposits from marine environments and from terrestrial environments low in human food and resources, so few humans would travel through or live there.

According to creationists but not evolutionists, then, a few human remains or artifacts could be found in middle and lower layers of the geologic column — and they are. No matter how well documented, such "out-of-place fossils" are either hotly disputed or just ignored by Darwin's followers. Such information is usually found only in special references, and the best references will include evidence to back up claims.

Among the better-documented human artifacts found "millions of mythical years" before mankind supposedly evolved are a brass bell and metal bowl found in coal (about 300 million evolutionary years in age) and a wooden-handled metallic hammer (nearly half a billion years in evolutionary age). One of the best documented "out of place" human fossils is the "Malachite Man" found in the "dinosaur age" Morrison Formation in Utah. It's well worth looking into the references, both Christian and secular, that detail many, many more examples.

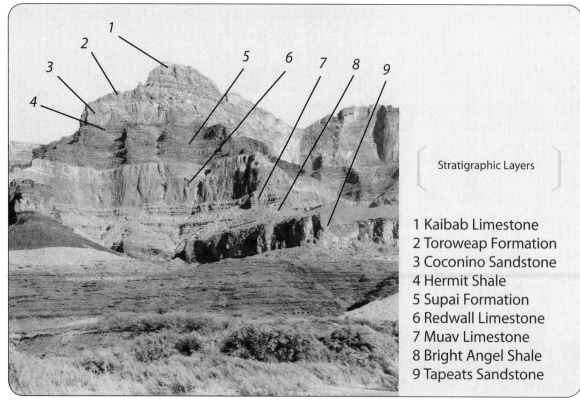

Stratigraphic Layers

1 Kaibab Limestone
2 Toroweap Formation
3 Coconino Sandstone
4 Hermit Shale
5 Supai Formation
6 Redwall Limestone
7 Muav Limestone
8 Bright Angel Shale
9 Tapeats Sandstone

Many evolutionists are willing to concede at least that the fossil human footprints found by Mary Leakey at Laetoli stratigraphically eliminate all fossils so far claimed to be mankind's ancestor.

Molecular Dating

Neither radiometric nor stratigraphic "dating" has been kind to evolutionists. The hot, new attempt is to use proteins and DNA as "molecular clocks."

Man and chimp each make over 30,000 different proteins. But when amino acid sequences were first determined for just five proteins in man and chimpanzees, some evolutionists got overly excited. In a university debate, one evolutionist said that if a chimp asked to take his daughter on a date, he was not sure he could say no! (Hopefully his daughter could!) Another evolutionist debater said he was concerned about separating man and chimp until the fifth protein showed a difference! Creationists would actually expect many proteins in man, chimp, and other animals to be similar or even identical, since they were designed by the same God to digest the same foods, build bones and use muscles the same way,

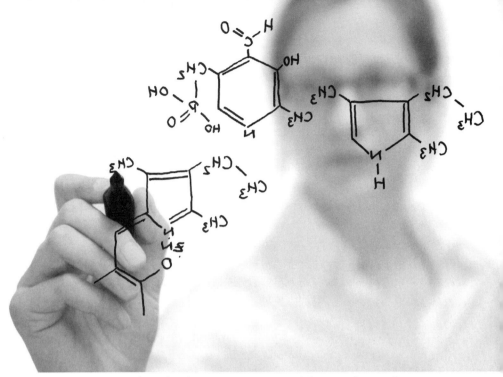

breathe the same oxygen, etc. There is plenty of room in the other 29,995 proteins for differences.

Textbooks, teachers, museums, and the media bombard students and the public with the claim that the DNAs of mankind and of chimpanzees are over 98 percent identical. That sounds "wow," but what does it mean? Practically nothing at all, for several reasons.

A cloud is 100 percent water, while a watermelon and a jellyfish are each about 98 percent water; that certainly does not mean they are nearly identical, or that two evolved from the other one! Or, what if the 2 percent different DNA organized the other 98 percent in different ways. The bricks used for building a house, a grill, or a garden wall may be 100 percent identical, but they are arranged to serve different functions or purposes.

More to the point, human DNA contains about 3 billion base letters in its genetic "alphabet." A 2 percent difference means there are 60 million differences between the DNAs of man and chimp! That means each of the 30,000 genes (current estimate) in man and chimp could have numerous differences in their genetic codes, even to the point (statistically) that no two genes were alike! Indeed, detailed studies comparing a small chromosome in man and chimp showed over 80 percent of proteins produced were

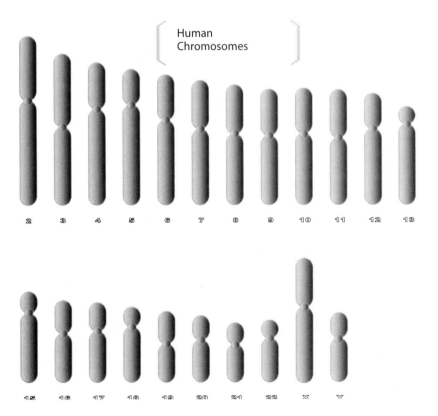

Human Chromosomes

2 3 4 5 6 7 8 9 10 11 12 13

15 16 17 18 19 20 21 22 X Y

141

significantly different. Besides that, you are only about 93 percent similar to yourself — that is, the genes a person inherits from one parent are, on average, only about 93 percent the same as genes inherited from the other parent.

Furthermore, small differences in DNA can produce huge effects. A difference of one letter in over 1,500 in the genetic code for hemoglobin produces the potentially deadly sickle cell hemoglobin.

As all *CSI* watchers know, subtle differences in DNA give each person a unique "DNA fingerprint." Using only 13 genetic markers, forensic scientists have no difficulty using DNA to tell the difference between brothers and sisters. It certainly seems that objective scientists would have no trouble telling the difference between chimp and human DNA!

The human/chimp DNA similarity has been a very effective propaganda ploy for evolutionists, but it is not very good science.

Actually, evolutionists attempting to use proteins and DNA as molecular "clocks" are not measuring time at all. They are measuring differences in the sequences of amino acids linked to form protein molecules, or of bases (nucleotides) linked to form DNA (Figure 19.1). To convert those sequence differences into "guestimates" of time, evolutionists must make a series of compounded and not particularly reasonable assumptions.

In a classic case of unjustified circular reasoning, an evolutionist will pick a molecule in a chimp and one in a human, for example, and then assume the amino acid

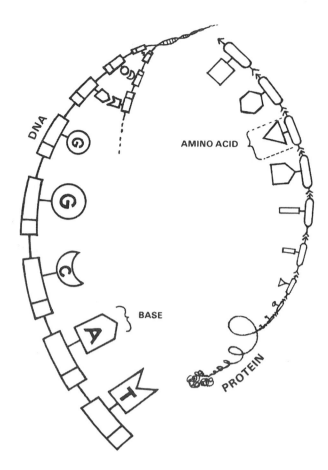

Figure 19.1: DNA is built like a string of pearls whose links (specifically the bases G, C, A, and T) act like alphabet letters that "spell out" hereditary instructions. Proteins are chains of amino acids. Each chain coils into a special shape that has some special function: muscle, contraction, digestion, oxygen transport, holding skin together, etc.

ACAAGATGCCATTGTCCCCCGGCCTCCTGCTGCTGCTGCTCTCCGGGGCCACGGCCACCGCTGCCCTGCC
CCTGGAGGGTGGCCCCACCGGCCGAGACAGCGAGCATATGCAGGAAGCGGCAGGAATAAGGAAAAGCAGC
CTCCTGACTTTCCTCGCTTGGTGGTTTGAGTGGACCTCCCAGGCCAGTGCCGGGCCCCTCATAGGAGAGG
CTGCAGGAACTTCTTCTGGAAGACCTTCTCCTCCTGCAAATAAAACCTCACCCATGAATGCTCACGCAAG
ACAAGATGCCATTGTCCCCCGGCCTCCTGCTGCTGCTGCTCTCCGGGGCCACGGCCACCGCTGCCCTGCC
CCTGGAGGGTGGCCCCACCGGCCGAGACAGCGAGCATATGCAGGAAGCGGCAGGAATAAGGAAAAGCAGC
AAGCTCGGGAGGTGGCCAGGCGGCAGGAAGGCGCACCCCCCCAGCAATCCGCGCGCCGGGACAGAATGCC
CTCCTGACTTTCCTCGCTTGGTGGTTTGAGTGGACCTCCCAGGCCAGTGCCGGGCCCCTCATAGGAGAGG
AAGCTCGGGAGGTGGCCAGGCGGCAGGAAGGCGCACCCCCCCAGCAATCCGCGCGCCGGGACAGAATGCC
ACAAGATGCCATTGTCCCCCGGCCTCCTGCTGCTGCTGCTCTCCGGGGCCACGGCCACCGCTGCCCTGCC
CCTGGAGGGTGGCCCCACCGGCCGAGACAGCGAGCATATGCAGGAAGCGGCAGGAATAAGGAAAAGCAGC
CTCCTGACTTTCCTCGCTTGGTGGTTTGAGTGGACCTCCCAGGCCAGTGCCGGGCCCCTCATAGGAGAGG
AAGCTCGGGAGGTGGCCAGGCGGCAGGAAGGCGCGCGCCGGGACAGAATGCC
CTGCAGGAACTTCTTCTGGAAGACCTTCTCCTCCATGAATGCTCACGCAAG
ACAAGATGCCATTGTCCCCCGGCCTCCTGCTGCTCCCACC
CCTGGAGGGTGGCCCCACCGGCCGAGACAGCGAGGAATAA
CTCCTGACTTTCCTCGCTTGGTGGTTTGAGTGGACCCCCT
AAGCTCGGGAGGTGGCCAGGCGGCAGGAAGGCGCACGCGCG
CTGCAGGAACTTCTTCTGGAAGACCTTCTCCTCCTGCATGAAT
ACAAGATGCCATTGTCCCCCGGCCTCCTGCTGCTGCTGCCACC
CCTGGAGGGTGGCCCCACCGGCCGAGACAGCGAGCATATGAATAA
CTCCTGACTTTCCTCGCTTGGTGGTTTGAGTGGACCTCCCCCT
AAGCTCGGGAGGTGGCCAGGCGGCAGGAAGGCGCACCCCCCCGCCG

A =	adenine
C =	cytosine
G =	guanine
T =	thymine
U =	uracil
R =	G A (purine)
Y =	T C (pyrimidine)
K =	G T (keto)
M =	A C (amino)
S =	G C
W =	A T
B =	G T C
D =	G A T
H =	A C T
V =	G C A
N =	A G C T (any)

C T T T A C C A A A T A A A A A A A C **G** C T A A A A T C A C C T

c t t t a c c a a a t a a a a a a a c **A** c t a a a a t c a c c t

DNA mutation

or base sequences were identical in the assumed ancestor! Sometimes this assumption also requires assuming certain links in the chain, especially at the beginning and end, do not "count" and can be ignored. Then evolutionists assume differences in the two chains assumed to match were caused by mutations; these mutations are assumed, not observed, and because of subjective prejudice, they "deliberately ignore" differences that could have had an original design purpose. Since more than one mutation could have produced only one difference, and because a later mutation could eliminate an earlier difference, evolutionists assume all sorts of statistical "corrections" to relate observed differences to hypothetical rates of change. The hypothetical rate of change is not the mutation rate (which is observable and far too fast), but the assumed rate at which the mutation worked its way from a level of nearly 0 percent to nearly 100 percent during the assumed struggle for survival among missing links in the evolutionary chain. Since evolutionists have not seen that happen in wild populations, evolutionists assumed the PAM (point accepted mutation) rate can be assumed from assumptions about stratigraphic dating and radiometric dating discussed above! Finally, they assume that no investigative reporters will investigate them, and they assume no evolutionist will criticize them for fear of being branded a creationist. Therefore, they are free to assume they can claim molecular "clocks" give the best "measure" of evolutionary time!

Based on these compound assumptions, evolutionists looked at certain DNA sequences in mitochondria, cellular energy organelles humans inherit from their mothers, and announced that all human beings descended from one woman, popularly called "mitochondrial Eve." Creationists were happy enough with one woman named Eve, of course, but not with the date for Eve's origin, originally given as about 160,000 years.

The plot thickens. Knowing that human males inherit Y chromosomes from their fathers, another evolutionist used Y chromosome DNA sequence comparisons to trace mankind back to one man. The date for that one man was initially given at about 270,000 years! Imagine sitting around on a Saturday night waiting for your girlfriend to call — 110,000 years is a long time! The molecular "clock," "falsely so-called," is so subjective and unscientific, however, that it could easily be stretched and/or shrunk to put the first man and woman on earth perhaps 200,000 "mythical molecular years ago." (That does not tell us what would happen, of course, if one evolved by chance in Africa and the other in Asia, etc.!)

Actually, many evolutionists think "molecular dating" is worthless, and stand on "radiometric dating." Others think radiometric dating, especially K/Ar, is full of errors, and stick to "stratigraphic dating." Both molecular and

radiometric daters think stratigraphic dating must be wrong, because man comes before man's ancestors.

Creationists simply point out that all the evolutionary dating methods are both inaccurate and unscientific. Because objectively repeatable and verifiable measurements of past rates cannot be made, the scientific method that works so fabulously in the present cannot give us the time in the past when the first man and woman appeared on earth. To find that time, we would need an accurate, reliable historical record — such as the Bible!

The Bible tells us God created mankind two days after He created the sun, moon, and stars, and the day after He created swimming and flying creatures. The Bible tells us

the time from one human generation to the next, from Adam and Eve through Noah and into the time covered by secular historical records. Biblical/historical records, which — unlike science — can reach into the past, suggest the first man and woman appeared on earth about 6,000 years ago (and they appeared in the same place, designed for each other, and introduced by God himself).

As we shall see in later volumes, radiometric, stratigraphic, molecular, and other evidences that contradict evolutionary belief in great age fit much more easily with the biblical/historical record of a young earth and recent human creation.

Form your foundation.

"Since we can't know starting conditions or past changes in rates or amounts, we can't tell you how long it took to form earth and life," a scientist would say, "so you really need an eyewitness to tell you." The Ultimate Eyewitness, God himself, says it took six days at the dawn of human history, about 6,000 years ago!

Building Inspection

1. Asked to date a rock or a fossil, a "real scientist" would give three unknowns that make it impossible for "real science" (empirical science) to date events in the unrecorded past.

   _____

   _____

2. "Radioactive decay dating" is based on measurements of (the passage of time/amounts of certain elements) _____. Converting measurements of elements into "guesstimates" of time for dating requires making assumptions such as (circle one):
   a. the starting amounts of parent and daughter elements are known;
   b. no relevant elements have been added to or subtracted from the sample;
   c. the rate of change from parent to daughter has never changed in unknown ways;
   d. all the assumptions above must be made; or
   e. no assumptions need be made, since radioactive decay dates are simply facts that can be directly observed.

3. Potassium-argon (K/Ar) dating is often used for ape and human fossils, but it is a very bad (or "very flexible") method because argon (an inert gas) moves easily in and out of pore spaces in rocks and studies of the atmosphere on Venus show we have no reasonable idea about how much argon was present at the start. True or false? _____.

4. In the absence of evidence for rock movement, it makes sense that rock layers (strata) on the bottom are (older — deposited first/younger — deposited later) _____. The difference in age (time since deposition), however, (may be only minutes/must be millions of years) _____. Creationist Flood geologists and evolutionists agree that Jurassic dinosaur fossils are usually older than human fossils, but creationists suggest they are (only weeks/millions of years) _____ older and that both were living on earth at the same time before they were buried rapidly after one another during _____.

5. In molecular dating, subunit sequences of proteins, RNA, and DNA are studied by scientists who can see (time elapsing/changes occurring/differences existing)_____. Converting subunit sequence differences into "guesstimates" of time for dating requires making assumptions such as (circle one):
   a. the sequences were the same in a common ancestor;
   b. differences were caused by mutations, and were not present at the beginning as differences designed for different purposes;
   c. statistical corrections are needed since one difference can result from multiple changes, and some changes eliminate differences;
   d. observed mutations rates are not used to estimate rates of change, but rates of presumed evolutionary changes are;
   e. evolution must be assumed in order to use molecular dating to support evolution;
   f. all of the assumptions above must be made; or
   g. no assumptions are required since molecular dates are simple facts of observation.

In God's Image

In one of its most dramatic and widely quoted statements, the Bible makes it crystal clear that people were created both distinct from all the other kinds of creatures and created in the image of their Creator (Gen. 1:27):

So God created man in his own image, in the image of God created he him; male and female created he them (Gen. 1:27).

Wow! People are created in God's image! That really ought to make us treat each other, and ourselves, as something very special!

What does it mean to be created in God's image? Under the title of "God's Image," one cartoon pictured a fat, balding, stubbly-faced man slouched in a lounge chair surrounded by empty beer cans and pretzel crumbs staring through bloodshot eyes at TV porn! The "cartoonist" forgot that modern man is sinful, and that sin both (1) distorts the image God created into our first parents, and (2) blinds the sinful, "natural man" so that he cannot and will not see beyond the temporal, physical reality to eternal, spiritual reality.

We do not see God's image in us by looking in the mirror. Those born again in Christ see it by looking into their hearts, minds, and spirits. God's image is not what we look like; it's who we are and how we act.

God is Creator, and in His image He made mankind creative. The arts (painting, literature, sculpture, music, theater, etc.), the sciences (pure and applied), building (architecture and construction), parenting and teaching, commerce and government, plant and animal care and development, etc. — all these things and many more are expressions (images) of God's creativity reflected in us.

God has a high view of mankind's creativity — even when sinful people in a corrupted creation use their creative abilities in the wrong ways. God told Noah's descendants to scatter out after the Flood; instead, they huddled together and built a tall tower (Babel) to reach the heavens. When God examined their disobedient but ambitious building

project, you might think He would laugh at their "puny" efforts. Exactly the opposite; disliking the misuse of their gifts, God nevertheless acknowledged their ability:

This is only the beginning of what they will do; and nothing that they propose to do will now be impossible for them (Gen. 11:6; RSV).

Think about that statement of God in terms of mankind's creative use of cloning, genetic engineering, and atomic energy! In our sin-corrupted world, we need God's love and wisdom to guide our use of the awesome creativity our Creator created within us!

Most wonderfully, the Bible tells us "God is love." Our reflection of God's love is perhaps the highest expression of God's image in us.

As it was written in Greek, the New Testament uses three different words for three different kinds of love. *Eros* is the physical love in marriage, the rich depth of feeling God designed to bind husband and wife together in lasting care for each other and their family, "until death do us part." *Philos* is love between friends, which can become so strong that one might give his/her life for a friend (John 15:13). The highest form of self-sacrificing love is love for your enemies or love for the unlovely, agape, the love Jesus Christ demonstrated when He died for us "while we were yet sinners" (Rom. 5:8). Jesus loved us when we hated

Him, and gave himself for us when we wanted nothing to do with Him (Rom. 5:7–8):

For scarcely for a righteous man will one die: yet peradventure for a good man some would even dare to die. But God commendeth his love toward us, in that, while we were yet sinners, Christ died for us.

Biblical love involves feelings — deep, enriching, and fulfilling — but it's nothing at all like the "chemistry" of self-gratification and "how this makes me feel" attitude touted in Hollywood films or teen gossip sessions. All three kinds of biblical love, the soul-satisfying love that reflects God's image in us, involve commitment and caring: a greater concern for your beloved — spouse, friend, or enemy — than for yourself. Love is about giving, not getting. If your foremost concern is about you and your feelings and what this relationships means to you, it's not love — Hollywood love or puppy love maybe, but not biblical love — not the image of God's love.

God's love, and our reflection of it, extends to all of creation. God placed Adam and Eve in charge of His creation, commanding them "to till and keep" it as a Garden of Delight (the meaning of Eden). To "till" means to "cultivate," to bring out the full potential, to cause to blossom and bear fruit. We get our word "culture" from it. Art, science, literature, construction, music, farming, commerce, conservation — all these things and more are expressions of both creativity and love, God's image in us.

When the love of God controls the creativity God put in us, the whole world and everyone around us benefit. Love brings joy. The love of God for all His creation, the love of Christian leaders for all in their care, sets the God of the Bible in a different category — a different dimension — from all others who would claim authority. Of himself, Jesus said:

For even the Son of man came not to be ministered unto, but to minister, and to give his life a ransom for many (Mark 10:45).

The "gods" made in man's image love to be served, and bosses whose highest authority is human opinion love to have others serve them. But, concerning those who would exercise leadership in God's image, Jesus said (Mark 10:42–44):

Ye know that they which are accounted to rule over the Gentiles exercise lordship over them; and their great ones exercise authority upon them. But so shall it not be among you: but whosoever will be great among you, shall be your minister: and whosoever of you will be the chiefest, shall be servant of all.

Jesus extended servant leadership or loving leadership to husband, wife, and family with these words:

Husbands, love your wives, even as Christ also loved the church, and gave himself for it (Eph. 5:25).

To communicate love and creativity person-to-person, culture-to-culture, and generation-to-generation, human beings use complex language. God and mankind also commune through words, and both the Bible and Jesus Christ are called the Word of God.

In the beginning was the Word, and the Word was with God, and the Word was God. The same was in the beginning with God. All things were made by him; and without him was not any thing made that was made. . . . And the Word was made flesh, and dwelt among us, (and we

beheld his glory, the glory as of the only begotten of the Father,) full of grace and truth (John 1:1–14).

At this point, evolutionists might be tempted to say, "What is so special about the 'image of God?' Consider the creativity demonstrated in building a bird's nest, the love expressed by a pet dog, and the language of whales. Man just has a more highly evolved form of traits found in other animals."

Man is a creature, and shares many features with the other living things God created. Indeed, Jesus and Bible authors use many animals and plants to teach object lessons to people. But the creativity, love, and language expressed by human beings are different in quality and kind, not just quantity and degree, from analogous things in animals.

From bird nests to salmon navigation to farmer ants milking aphids, animals perform amazingly complex feats. These intricate behaviors, however, are largely instinctive — programmed by God into their genetic make-up

Instinctive animal behavior

at conception, barely modified by experience or situation, and passed unchanged through multiple generations. God programmed man's creativity in an entirely different manner. He programmed animals to achieve predetermined, God-given goals; He programmed man for choice, both choice of goals and choice of means to achieve them. A person may be born with genetic predisposition for musical talent, for example, but the notes and words are not preprogrammed (like a bird's song is), and musical expression is modified considerably by experience and situations, and changes dramatically through the generations.

Hopefully, you've experienced the loving attention of a pet cat or dog, and watched their changing "emotions." Perhaps you've heard of a mother hen literally taking her chicks under her wing, protecting them even while she herself is killed in a fire. Porpoises have saved shipwrecked sailors. Is human love "in God's image" just a more (or less) highly evolved form of animal "love"? Absolutely not. Animals that do things that seem loving are only doing what comes naturally; God has programmed their behavior as an expression of His love.

God has programmed humans for love on an entirely different basis. Human love is based on choice, not instinct or breeding. In fact, in our fallen, sin-cursed world, love is contrary to human nature. So often it takes either "super-human" strength or the power of God's Spirit to overcome self and offer selfless, Christ-like love "for richer, for poorer, in sickness and in health, 'til death do us part." Furthermore, human love in the image of Jesus' love can extend far beyond relationships among family and friends. It can extend to enemies, country, endangered species, democracy, emancipation of slaves, the unborn child, exploration of space, conservation, literacy, and on and on!

A soldier who willingly lays down his life to win freedom for others, even for the man who may someday have the children he wanted with the girl of his dreams, is nothing like the soldier ant that dies in defense of the colony.

Activation of the ant's complex defense behaviors requires no courage, no sense of what it is losing, and no concept of values worth dying for.

In a Nobel address, biochemist Jacques Monod contrasted two views of ultimate causality in the universe: determinism and indeterminism. According to the first view, every act — including every human thought and emotion — is completely determined by the past and is merely the next link in a chain of causality resulting from the inexorable and unchanging laws of science operating on the properties of matter. According to the second view, there are subatomic fluctuations in the properties of matter and, consequently, the laws of science are only statistical; therefore, the chain of causality — including human thoughts and emotions — are fundamentally a consequence of chance events in the present.

Neither of these fatalistic views reaches the biblical understanding of human thought and actions. It's not "Chance or Necessity" (Monod's title) but *choice* that distinguishes God's image in man. It's neither the past nor the present that distinguishes distinctively human thought and deeds, but the future. In our defining moments, it's neither causes from the past nor chance events in the present that make us who we are; it's choices we make about the future. It's choices we make about expected consequences in the future that set us apart as human beings. In our highest moments, we choose our thoughts, words, and deeds in accord with the dreams we have for our family, our friends, and our world.

It's choice of consequences that leaves mankind "suspended" between the creature below and the Creator above. Like other creatures made of atoms from the earth,

many of our
actions (e.g., eating,
walking, sleeping) follow
from past programming operating in present circumstances. But like our Creator, we work with purpose and goals and a plan for the future.

There is, of course, a BIG difference between us and the Creator whose image we so feebly reflect. God doesn't have to guess or hope or wonder what the future holds. Jesus is outside time, the "everlasting Father" (Isa. 9:6), "Alpha and Omega, the beginning and the ending . . . which is, and which was, and which is to come" (Rev. 1:8).

He hath has also set eternity in the hearts of men; yet they cannot fathom what God has done from beginning to end (Eccles. 3:11; RSV).

In the image of our Creator's mind, our minds stretch toward eternity and consider cosmic consequences. Animals don't do that.

Human beings communicate on a plane as far below the Creator's as it is above the plane of other creatures. We can think about eternity; God lives in eternity. We can plan for the future; God controls the future. We speak what we believe; God speaks what He knows! In short, God's Word is based on absolute, unchangeable, eternal truth; people are finite, and their choices and decisions must be based on faith. The *life of faith* separates mankind both from other creatures below and the Creator above.

But in whom or what shall we put our ultimate faith? As human beings, no matter how much we know, there will always be things we don't know. And we don't know if new things we discover will change what we thought we knew. So we can really never be absolutely sure how much we know or don't know — unless we know Someone who knows everything and tells us things we can know absolutely for certain! Only God has infinite and absolute knowledge of the eternal truth, and — praise God! — He has chosen to reveal some of that truth through His written Word (the Bible), the Word made flesh (Jesus Christ), and the things made (God's world seen through God's eyes).

Our ultimate choice, then, is the one Adam and Eve faced in the Garden. Will you, like they, put your ultimate faith in your own opinion? Will you, as the "natural man" has done since sin, put your faith in the words of human "experts" who weren't there at the beginning, who don't know everything, who've made a great many mistakes, and who scarcely care for you at all? Or will you put your faith in the Word of God who was there in the beginning, who does know everything, who doesn't make mistakes, and who cares so much for you that He died that you might have life, rich and abundant, forever with Him? What we see in God's world encourages us to put our trust in God's Word!

The ultimate choice we make, for or against God, is perhaps the most uniquely defining human trait. It introduces the dimension of morality into human choices that has no analog or evolutionary ancestor among animals. Those choices we make based on faith in God, the principles of God's written Word, and the example of Christ we call good and right (regardless of their survival value, feeling, or material benefit to us). Christian morality is called absolute, because good and right are based on the eternal, unchanging wisdom and love of God, constant principles applied to ever-changing circumstances.

Those choosing human wisdom over God's wisdom must accept some sort of relative morality (which has nothing to do with Einstein's relativity) in which good and right vary with time, culture, and situation. Believers in relative morality have no basis for rejecting the claims of some groups, for example, that their morality entitles them to kill or make slaves of "inferior" groups. They may wish the best for mankind, but history is rife with repeated and dramatic failures of those trying to judge the con-

sequences of their actions apart from God's guidance. In these days of cloning, genetic engineering, nuclear energy, terrorism, and space exploration, we need truly supernatural intelligence — and love — far beyond anything the human mind and this universe has to offer!

What we see in God's world (science) encourages us to put our faith in God's Word (Scripture). A century and a half of searching the fossil evidence has disproved every suggestion that mankind evolved from ape-like ancestors. The fossils we do find, and the study of human creativity, love, language, faith, and morality all support the biblical record that people are uniquely created in the image of their Creator. Our first parents rejected God's wisdom and love, as we still do today, but we can be *reborn* to the full image of God, and to life eternal, through the perfect life, sacrificial death, and conquering resurrection of our Creator, Sustainer, Judge, and Blessed Redeemer, the Lord Jesus Christ.

Even so, come, Lord Jesus (Rev. 22:20).

Form your foundation.

We share many features with other living things God created, but our creativity, how we use language, our God-given stewardship over God's creation, moral choice, goal orientation, self-sacrificing love, and faith life all reflect God's wondrous image in each of us! Praise God!

Bonus Project

A. Hopefully you will get to visit the Grand Canyon some day. (Dr. Parker has led over 40 week-long hikes there!) Volume III in this Creation Foundation Series deals with *Building Blocks in Geology [Earth Science]*. What questions would you like to see answered at the Grand Canyon? How do you think creationist and evolutionist views might differ?

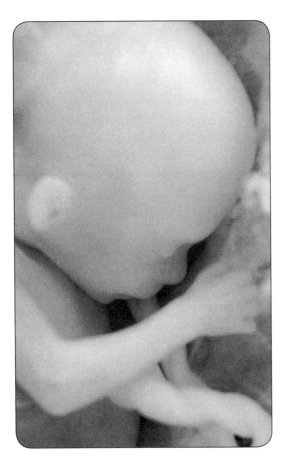

B. We touched on fossils and human origins in this volume, but Volume II, *Building Blocks in Life Science*, will look at much more evidence related to human beginnings: life before birth (embryonic development), DNA and the origin of living cells, genetics and reproduction, Design vs. Darwin in the structure and function of people and other creatures, etc. What questions about the structure, function, reproduction, and origin of living things would you like answered?

C. How old is the earth, and how do we know? What about carbon-14 and uranium dating? How long would it take for light to reach earth from distant galaxies? Does the universal law of entropy (increasing disorder) disprove cosmic evolution? What about a "big bang"? Explore these questions in Volume IV as you continue to build your world view — and discover how much God's Word helps us understand God's world!

1. Do we see God's image when we look in a mirror? _____ or do we see a barroom brawl or a drug deal gone bad? _____. Where/how do we see God's image in us?

2. How do nest building by birds and house building by people differ? Is it a difference in kind, or just degree? Would these building skills likely evolve from a common ancestor? Is human architecture a reflection of God's image? Explain.

   _____

   _____

   _____

3. Is a U.S. Marine's defense of democracy in war just an extension of a soldier ant's defense of its colony? Both are expressions of God's creation, but is only one an expression of God's image? Explain.

   _____

   _____

   _____

4. How is human language an expression of God's image in us, unlike animal communication?

   _____

   _____

   _____

5. The choices that help to define God's image in us result from neither fatalistic causes in the past or random events in the present but from dreams about the future. Explain.

   _____

   _____

   _____

6. "People must live by faith; they can do no other." Explain how the life of faith reflects God's image in us, separating us both from our Creator above and other creatures below.

   _____

   _____

   _____

7. How do faith, fact, and feeling relate in the person who is truly happy or blessed?

   _____

   _____

   _____

Chapter
20

Index

AaBb, 112, 115, 136, 159

ACLU, 117, 120, 122–123

Acts 17:26, 31, 110, 115, 136

Adam, 11, 26, 31, 45, 110, 112, 115, 118, 126, 136, 144, 147, 151, 159

"Age of Dinosaurs," 34, 62, 77, 80–81, 84–86

agnostic, 119

airplane, 13, 17, 157

Alaskan dinosaurs, 96

alligator, 50, 56

ammonites, 86

amniote, 69

Amphibia, 70

amphibians, 57, 62, 69, 85, 99–100, 107

animal instincts, 41, 101, 107, 160

anthropoid, 100

Apatosaurus, 46, 64, 88

apes, 22, 32, 35, 99–100, 104, 106, 113–114, 124–125, 128–135, 137–138, 160

Ararat, 29, 31

Archaeopteryx, 34, 76–79, 159

"Archaeoraptor," 75, 79

ark, 5, 11, 14–15, 28–29, 33, 39, 55–57, 59, 61, 80, 84, 86–87, 89, 96, 112, 158

arrowhead, 12–13, 17 157

artists, 65–67, 102, 128

assertion, 39, 74, 95

assumption, 39, 138, 143, 157

Assumptions, Assertions, and Implications, 24, 39, 43

asteroid, 32, 34, 54, 62, 67, 80, 85, 87, 158–159

atheist, 39

Australian Aboriginals, 109, 113–115, 124

australopithecine, 124, 126, 131, 160

Australopithecus, 35, 124–126, 160

Aves, 70, 72

"away from evolution,"130

ballast, 51

behemoth, 46–47, 51–53, 56, 158

belief, 11, 22–23, 25, 45, 73–74, 76, 80, 84–85, 88–89, 93, 96, 99–100, 102–103, 105–108, 110–111, 114, 117, 120, 126–131, 137, 144, 159–160

Bible, 5–6, 8, 10–11, 13–15, 20, 24, 37, 39, 45–47, 50, 52–55, 58, 63–64, 66–67, 78, 84, 89–90, 92, 96–97, 102–103, 105, 107, 110–112, 114–115, 117–123, 126, 134, 136, 144, 146–148, 150, 157–159

biblical record, 7, 50, 84–85, 96, 144, 151

big bang, 10, 31–32, 152

blacks, 108–111, 113–115, 123–124, 131

Bliss, Richard, 38

blood, 19, 50, 55, 60–61, 110, 158

bombardier beetle, 92, 159

bonobo, 127–129, 160

brachiation, 135

brain volume, 103, 107, 125, 128, 135, 137

Broca's area, 103–104, 107

"Brontosaurus," 64, 67

Bryan, William Jennings, 117–120, 123

Cambrian, 14, 28, 32, 34, 81, 83

Cambrian Explosion, 14, 28, 32, 34, 83

Canaan, 110–111

carbon dioxide (CO_2), 56, 69

carbon-14, 5, 15, 55, 61, 86, 96, 138–140, 152, 158

carnivore, 48, 51, 53, 91

carnivorous, 48, 53, 93, 158

Catastrophe, 14–15, 17, 28, 31, 33, 54, 58–59, 61–62, 80, 84–85, 87, 96–97, 118, 120, 134, 157–158

cave art, 90, 102–103, 107, 159

"cave men," 76, 100, 102, 104, 106–107, 124, 129

CBC, 99, 102, 107

censorship, 43

chill, 31, 33, 154

chimp/chimpanzee, 35, 50, 100, 103, 109, 116, 125–129, 134–135, 137, 141–142, 160

choice, 13, 17, 19, 23, 149, 151, 160

Christ, 5, 11, 15, 17, 19, 26, 31, 33, 41, 58–59, 61–62, 78, 84, 94, 96–97, 102, 110, 118–123, 146–148, 150–151, 157–160

Christian, 5, 8, 11, 20, 39, 41, 45, 66, 76, 95, 107, 110, 117–120, 122, 125–126, 128, 132–133, 140, 148, 151

circumstantial, 23–25, 36, 39, 43, 64, 67, 157

classic creation(ist), 10, 15, 26, 31, 43

classic evolution(ist), 11, 15, 24, 31–32, 43, 107, 158

Classic Positions of Creationists and Evolutionists, 16

climate change, 56, 87, 96, 158

coal, 14, 30, 56, 81, 86, 92, 94, 140

coelacanth, 92, 97

cold-blooded (ectothermal), 56, 87

Columbine, 122

coming again, 31, 33, 157

composite, 75

Compsognathus, 75–76

confusion, 28, 31, 33, 157

Congo dinosaur, 88

consequences, 15, 22, 107, 111, 149–151

consummation, 33, 157

Cooper, Bill, 58, 90

coprolite, 50–51, 158

cool down, 28, 33, 157

Corruption, 14–15, 17, 26, 33, 58–59, 61, 84, 96–97, 118, 120, 134, 157–158

Creation, 5–7, 9, 11–15, 17, 20, 22–26, 29–33, 36–39, 41, 43, 46, 50–51, 53–54, 57–59, 61–63, 78–79, 81, 84–85, 96–97, 99, 102, 107, 110, 113, 117–118, 120–123, 126, 130–131, 133–134, 144, 146–148, 151–153, 157–160

creation days, 118, 120

Creation Adventures Museum, 36, 57

Creation Foundations Series, 5, 7, 15, 24, 38, 41, 85

creation week, 29, 33, 37

creative intelligence, 12–13

Cretaceous, 81, 85–87, 94

crocodile, 65, 68–69, 73

Cro-Magnon, 104, 107

Cross, 31, 33, 37, 118, 120, 157

CSI, 65–67, 142, 159

"curse on Ham," 110

cycads, 62, 86, 93

Darrow, Clarence, 117, 120

Darwin, Charles, 8–11, 14, 28, 33–34, 38, 45, 50, 59, 66, 75–78, 85, 89, 96, 99–102, 106–108, 114–115, 117, 120–122, 131–132, 136, 140, 152, 157–159

"Darwin's Bulldog," 76, 117, 121

Darwin's followers, 66, 78, 89, 99–101, 106, 136, 140, 157, 159

days of creation, 118

death wins, 15, 41, 62

debate, 6–8, 11, 23, 39, 41, 121, 130, 141

Descent of Man, 108, 115

design, 9, 12–13, 21, 33, 45, 71, 84, 96, 143, 152

Designer, 9, 45, 157

diet, 48, 50–51, 87, 159

different kinds of evidence, 17, 23–25, 36, 43, 67, 119, 157–160

"dino-bird," 74, 76–78, 159

"dinosaur-bird" link, 74, 76–78, 159

dinosaur blood, 61

dinosaur reconstruction, 64, 67

dinosaurs, 5, 10–11, 28, 32, 34–35, 37, 44–47, 50–81, 84–97, 100–101, 157–159

"dinosaur wars," 45

Diplodocus, 46–47, 56, 64, 88

DNA, 9–11, 13–14, 17–18, 20, 33, 35, 38, 55, 96, 100, 105–106, 141–143, 145, 152

"DNA fingerprint," 142

dragon, 68, 73, 90–92, 97

duck-billed dinosaurs, 65

ecological zones, 86–87

ectothermal, 87

Eden, 26, 102, 147

Einstein, Albert, 19, 151

elephant, 46, 53, 56–57, 158

empirical, 19–20, 22–25, 36, 38, 41, 43, 67, 69, 145, 157

empirical science, 19–20, 22–23, 25, 36, 38, 41, 145

endothermic, 57, 87

errors of evolution, 85, 102, 121

eternal life, 78, 119, 151, 160

154

evolutionary racism, 108–112, 114–115, 117, 136

extinction, 35, 52, 55, 61–62, 69, 80–81, 85–89, 96, 102, 158–159

Eve, 11, 26, 31, 110, 112, 115, 118, 126, 136, 143–144, 147, 151, 159

evidence of creation, 12–13, 17, 121

"evo-logical," 128

evolutionary humanism, 5, 7, 117

"exherent" order, 13

experiment, 21, 64, 86

fact, 8–9, 14, 17, 20–21, 23, 39, 47, 88–89, 115–116, 126, 139, 149, 153, 157, 159

faith, 5–6, 11, 20–21, 23, 41, 45, 75, 78, 85, 88, 110, 117–120, 128–129, 131–132, 135, 137, 150–151, 153, 160

Fall, 21–22, 28, 33, 46, 49, 125

feather, 63, 69–70, 74–79, 159

"Feathers for T. rex," 75

fire-breathing, 91–92

first dinosaur, 84

1 Peter 3:15, 11, 122–123, 157

1 Timothy 6:20, 11, 157

Flood, 14–15, 17, 28–31, 33, 37–38, 46, 50, 52, 54–59, 61, 63, 78, 80–90, 94, 96, 102–103, 110, 120, 134, 140, 145–146, 158–160

flood conditions, 15, 17, 54

Florida, 36, 57, 59, 68, 73, 85–86, 88

flowering plants, 29, 56, 62, 86

flow-through lung, 70, 159

flying fox, 48

forensic, 65–67, 142

fossil, 10, 14–15, 22, 32, 34–35, 45, 47, 53, 60, 64–67, 69, 71–73, 75–79, 81, 83–84, 86, 88–89, 91, 93–94, 104, 116, 123, 125, 127–132, 134–135, 137–139, 141, 145, 151, 159–160

fossil boy, 135

fountains of the great deep, 14, 17, 28

four Cs, 15, 17, 61, 97

4.6 billion years, 9, 35

"four hands," 135

frog-to-prince, 102, 106

fruit bat, 48

fundamentalist, 118–119, 123

Galapagos, 8

gastroliths, 51

GCD, 81, 83–85, 89

Genesis 1:1, 11, 157

geologic column, 10, 15, 69–70, 81–83, 88–89, 127, 133, 140, 159

geologic system, 83, 94, 159

"Germany's Darwin," 108, 114–115

giant ground sloth, 56, 88

Gish, Duane T., 121, 127

gizzard stones, 51

goal, 18, 24, 39, 107, 119, 151, 157

goanna, 73

God, 5–15, 17, 21–22, 24, 26, 28–29, 31–33, 35, 37–39, 41, 43, 45–47, 50–51, 53–54, 56, 58–59, 78, 81, 84, 96, 99, 101–102, 107, 110, 112, 115, 117–123, 128, 130–133, 135–136, 141, 144, 146–153, 157–158, 160

"god," 5, 6, 10, 16, 35, 42, 101, 107, 117, 119, 148, 158

"God is love," 147

God's image, 110, 136, 146–149, 153

God's Word, 7, 15, 17, 22, 24, 41, 47, 78, 96, 107, 117–121, 130, 132, 135, 150–152, 157, 160

God's world, 7, 15, 17, 41, 53, 78, 96, 118, 120–121, 128, 130, 132, 135, 150–152

Gould, S.J., 102, 109

Grand Canyon, 9, 14, 83, 152

graptolite, 93

graveyards, 15, 54, 59, 96

Great Dinosaur Mystery and the Bible, 58, 90

greenhouse, 30, 56, 91

hadrosaurs, 65

Haeckel, Ernst, 108–109, 114–115, 136

happiness, 6, 160

healing, 120, 157

herbivore, 51, 53, 62, 91

historian, 23–24, 35, 60, 92, 97, 157

historical, 3, 15, 22–24, 26, 29, 31–32, 39, 41, 50–51, 58, 63–64, 66, 84, 87–88, 90–93, 95–96, 102, 118, 121, 144, 157–159

historical science, 23

Historical Time-lines, 24, 31–32, 39, 41

"History Book of the Universe," 84

Holy Spirit, 26, 41, 160

hominid, 100

hominoid, 100

Homo erectus, 114, 125, 135, 137–138

Homo sapiens, 35, 80, 100, 104–107, 109, 114–115, 119, 131, 133, 135–138

Horner, Jack, 49, 55

human opinion, 22, 24, 96, 119, 148, 157

Huxley, Thomas, 76–77, 117, 120–121

hypothesis, 19, 80, 95, 132

"I AM," 26, 32, 157

Ice Age, 31, 33, 37, 56–57, 59, 87–88, 96, 105

ICR (Institute for Creation Research), 57, 121

iguana, 68

implication, 7, 24, 39, 41–43, 134

in-between traits, 78, 159

inherent order, 13

Inherit the Wind, 120

Institute for Creation Research (ICR), 57, 121

intelligent design, 13

interdisciplinary, 24–25, 157

interpretation, 24–25, 75, 81, 107, 129, 157–158

isotopes, 138–140

Java Man, 114–115, 123–124

jaw, 36, 69, 103, 113, 115, 124, 134–135, 137

Job, 19, 41, 46–47, 51, 53, 57, 59–60, 80, 92, 106, 119, 133, 158

John 1:1–14, 26, 37, 148

Judge, 118, 151

Jurassic, 48–49, 52, 65, 77, 81, 85–87, 93, 145

Jurassic Park, 48–49, 52, 65

K/Ar, 139–140, 143, 145

Kelly, Tom, 99

knee, 125–126, 128–129, 135

komodo dragon, 68, 73

Laetoli, 127–129, 135, 137, 141

land bridge, 57

lawyer, 9, 23–25, 43, 45, 63–64, 117, 120, 123, 157

Leakey, Louis, 135

Leakey, Mary, 124, 127–129, 135, 137, 139, 141, 156

Leakey, Richard, 124, 127–128, 135, 137, 139

leviathan, 52

life wins, 15, 62

limits of science, 23

living cell, 13, 17, 20

"living fossils," 11, 93, 96

love, 5–6, 14, 19, 21, 26, 43, 81, 120, 147–149, 151

"Lucy," 10, 35, 125–130, 135, 137, 139, 160

Lyell, Charles, 9–10, 45

macroevolution, 22, 25, 157

Malachite Man, 94, 140

Mammalia, 70

mammoths, 57, 59, 88, 158

man's meal, 125, 129, 131

Mars, 6, 9, 12, 33, 109–110, 115

mass extinction, 80, 85–87, 89, 159

melanin, 111–112, 114–115, 136, 157, 159

Mesozoic, 34, 62, 77, 81–82, 85–87, 89

mind, 6, 13, 17, 41, 43, 109, 132, 150–151, 157–158

missing link, 34, 74–79, 114, 130–131, 137, 139, 159

"missionary lizards," 58

"missionary reptiles," 58–59, 61

mitochondria, 105–106, 143

"mitochondrial Eve," 143

model, 14, 24, 26, 31–33, 47, 76, 102, 104, 134

mokele mbembe, 88–89

molecular clocks, 141–143

molecular dating assumptions, 141, 143, 145

molecules-to-man, 22, 25

"monkey" trial, 116–123

Morris, Henry M., 121

Morrison Formation, 94, 140

Mount St. Helens, 14, 83

mutations, 9, 14, 17, 28, 30, 32–33, 50, 84, 87, 100, 134, 143, 145

myth, 39, 75, 88, 102

mythical, 10, 45, 97, 100–101, 120, 140, 143

National Geographic, 48, 75, 78–79, 124, 128, 159

natural selection, 9, 14, 17, 32, 34, 45, 62, 108

Neanderthal, 102–107, 123–124

Neanderthal DNA, 105–106

Nebraska Man, 116, 122–124, 129, 131, 159

new life, 5, 15, 18, 31, 33, 41, 58–59, 102, 120, 158

New Zealand, 69, 73, 126

Noah's flood, 14–15, 28, 37–38, 50, 52, 54–56, 59, 61, 63, 78, 80–82, 84–88, 94, 96, 102, 134, 140, 158–160

"Nutcracker Man," 124–125, 127, 135

objective, 19–20, 66, 69, 125, 127, 142, 157

observation, 12–13, 17, 21, 38, 65, 132, 145, 157

oil, 15, 30, 56

"one blood," 110

operation, 13, 21

opinion, 22, 24, 39, 43, 96, 117, 119, 125, 148, 151, 157

origin, 6, 9, 11, 13–15, 17, 19–21, 23–24, 33–34, 39, 45, 72, 75, 102, 108, 125, 132, 143, 152, 157–158

Origin of Species, 9, 34, 75, 108

Osborne, H.F., 109–110, 114, 116

overhunting, 56, 89, 96, 158

oviparous, 70

ovoviviparous, 70

Owen, Sir Richard, 66, 159

owl pellet, 65

Oxnard, Charles, 125–126, 129

paleosystem, 83, 159

Paluxy tracks, 95

patterns of order, 12, 18, 21, 39, 138

Peking Man, 125, 129, 131

pelvis, 126, 128–129, 135, 160

persuasion, 41, 43, 160

petrified "poo", 50, 158

petroglyphs, 58, 66, 88, 90–91, 96–97

philosophic, 5, 7, 24–25, 39, 41, 103

philosophic naturalism, 5, 7, 24

pictographs, 66, 88, 90, 96

pig's tooth, 122–123, 159

Piltdown hoax, 122, 135, 159

Piltdown Man, 113, 115, 123–124

"Pithecanthropus," 114–115, 119

plesiosaur, 91–93

post-Fall, 28

post-Flood, 29–30, 56–57, 59, 86, 103, 158

potassium-argon, 145

predator, 49–50, 69, 92

predictions, 18, 20, 24, 38, 41, 99, 157

pre-Flood, 28–30, 56, 81, 83, 86–88, 103, 140

presuppositions, 24, 39, 41, 64

primate, 100, 132–134, 137

propaganda, 22–23, 25, 43, 47, 52, 63, 75–76, 102, 106, 114, 116–117, 119, 122–123, 126, 142, 157, 160

properties of matter, 10, 13, 17, 33, 149, 157

properties of organization, 13, 17

Pteranodon, 71, 90, 92, 159

pterodactyl, 58, 71–72, 74, 76, 90–92, 97, 159

purpose, 6, 10, 12–13, 17, 56, 84, 99, 101, 106–107, 143, 150, 157

race, 31, 108, 110, 114–115, 123, 136

racism, 108–112, 114–115, 117, 122, 136

radiometric dating, 138, 141, 143

Ramapithecus, 134, 137

"real science," 19, 63, 145, 160

reasonable doubt, 22–23, 157

Redeemer, 118, 151

religion, 22, 25, 118, 122, 160

repeatable, 17–18, 20, 38, 64, 66, 132, 135, 144, 157

Reptilia, 70

restoration, 62, 97, 157

ridicule, 91, 95, 117, 119, 121

rock art, 97, 159

sagittal crest, 135

Sagan, Carl, 6, 9, 12–13, 87

salvation, 110, 118, 157

sauropod, 46–47, 51–53, 65, 74, 88

Savior, 31, 115

scavenger, 29, 49, 57

scenario, 23–25, 35, 63, 100, 125

"science falsely so-called," 5, 11, 109, 111, 115–116, 120, 126, 132, 135, 137

scientific method, 18–19, 21–23, 25, 63–64, 144

Scientifically Testable Predictions, 24, 38

scientific malpractice, 75, 131

Scopes trial, 116–118, 122–123, 160

Scripture, 46, 55, 78, 85, 89, 107, 110, 112, 115, 123, 136, 151

scuba, 51, 85–86

sea to land, 37, 158

sediment, 9, 14, 17, 29, 59

sedimentary rock, 60

servant leadership, 148

SETI, 13, 24–25, 157

seven Cs, 37

simple to complex, 37, 158

sin, 10–11, 15, 17, 28–29, 31, 33, 35, 45, 50, 52–54, 58–59, 62–63, 78, 81, 84, 96, 101–102, 107, 110, 115, 134, 146, 151, 158

six days, 26, 144

6,000 years, 5, 9–10, 33, 144

skin color, 65, 67, 111–112, 114–115, 136

steward(s), 26, 151, 158

St. George, 90, 159

stratigraphic dating, 140–141, 143–144

struggle and death, 5–6, 10–11, 15, 20, 31–33, 37–38, 41, 45, 50, 52–53, 58–59, 62, 67, 81, 84–85, 96, 99–102, 107, 128, 158

struggle for survival, 8–9, 11, 14, 32–35, 85, 100–102, 107, 143, 157–158

subjective, 18, 23–24, 69, 125, 129, 132, 143

survival of the fittest, 9, 17, 32, 34, 70, 86, 108, 157

Sustainer, 118, 151

tadpole, 62, 69, 100

Tasmania, 109

Taylor, Paul, 58, 90

TCSD (time, chance, struggle, and death), 20, 32–33, 38, 58, 62, 84, 96, 99–102, 107

tentative, 19

testable, 18, 23–24, 38, 132

textbooks, 19, 23, 47, 52, 88, 102, 106, 113–114, 125, 128–131, 141

theory, 9, 18, 21–23, 25, 32, 34, 75–76, 96, 115, 129, 160

time, chance, struggle, and death, 20, 32–33, 38, 58, 62, 84, 96, 99–102, 107

time-line, 22, 31–32, 38–39

Tower of Babel, 31, 33, 37

transcendent, 6, 12, 26

transitional traits, 78

T. rex, 48–51, 53, 55–57, 69, 72–75, 88, 93, 159

trilobite, 34, 81, 94

tuatara, 69, 73

two winners, 41, 43

unfossilized dinosaurs, 57

universe, 6, 9–12, 18, 20, 24, 26, 32–33, 35, 84, 117, 149, 151

values, 23, 149, 160

variation, 17, 28, 30–31, 33–34, 38, 100, 112, 125, 136

vegetarian, 29, 33, 49–50, 53–54, 65, 68, 73

vitamin D deficiency, 103, 107

viviparous, 70

warm-blooded (endothermic), 57, 87

"war of nature," 9–10, 14, 28, 33–34, 38, 45, 50, 58, 85, 96, 99, 102

"war of the world views," 6–7, 43, 102, 117, 123, 160

wisdom, 147, 151

Woolemi pine, 93, 97

Word, 7, 15, 17, 19, 22, 24, 26, 32, 37, 41, 46–47, 53, 66, 78, 90, 96, 102, 107, 110, 115, 117–121, 130, 132, 135, 147–148, 150–152, 160

world view, 24–25, 39, 41, 43, 64, 67, 126, 128, 132, 152

worldwide, 15, 28, 31, 33, 54, 59, 62, 80–81, 83–85, 87, 90, 96

Y chromosome, 143

"Zone of Dinosaurs," 81, 88

Zuckerman, Lord, 126, 129

Answers to Questions

Chapter 1

1. All
2. Free coffee . . .
3. a. Genesis 1:1
   b. 1 Timothy 6:20
   c. 1 Peter 3:15
4. "War of nature"; "struggle for survival"; variation/variety; "survival of the fittest"
5. The human body . . .
6. Made itself; an outside force/transcendent God.

Chapter 2

1. Sample: Contrary to a pattern produced by time, chance, and the properties of matter, chip marks in an arrowhead can go with or against the grain and can cut through hard and soft rock equally — a visible (scientific) pattern of organization reflecting the plan, purpose, and special creative acts of a (usually unseen) creator (whether human, "Martian," or God).
2. Sample: The parts of an airplane can't fly until they are organized by the plan of an intelligent creator to accomplish the purpose the designer (not the parts) has in mind. Similarly, it takes plan, purpose, and special acts of creation to produce the organization of non-living molecules required for life.
3. a. Creation
   b. Christ (salvation, restoration)
   c. Corruption
   d. Catastrophe
   e. Catastrophe
   f. Corruption
   g. Christ (healing/restoration)
   h. Creation
4. a. B, b. E, c. B, d. B/C, e. N

Chapter 3

1. Scientists; theories
2. D
3. a. T, b. T, c. F, d. F, e. T, f. F
4. a. S, b. S, c. N, d. S, e. N, f. N, g. N
5. (Your choices)

Chapter 4

1. C
2. Samples (any order of at least three): (1) Observability: Almost none of the key events in the evolutionary story line was ever seen or recorded, and science limits itself to ideas that can be tested by repeatable observation.
   (2) Domain: Evolutionists attempt to establish a time sequence of events that occurred in the unrecorded past; scientists attempt to establish theories that predict the behavior of nature in the present.
   (3) Goal: Scientists want to cure diseases, invent machines, send probes to other planets, etc.; evolutionists want people to accept evolution, not God, as the basis for culturally

relative values and man's opinion, not God's Word, as the source of truth.
(*) Historical records: Evolutionists believe there are no reliable records of earth's early history, so there are no limits on human opinion. Creationists believe the Bible is an accurate eyewitness record of real history whose statements can be checked against scientific observations in the present.

3. E
4. Sample: Empirical evidence can be directly and repeatedly observed; circumstantial evidences are tidbits of information thought to be related to the question at hand, but the evidence is subject to more than one interpretation. Historians, lawyers, and those interested in the origin and history of life are limited to circumstantial evidence, and their ideas can be compared subjectively for consistency and "reasonable doubt," but they cannot be decided by objective, experimental tests like tests of empirical ideas.
5. Interdisciplinary; greater than
6. Sample: Gravitational and atomic theories can be tested by repeated observation of present processes, completely unlike "macro-evolution's" beliefs about the past. Darwin's followers like to make the false comparison of evolution with gravity or atomic theory as a propaganda technique — associating a weak theory about the past with a strong theory about the present.
7. Sample: (1) Both creationists and evolutionists make predictions about processes and patterns in the present that can be tested scientifically.
   (2) As SETI shows, all scientists know they can detect differences between patterns produced by time and chance (evolution) and those resulting from plan and purpose (creation).
   (3) Free and open discussion of all relevant evidence (a) promotes respect and understanding of different ideas, (b) illustrates both the strengths and limits of scientific inquiry, (c) helps separate fact from assumption in decision-making, and (d) makes education exciting!

Chapter 5

1. I AM
2. Jesus the Christ
3. a. 4, b. 3, c. 5, d. 1, e. 2, f. 6
4. (1) Creation   a. (4)
   (2) Corruption   b. (5)
   (3) Catastrophe   c. (2)
   (4) Chill (Cool Down) d. (6)
   (5) Confusion   e. (1)
   (6) Christ (Cross)   f. (3)
   (7) Consummation   g. (7)
       (Christ, Coming Again)

5.
creation	evolution
continent	stars
fruits	continent
stars	death
birds	dinosaurs
dinosaurs	birds
death	fruits

6.

creation	evolution
a. worse	better
b. end	beginning
disorder	order
c. but never	and also
d. torn apart	put together
e. (1) complex	simple
(2) sea to land	simple to complex
(3) 1	500,000,000
f. always disproven	sometimes found
g. sin against God	struggle for survival
h. future; new and everlasting life	past: struggle and death

Chapter 6

1. a. T, b. T, c. T, d. F, e. F
2. Sample: Evolutionists limit themselves to small, slow processes in the present and human opinions about what might have happened in the past, while creationists start with an infallible eyewitness account in the Bible that records what really did happen in earth history — so differences in world view strongly affect interpretation of evidence in the present and the types of experiments run.
3. Sample: They agree that nature has an order understandable to the human mind, but disagree on whether man is "just another" product of nature or God's steward to take of (and heal and restore) His world.
4. Sample: In classic evolution, "god" evolved as a product of the human imagination, and one idea of god (or no god) is just as good (or bad) as any other.
5. Samples: (1) Creation — completed supernatural acts in the past, establishing multiplication after kind, etc. (2) Corruption — the entrance of death and struggle ("Darwin's war") into God's perfect word, following man's sin. (3) Catastrophe — the worldwide flood at Noah's time.
6. in the Bible
7. d
8. Sample: If creationists win, evolutionists will win, too, because students in science classes will be able to explore all the scientific evidences and past events related to the origin, history, and destiny of life on earth — an exciting adventure in good science and good education.
9. Review later!

Chapter 7

1. Sample: Dinosaurs have been used to lure people away from trust in the Bible by suggesting millions of years of struggle and death, but the truth about dinosaurs illustrates the biblical truths of God's perfect world, ruined by man's sin, destroyed by Noah's flood, restored to new life in Christ.
2. Sample: The word "dinosaur" wasn't made up until after the Bible was written, but animals like dinosaurs are described in the Bible (e.g., Job 40 and 41).
3. Sample: Because behemoth had a tail like a cedar (a symbol of strength and power in the Bible), it could not be an elephant or hippo, which have tiny tails. The rest of the description sounds like a longneck dinosaur: strength in the muscles of its belly, able to stand against flood waters, bones like bars of iron, etc.
4. Yes — carefully, when it first hatched out of its egg.
5. Plants — because all animals God created were originally designed to eat only plants, as God tells us (Gen. 1:30–31)

— and an eyewitness account by a Reliable Witness (God himself) is much better than any man's guess based on what he sees today!
6. Mankind's sin; Noah's flood
7. Samples of plant eaters with "carnivorous" (falsely so-called) teeth: fruit bats, pandas, parrots, silver langur monkey, uakari, etc.
8. Coprolite — "petrified poo"
9. Scientists would find it easy to explain the biblical change from plant to meat eating among some animals, since the change would be loss, the opposite of evolution, and the plant environments and nutrition probably declined after the Flood. No new structures were involved, since so-called "carnivorous" teeth, claws, hooked beaks, and talons can be used to eat either plants or meat.
10. All of these; yes; pony-sized; cattle, racehorse, elephant, etc.; great blue whale; size to hold in your hand and pet (!), or football-sized.

Chapter 8

1. Same (day 6)
2. Sample: It would be easy to live with dinosaurs. They came in all sizes, rats to half as big as a blue whale, the average only pony size. Elephants, bigger than the average dinosaur, can be tamed. Most dinosaurs were vegetarian, and people often kill ferocious, large animals.
3. An asteroid; Noah's flood
4. Sample: Alaskan fossils of dinosaurs are so fresh they could not have survived for 65 million years, and blood cells and even stretchable blood vessels in T. rex bones show the fossils were formed rapidly and recently. Carbon-14, found abundantly in fossils with dinosaurs, would disappear in less than 100,000 years, so dinosaur fossils could not be even 1 million years old — 4,500 years is more likely, the date for Noah's flood. Still, the Flood would not cause extinction of dinosaurs, because two of every kind would be on the ark!
5. There was plenty of room for two of every kind of land dinosaur on the ark. God would not have brought Noah either the eggs or the larger older specimens, but young adults ready to reproduce — some rat, cat, dog, and pony sizes, but the young adults of even the largest would be smaller than the elephants and giraffes on the ark.
6. (1) The climate change, including ice build-up, would be hard on the dinosaurs, and many of their plant foods may have done poorly in post-Flood soils and atmospheric conditions. (2) Over-hunting by people may have done in the last of some dinosaurs; scientists think man may have killed off mammoths and mastodons perhaps 4,000 years ago. Cultures around the world record many heroes killing dragons and man has recently brought many large animals to near-extinction.
7. Sample: Creation: Dinosaurs appear complete and complex as fossils, with no links between kinds. Corruption: Mangled, bitten, and diseased dinosaur bones show the struggle and death that followed man's sin. Catastrophe: Herds of dinosaurs buried deep and fast and turned to stone before they could rot point back to Noah's flood, and dino blood and C-14 say that must have been recent. Christ: God provided a way of escape for dinosaurs aboard the ark, and some of those multiplied into historical times.

Chapter 9

1. f
2. Present; dinosaur fossils exist in the present and can be studied scientifically; a "Dinosaur Age" is a belief about the past (that seems to contradict much evidence in the present).
3. a. E, b. C, c. C, d. C, e. C (but historical, vs. conjecture)
4. a. T, b. T, c. T, d. T, e. T
5. Sample: The CSI has a large database relating numerous bone samples to many different soft-part traits (color, hair, lips, ears, etc.); the paleontologist has to guess at external appearance (unless he or she is willing to accept biblical descriptions, "cave art," or descriptions in various cultures).
6. Sir Richard Owen; "terrible lizard"

Chapter 10

1. c, a, b, d, e
2. Sample: Lizards, crocodiles, and turtles all appear in the sequence of fossil rock before dinosaurs, all lived with dinosaurs, and many are still living — largely unchanged — today, so dinosaurs came "late" and left "early," leaving lizards, crocodiles, and turtles as the real "winners" and "stronger" reptiles!
3. Reptiles; d
4. Skulls are not common fossils, and are often crushed and distorted when found — and the bony passages have no major function related to survival (so it's like classifying humans on earlobe shape).
5. Plesiosaurs (the "Loch Ness" type) or mosasaurs or ichthyosaurs; pterodactyls (e.g., Pteranodon or Rhamphorhynchus)
6. Dragons!

Chapter 11

1. Feathers; birds
2. Dinosaur; *T. rex*
3. Fake
    (a) ". . . sensationalistic, unsubstantiated, tabloid journalism. . . ."
    (b) "The Missing Link That Wasn't"
4. a. long bony tail, unfused backbones, teeth in the bill, claws on the wings.
    b. Yes: penguin has bony tail and unfused backbones; some fossil birds had teeth (and not all reptiles do, e.g., turtles); wing claws are found on ostrich, hoatzin, and turaco.
    c. Feathers (including flight feathers like those of strong flyers); flow-through lung
    d. None of the traits are "half-way," "in-between," or transitional — no half-scale/half-feather, no half-leg/half-wing, etc. All traits are complete and complex — as a creationist would expect.
    e. *Archaeopteryx* (GCD9) is found above fossils of regular birds (GCD8), so it could not be the ancestor of birds, since birds were already living, dying, and being fossilized before *Archaeopteryx* was — supporting creation.
5. Sample: Be skeptical! Wait for other scientists to check it out. Then hang in there and wait for science to catch up and show the Bible has been right all along!

Chapter 12

1. Geologic system (or paleosystem); geologic column (diagram); Noah's flood; evolution
2. Flood geologists; Darwin's followers; Flood geologists
3. Fact of science; belief about the past; the Bible
4. "Age," "Zone"
5. Mass (extinction); Noah's flood; an asteroid; Noah's flood
6. Dinosaurs; dinosaurs
7. (1) Drop in temperature, including ice sheet build-up
    (2) Decline or extinction of plants crucial to dinosaur diet
    (3) Reduced soil and mineral nutrition
8. (1) Records of heroes killing dragons, as St. George
    (2) Rock art and etchings
    (3) Man killing off many large animals

Chapter 13

1. Dragons
2. Dinosaurs
3. Sample: Many animals and people produce the flammable gas, methane. Some dinos had tubes leading from skull chambers to the mouth. If these tubes injected an accelerating enzyme into a mouth full of methane belched up by a dinosaur, the methane enzyme would burst into flame as it hit oxygen in the air when the "fire breather" hissed. (A peroxide-enzyme combo enables the bombardier beetle today to eject hot gas!)
4. a. B   g. H
    b. A   h. G
    c. C   i. K
    d. F   j. I
    e. E   k. J
    f. D   l. L
    m. N
5. See answer to #7 for Chapter 8
6. Sample: Wait for other scientists to check it out, then hang in there until science catches up and shows the Bible has been right all along (about 40 years for the Piltdown hoax, about four months for the dino-bird fake in *National Geographic*).

Chapter 14

1. X: a, b, c, d, e
2. a. T, b. T, c. T, d. T, e. T, f. T
3. B

Chapter 15

1. X: a, b, c, d
2. Adam, Eve; Jesus Christ; melanin
3. AABB; aabb; medium; could; thousands or millions of years; one generation
4. a. T, b. T, c. T
5. a. T, b. T, c. T

Chapter 16

1. Sample: "Nebraska Man" (skeleton, flesh, hair, family, and culture) was made up from a single tooth that turned out to be a pig's tooth (biggest scientific blunder!) but it was a significant part of the evidence — all now discarded — used

to convince the public of human evolution at the Scopes trial (greatest propaganda triumph).

2.   a. F, A. T, b. F, B. T, c. F, C. T, d. T, e. T
3.   a. D, b. E, c. C, d. B, e. A
4.   Sample: To avoid dealing with the scientific evidence related to origins, evolutionists have resorted to censoring contrary evidence from the classroom, lowering grades of students who present creation evidences, firing teachers who permit open discussion of creation/evolution, threatening school boards with lawsuits, ridiculing creation ideas on TV and in museums, getting famous scientists to denounce creation, screaming "separation of church and state," branding creation as religion and claiming evolution is science, and other propaganda techniques.
5.   Sample: God tells Christians to be always ready to give an answer to anyone who asks a reason for their hope in Christ, but in gentleness and meekness (1 Pet. 3:15). Many Christians know what it was like before they accepted Jesus, and that should help them wage the "war of the world views" with clear but gentle persuasion, respecting other persons and knowing that they must make their own informed choices for their own reasons — leaving the Holy Spirit to convict and convert.
6.   Your report on apologetics, studying to give answers the Holy Spirit can use to give others eternal life in Christ!

Chapter 17

1.   australopithecines; gorilla-like; tools; Leakey; on; meal
2.   Johanson; "Lucy"; *Australopithecus*; apes; mankind
3 a.   disproved; less
3 b.   cut and glued the pelvis to make it fit
3 c.   little different from the living pygmy chimp or bonobo
3 d.   different; discredited; no; no; blind faith
4.   Sample: Belief in human evolution cannot be called "good science," because good science would have given up a theory contradicted by so much evidence and supported by so little (or none). People continue to believe in human evolution simply because they don't want to believe in God. (More than one leading evolutionist has claimed in nearly exactly these words, "The only alternative to evolution is special creation, which is unthinkable" — unthinkable if you refuse to think about the evidence available!)
5.   Sample: When it comes to human origins and history, both evolutionists and creationists must build their ideas on faith. But it doesn't have to be a "blind faith" contradicted by the evidence at hand (evolution); it can be a faith that fits together the facts discovered (creation) — the evidence that shows mankind and the various apes have been separate kinds as far back as you can go.

Chapter 18

1.   Phantom creatures; rule; frustrated; away from
2.   Sample: To go looking for missing links, an evolutionist must believe missing links are still "out there somewhere." After 150 years of finding none, that requires an incredible blind faith! Before evolutionists introduced belief in missing links, we were just finding lots of separate and complex kinds of life as fossils. The millions of tons of fossils actually found support the idea different kinds were separately created; evolutionists are still looking for their first ton of missing links to support their faith. It is NOT starting with faith that makes evolution unscientific; it's

persisting in a faith shown to be contrary to the evidence over and over and over again.

Chapter 19

1.   Sample: A rock or fossil cannot be dated by "real science" because a "real scientist" would not know (1) the starting amounts of parent and daughter elements, (2) what elements might have been added or subtracted, or (3) whether the current rate of change was the same in the past.
2.   Amounts of certain elements; d
3.   True
4.   Older—deposited first; may be only minutes; only weeks; the year of Noah's flood
5.   Differences existing; f

Chapter 20

1.   No; no; in who we are, how we act, and what choices we make
2.   Sample: God programmed some birds with incredibly intricate instincts for nest building, but no learning is required and the plan cannot be modified and adapted to changing environments or goals. Human architecture, an image of God's creativity in us, is learned, personally and culturally modified, adaptable to changing needs and choices, makes use of varied and novel materials, reflects goals for the future, contains both functional and artistic elements, and represents a reasoning process that could not derive from nor reduce to nest building in birds, a marvelous feat that differs in kind, not just degree, from human building.
3.   Sample: Again, the soldier ant's instinct is a marvelous creation, but radically different in kind from a marine's courage and choice to defend ideas and goals larger than him/herself for people valued in the abstract as well as personally even more, on occasion, than he/she values his/her own life and dreams.
4.   Sample: It's not just human talk that's different in kind from animal communication; it's what we talk about. Unlike animal instinct, human language is learned and culturally conditioned, yet it lifts us to thoughts of eternity that transcend the limits of space, time, and culture. Motivational words are passed through the centuries, and God's Word has been continuously applied to solving human problems for millennia, never-changing but always new!
5.   Sample: Unlike God, we don't know or control the future, so we (like all finite people) must live by faith (as "the substance of things hoped for, the evidence of things not seen," Heb. 11:1). Unlike the other creatures, however, we can live by a faith that lifts us above the limits of space and time and events past and present. Faith-life suspends each of us between the God above and creatures below, with a unique place in His plan.
6.   Sample: It seems deep and abiding happiness and joy are found in those for whom faith, facts, and feeling are all in harmony, a rich spiritual blessing reserved for those who are found in Christ "in whom all things hold together" (Col. 1:17), now and forevermore! "Even so, come, Lord Jesus" (Rev. 22:20).